Defending the Faith
Through Counseling

A quick reference guide with

Bible answers to 101 topics

Nelson T. Newman

ariseanddeclare.com

Dedication

I affectionately dedicate this book to my four dear children. I thank God for them and cherish them greatly. After foolishly trying to decide which earthly treasures to invest in it dawned on me that I need to be investing in my children. Our children are our greatest investment besides furthering God's Kingdom. May we all cherish and love the children God has blessed us with. Pearl, Reed, Lilli, and Levi, I love you and if you grow up to have a deep love for our Savior Jesus Christ, live your life for Him, and understand and believe the truths found in this book I will have considered my investment a success.

Table of Contents

Foreword

One of the most needed things in our complicated world of the twenty-first century is a treatise on how to cope with the multiplicity of emotional, spiritual, financial, and physical problems in these days of confusion. Nelson Newman has done a magnificent job in covering all phases of life's experiences in his mammoth work entitled *Defending the Faith Through Counseling.*

Brother Newman has covered all the basics of human emotions in an effort to set forth principles from the Scriptures to guide the reader along the pathway of life. His wise handling of the Word of God is an indication, not only of his knowledge of the Bible, but the wisdom God has given him to apply these principles of the Scriptures to everyday life. Such a treatise is needed as never before in a day when the masses of people are looking in all directions for the solution to their problems. Brother Newman has provided Bible-based answers to the most pressing questions and solutions to the most complicated problems people in all walks of life confront each day.

Pastors and laymen can gain tremendous help for themselves, as well as for those whom they seek to serve in the work of the Lord.

I commend this book to all who desire to be better equipped to serve God in a most effective way. *To God be the glory!*

Dr. Raymond W. Barber

Pastor Emeritus, Worth Baptist Church, Fort Worth, Texas

Founder/President Emeritus, Norris Bible Baptist

Seminary, Fort Worth, Texas

Preface

I believe there is a great need today for Christians to know and understand what the Bible says on key issues in life. *Defending the Faith through Counseling* was written to give answers to the Christian who wants to know what the Bible says on a certain topic. I also believe that we as Christians are lacking in the area of counseling and discipleship. Outside of the pastor counseling his people within the local church (when the people are brave enough to consult their pastor) there is not much counseling going on. I believe there is a reason for this; most Christians themselves don't know where they stand on certain issues and topics in life. Therefore, they are not able to counsel others that may have questions or concerns with issues they may be facing in their life. *Defending the Faith through Counseling* will be a great help in not only helping the reader to see where the Bible stands on certain topics but also give them the confidence to counsel others when questions arise.

When looking for an answer, most people don't want to read a 200-page book or even a 20-page pamphlet to find it. I wanted to write a resource book that condenses all of the information from many different books and pamphlets into one easy to use book. I have defined and explained what the Bible says on each topic in approximately 600 words. My desire was to address each topic in two ways, concisely but thoroughly, answering the reader's questions and then supporting each topic with supporting verses from Scripture. I went through many lists and resources to find what I felt were the top 101 topics Christians are facing in life. Whether this is your first Christian resource/reference book or whether you have a vast library, I believe this book will be a blessing to you in helping you quickly find and address questions for yourself and/or in counseling others.

This book would not have been possible without the work from some other very dear people. I would like to take this opportunity to thank those who invested their time in reading over my manuscript and provided personal input on the material. Special thanks goes to my wife, Brandi Newman (typesetting), Cassandra Caudle (grammatical proofreading), and Dr. Roger Salomon (doctrinal proofreading). The time and energy you put into this project is greatly appreciated!

Introduction

There are two parts to the subtitle of the book further explaining its use and reliability. 'A Quick Reference Guide' is what it says it is. *Defending the Faith through Counseling* is a quick reference guide that the pastor, Christian worker, Christian counselor, or layperson can use to answer their own questions or to counsel others. The user will be able to find the answer to their topic quickly and easily and the answer will be given in a concise yet thorough manner.

The last part of the subtitle says 'With Bible Answers to 101 Topics.' *Defending the Faith through Counseling* is not merely a book of ideas from the author and where I stand, but rather what the Bible has to say and where it stands on key issues and topics. In our ever-changing society, things that would have never been accepted in previous generations are becoming acceptable today. Many will read this book and argue that the material is bizarre and outdated. The reality is, however, that society is the one who has changed and gradually made a shift away from God and His Word, but God never changes. (Hebrews 13:8) As Christians we must base our beliefs on the Bible. Anytime we seek or give counsel, it should come from the Bible. When using *Defending the Faith through Counseling* you can be sure that you are receiving Bible counseling as every topic is supported with Scripture.

There are a few things about the book that will explain how it was written and laid out. I strove to keep the descriptions informative, not a story of personal experiences. The topics are explained according to God's Word and each is supported with 5-6 verses/passages. Many of the supporting verses are explained on the left side in the description but not always in order to stick to the desired 600-word format. The topics are listed alphabetically in the table of contents and throughout the book for ease in finding the desired topic. Definitions come from the Webster's 1828 dictionary whenever possible. Finally, quotes used are from fundamental preachers or other well-respected Christians.

There is one key element that must be understood before one can effectively use this book. The salvation of the one seeking answers should be sought first and foremost. As I Corinthians 2:14 reveals, those who are not saved will not be able to fully grasp the truths found herein.

I pray this resource will help you become more knowledgeable on these key topics because the more knowledgeable we are as Christians, the better we will be in defending the faith.

12 Tips for Successful Christian Counseling

1) Identify opportunities to counsel – I Peter 3:15

   Counseling is not done solely on a professional basis. Each of us has a circle of influence. We must always be mindful of those around us and be ready to take advantage of opportunities to help those who are struggling. This is very difficult to do if we are not grounded in God's Word and have clear biblical convictions about what we believe on different topics in life.

2) The salvation of all parties is essential (counselor and counselee) – I Corinthians 2:14

   Ensuring the counselee's salvation is always the first line of business. The natural man (unsaved) will not understand the things of God, therefore, biblical counsel will be futile and of no effect. Only a saved counselor with a relationship with Christ Jesus will be able to impart biblical truths to another.

3) Spirit-filled counselor – I Corinthians 2:9-12; Ephesians 1:18

   It is the work of Holy Spirit to open the eyes and understanding of the believer to the truths found in God's Word, He illumines the Scriptures. We are only able to give counsel because of the Holy Spirit within us. Therefore, the counselor must not only have the Holy Spirit present but be filled with the Spirit in order to be most effective.

4) Saturated with prayer – James 5:16

   Prayer is our direct access to God and is an avenue to healing. Both the counselee and counselor should prepare their hearts and mind through personal prayer leading up to the counseling session. It is a good practice to begin counseling sessions with prayer to ask the Lord to guide the session so that it may be fruitful. Sessions should always be followed with prayer to ask God to help the counselee to be strong and to apply those things that were discussed during the session.

5) Counsel must come from the Bible – II Timothy 3:16

God has revealed Himself to us through His Word. He gave it *for doctrine, for reproof, for correction* and *instruction in righteousness* and it is God's instruction book for life. If we use the Scriptures as the foundation for our counseling, then our counsel will always remain Christ-centered.

6) Understand the goal of counseling –Psalm 51; James 4:17

There is a three-fold goal to Christian counseling. The counselor wants to get the counselee to realize the root of their problem, to repent of the sin that is causing their problem, and to restore fellowship between the counselee and the Lord and with other persons involved if necessary.

7) Follow-up – Acts 2:42

Counseling is interchangeable with discipleship. Proper discipleship is a process and requires repeat visits and follow-up. After Peter and the disciples had seen the thousands saved at Pentecost they didn't let them to their own devices. They *continued stedfastly in the apostles' doctrine and fellowship*. They continued to teach them doctrine and joined together in fellowship for encouragement and support.

8) Maintain confidentiality unless it would be illegal to do so – Proverbs 11:13

The one seeking counsel and help is putting their trust and confidence in the counselor. The counselor must resist the temptation to tell others what the counselee has shared with them. Spreading information would be gossip and would destroy the necessary trust within the counseling relationship. The only exception would be in cases of child abuse or other scenarios of illegal behavior that would make the counselor an accessory to the crime by their silence.

9) Safeguard appearances and temptation – I Thessalonians 5:22; Proverbs 26:20-21

Whenever the counsel is between those of the opposite sex it should be conducted in a public area or there should be a third person present. Rumors can start very rapidly and can destroy ministries and/or lives. This is why it is of the utmost importance that safeguards are put in place to eliminate any chance of false accusations. These safeguards will also prevent temptations that can lead to immorality.

10) Don't take others' offences personally – Proverbs 1:7, 23:9; John 8:47, 15:18

The Bible is clear there will be those who are *not of God* that will take offence and not listen to what you tell them. The Bible calls them *fools*. The counselor cannot let this prevent them from sharing God's Word with others or to take ridicule and rejection personally. It is ultimately the Lord whom they are rejecting and fighting against, not the counselor.

11) Don't get involved in debates – II Timothy 2:23; Romans 14:1-5

The counseling session cannot be turned into a debate over differences of opinion. The counselor is only able to present Scripture that applies to the circumstances at hand and give suggestions on how the counselee can apply them. If the two parties are not in agreement, they must decide to move on (or in severe cases parting ways may be necessary). Debates do not accomplish anything but provoke strife.

12) Know your limits – II Timothy 2:2

God expects His children to study and learn His Word so that they are *able to teach others also*. However, the counselor must be aware of what they are actually *able* to do. Sometimes a person's problems are deeper and go beyond that which an untrained professional can handle. Furthermore, sometimes there are sincere mental disorders that require the expertise of medical personnel and/or pharmacologic treatment.

"But sanctify the Lord God in your hearts:

and *be* ready always to *give* an answer

to every man that asketh you a reason

of the hope that is in you with meekness and fear:"

I Peter 3:15

"If you would be true to Christ

you must earnestly defend the faith

and must beware and teach others

to beware of false doctrine, false teachers."

John R. Rice

Abortion

Abortion is the deliberate termination of an unborn child. In 1973, the Supreme Court ruling in the case Roe vs. Wade made a landmark decision to extend a woman's right to have an abortion that set a precedent for future cases and began the birth of the 'pro-choice' movement. Since this ruling, over 50 million babies have been killed in the United States through abortion – that's six times the number of Jews killed by Adolf Hitler!

God is the creator of life as seen in the creation account in Genesis, particularly Genesis 1:27. We are then told in the Ten Commandments that we are not to take the life of another (this does not encompass areas such as capital punishment and war which is explained elsewhere in the book). I John 3:15 tells us that even feeling hatred towards another is the same as murder. It is the Lord who gives us everything, including life, and the Lord who taketh it away, as Job wisely says in Job 1:21. It is not our place to decide life as if we are God.

Those in the 'pro-choice' movement like to argue that what is growing in the mother's womb is nothing more than a fetus until it is viable or able to live on its own without its host. The Bible, however, is full of verses that support the fact that life begins at conception. In passages such as Exodus 21:22-23, Psalm 139:13-14, Isaiah 49:1, & Jeremiah 1:5 this is clearly proclaimed. In Exodus, the life growing in the woman's womb was referred to as a 'child' and was protected. In Psalms, the Psalmist refers to himself as a person while still in the womb, being owned by God and protected by Him. In Isaiah and Jeremiah, we see that God had plans for these men before they were born. Birth is not the origin of life; it is only the arrival of it on earth.

Abortion devalues life. It legalizes murder, yet we are surprised by all the violent crime in our nation today. The first socially accepted abortions (although still biblically wrong) were in the case of rape or for the physical safety of the mother. It has sadly evolved, however, to be almost a cosmetic procedure – a means to weed out undesirable children (from birth defects to the sex of the child). There is even a large group of people who feel abortion of a child with a 'defect' is a *duty* rather than an option because of the so-called burden the child would put on society. How far will we allow this to go? The new controversy is 'post birth abortion' which gives parents the right to 'abort' (murder) a born child within a few days of birth if they now decide that the child will be an unbearable burden to their lives (they change their minds). What is ironic is that those who think it is acceptable to end human life if the parents want to, are the same people who so dogmatically protect the rights of animals. Have we come so far as to put more concern on the rights of animals than on that of human children?

God's Word is clear that *children are an heritage of the Lord*. (Psalm 127:3) They are a gift from God no matter the means by which they were conceived. The ability to conceive a child is a cherished blessing; just ask the many couples that want to conceive children, but are unable to do so. A child is such a precious gift of God, and grave punishment is due to those who choose to have and perform abortions.

"For thou hast possessed my reins: thou hast covered me in my mother's womb. I will praise thee; for I am fearfully *and* wonderfully made: marvellous *are* thy works; and *that* my soul knoweth right well."

Psalm 139:13-14

"Listen, O isles, unto me; and hearken, ye people, from far; The Lord hath called me from the womb; from the bowels of my mother hath he made mention of my name."

Isaiah 49:1

"Before I formed thee in the belly I knew thee; and before thou camest forth out of the womb I sanctified thee, *and* I ordained thee a prophet unto the nations."

Jeremiah 1:5

"Lo, children *are* an heritage of the Lord: *and* the fruit of the womb *is his* reward."

Psalm 127:3

"Did not he that made me in the womb make him? and did not one fashion us in the womb?"

Job 31:15

"And he lifted up his eyes, and saw the women and the children; and said, Who *are* those with thee? And he said, The children which God hath graciously given thy servant."

Genesis 33:5

"While popular culture may consider abortion to be an option, it is not a biblical option. God's Word leaves no room for doubt concerning the inception of human life and the personhood of an unborn infant." – Paul Chappell

2

Abuse

Abuse is to maltreat; to use with bad motives or to wrong purposes; to violate; to defile by improper sexual intercourse; to treat rudely, or with reproachful language; to revile.[1] There are many different forms of abuse including child abuse, physical abuse, sexual abuse, emotional abuse, bullying, and sexual harassment. No matter what the form, abuse is usually the result of a weak person inflicting some type of abuse on another person in order to boost their own confidence.

Abuse is just one result of the sinful nature of mankind. Galatians 5:19-20 gives us a list of the types of behavior resulting from the sinful nature. Note that several of the behaviors listed could be associated with abuse. Abuse is one of the *offences* God speaks of in Matthew 18:7 that are unavoidable in this world; but He warns against being the one that is the source of the offences. Jesus himself suffered great abuse out of His love for us even though He was sinless. Isaiah 53:5 tells us, "But he was wounded for our transgressions, he was bruised for our iniquities: the chastisement of our peace was upon him; and with his stripes we are healed." Christ experienced horrible abuse and is there to comfort us in our time of pain and need.

Even though the abused may feel alone in their situation, God is always there for His children, and His Word tells us to call out to Him for comfort and strength. Psalm 46:1 tells us that *God is our refuge and strength, a very present help in trouble.* In Psalm 142, David was hiding in a cave from the harassment of King Saul. He prayed unto the Lord as his *refuge* and asked the Lord to *deliver me from my persecutors.* Another powerful promise is found in Psalm 107:19-20 when God hears the cry of the troubled and *saveth them.* Take special note in verse 21 that He delivered them through *his word.* The only way to find the help we need from the Lord is by being in His Word.

Although we are to seek the Lord for comfort, one cannot be afraid to get godly counsel if they are still struggling. There is no shame in asking advice from a trusted godly person. One must be careful, however, to go to someone that is going to give counsel from a biblical perspective. Often times, we can find it hard to know how to find God when we are in the midst of a trial. A good counselor will help lead a person to Him. We may not see the light at the end of the tunnel and/or understand what the Lord is doing, but we can be sure that He will give us strength to bear our trials.

Although God is our refuge and help in the time of such trials as abuse, there are times when abuse *must* be reported to the proper authorities. Any abuse involving a child, physical or sexual, needs to be reported. The law takes child abuse very seriously. In most cases, a person can be held liable for failure to report known child abuse. Often times children cannot, or will not, speak up for themselves and it is our responsibility to do it for them. Jesus Christ cherished children and let it be known that anyone who would harm them had His judgment on them. (Matthew 18:6) When abuse has occurred, go to the Lord for strength and comfort, and when necessary go to the proper authorities for justice and correction.

"Now the works of the flesh are manifest, which are *these*; Adultery, fornication, uncleanness, lasciviousness, Idolatry, witchcraft, hatred, variance, emulations, wrath, strife, seditions, heresies, Envyings, murders, drunkenness, revellings, and such like: of the which I tell you before, as I have also told *you* in time past, that they which do such things shall not inherit the kingdom of God."

Galatians 5:19-20

"Woe unto the world because of offences! for it must needs be that offences come; but woe to that man by whom the offence cometh!"

Matthew 18:7

"But whoso shall offend one of these little ones which believe in me, it were better for him that a millstone were hanged about his neck, and *that* he were drowned in the depth of the sea."

Matthew 18:6

"And he said unto me, My grace is sufficient for thee: for my strength is made perfect in weakness. Most gladly therefore will I rather glory in my infirmities, that the power of Christ may rest upon me. Therefore I take pleasure in infirmities, in reproaches, in necessities, in persecutions, in distresses for Christ's sake: for when I am weak, than am I strong."

II Corinthians 12:9-10

"Though God makes the sins of sinners to serve his purposes, that will not secure them from his wrath; and the guilt will be laid at the door of those who give the offense..." – Matthew Henry

Alcohol

Alcohol is any intoxicating beverage (wine/beer/drink coolers/etc.) that has any trace of alcoholic content in it. In God's Word, we see it referred to as drunkenness, strong drink, and wine. Many Christians try to use verses out of context to justify casual drinking, so long as they do not get drunk. An honest look at the Scriptures, however, will show that Scripture never justifies drinking. For example, we are told in the Ten Commandments 'thou shalt not kill' but that does not give us the right to beat someone up. The same concept applies with the consumption of alcohol. To the right are only 6 verses in the Bible that clearly show how God feels about the subject. Consider for just a moment that we are told in Proverbs 23:31 that we are not to even *look* at it. If we are not even to look, then surely we should not drink it.

I Corinthians 6:19-20 tells us that the body of the Christian is not his own. It was bought at a great price and is the temple of the Holy Spirit. Therefore, we should not be using substances that alter or harm our bodies. Even the smallest amount of alcohol consumption alters thought processes and judgment. Even our secular government recognizes the mind altering effects of alcohol, forbidding those under its influence from driving because of impaired ability. Not only does alcohol impair our thoughts and judgment, but it also takes a toll on a person's body. It has serious effects on the heart, liver, and pancreas, as well as affecting the immune system and causing several types of cancer. Alcohol is also very addictive. I Corinthians 6:12 tells us, "All things are lawful unto me, but all things are not expedient: all things are lawful for me, but I will not be brought under the power of any." In other words, drinking alcohol may not be against the law, but that does not mean that is it good for a person and one should not allow himself to become a slave to it.

There is one last misconception that needs to be addressed. Alcohol consumption affects more people than just the drinker. It robs the drinker and their family of money. It ruins families by causing the drinker to spend late nights in bars, and the fights and abuse that result from drunkenness. Worst of all, there are the thousands that are hurt or killed each year because of drunk drivers. And just as drinking alcohol affects more than the drinker, so the Bible address more than the drinker. The Bible is clear about God's judgment on those who sell alcohol and/or host events serving it such as in Habakkuk 2:15.

Alcohol is just one tool of the devil. He is the great deceiver, and Proverbs 20:1 tells us that those who drink are deceived. The devil likes to appeal to fleshly desires; he promises immediate pleasure but fails to reveal the tragic ends. Billy Sunday once said, "The saloon is a liar. It promises good cheer and sends sorrow. It promises health and causes disease. It promises prosperity and sends adversity. It promises happiness and sends misery. ...It is God's worst enemy and the devil's best friend." The devil is good at using TV commercials to portray drinking as a fun time with beautiful women, but the commercials don't portray the reality of people who are overweight and have other alcohol related health conditions, people who have lost their families and homes and everything they had, and families that are torn apart because of loved ones lost to a drunk driver.

"Who hath woe? who hath sorrow? who hath contentions? who hath babbling? who hath wounds without cause? who hath redness of eyes? They that tarry long at the wine; they that go to seek mixed wine. Look not thou upon the wine when it is red, when it giveth his colour in the cup, *when* it moveth itself aright. At the last it biteth like a serpent, and stingeth like an adder."

Proverbs 23:29-32

"What? know ye not that your body is the temple of the Holy Ghost *which is* in you, which ye have of God, and ye are not your own? For ye are bought with a price: therefore glorify God in your body, and in your spirit; which are God's."

I Corinthians 6:19-20

"Woe unto him that giveth his neighbour drink, that puttest thy bottle to *him*, and makest *him* drunken also, that thou mayest look on their nakedness!"

Habakkuk 2:15

"Wine *is* a mocker, strong drink *is* raging: and whosoever is deceived thereby is not wise."

Proverbs 20:1

"Woe unto them that rise up early in the morning, *that* they may follow strong drink; that continue until night, *till* wine inflame them!"

Isaiah 5:11

"And be not drunk with wine, wherein is excess; but be filled with the Spirit;"

Ephesians 5:18

"Some doctors foolishly claim that alcoholism is simply a disease. But if so, it is the only disease that is bottled and sold with the approval of the government! If so, it is a disease that everybody can avoid by not taking the first drink. Nobody ever became an alcoholic or wino without taking the first drink." – Curtis Hutson

Angels

Angels are heavenly beings created by God, "to act as His messengers to men and as agents who carry out His will."[2] We know they are God's creation because Colossians 1:16 tells us *for by him were all things created*. They were created on a level higher than man according to Hebrews 2:7. Job 38:1-7 reveals that they were created before the world. In this passage, God is asking Job if he knows the secrets of the foundation of the world and then speaks of the angels (referred to here as 'sons of God') praising Him. There are/were three great leaders among the angels: Michael, Gabriel, and Lucifer (a fallen angel now known as Satan that is covered later in the book).

The supernatural nature of angels makes it difficult for some to believe that angels are indeed real, but God's Word confirms that they are real, and is filled with direct references to them. They are spoken of in the Old Testament and the New Testament during Jesus' earthly life and prophesied about as to their future involvement in the Lord's second coming so there is no reason to believe that they do not still exist. Not only do they exist, but they are innumerable according to several passages such as Hebrews 12:22 and Revelation 5:11.

Angels are spiritual beings, not to be confused with seraphim and cherubim whose appearance is specifically different. The Bible mentions that seraphim and cherubim have wings but never describe angels as such, although they can fly. (Daniel 9:21) Their physical appearance can take on a wide variety of attributes. In Daniel 10:6 and Matthew 28:3 their appearance has been likened to *lightening* and with *raiment white as snow*. They are described as having eyes of fire and feet as polished brass. They can also appear as men just like you and I because Hebrews 13:2 tells us that we could be entertaining them unawares. As you can see, their physical appearance differs in different passages, but one thing is consistent: they are always referred to in the masculine sense. They do not marry according to Matthew 22:30 and they are very mighty according to verses such as Psalm 103:20, II Peter 2:11, and II Kings 19:35.

While the specific duties of angels can vary vastly, there is one main purpose for all angels, to serve God as described in Psalm 103:20. While serving God, the second purpose all angels' duties can be classified under is ministering to the saved. (Hebrews 1:14) Perhaps the duty we see most displayed in the Scriptures follows suit with their meaning of 'messenger.' There are many times angels were used to deliver a message of God such as: the birth of Jesus Christ, Samson, and John the Baptist; warning Joseph to escape Egypt; and serving as a medium of revelation to the prophets like Elijah in II Kings 1:15 and Philip in Acts 8:26. Angels served in the past by ministering to Jesus in the wilderness when tempted by Satan and also in Gethsemane, feeding and delivering Elijah, protecting Daniel by closing the mouths of the lions in the lions' den, and liberating the apostles from prison to name just a few. Today they minister to the saved by protecting them and accompanying them to heaven when they die. In the future, they will be with Jesus when He returns and help Him set up His kingdom. It will be an angel that binds Satan and casts him into the bottomless pit. What a great comfort to the saved to know that such beings are in our midst looking out for us.

"And I beheld, and I heard the voice of many angels round about the throne and the beasts and the elders: and the number of them was ten thousand times ten thousand, and thousands of thousands;"

Revelation 5:11

"His body also *was* like the beryl, and his face as the appearance of lightning, and his eyes as lamps of fire, and his arms and his feet like in colour to polished brass, and the voice of his words like the voice of a multitude."

Daniel 10:6

"Be not forgetful to entertain strangers: for therby some have entertained angels unawares."

Hebrews 13:2

"Bless the LORD, ye his angels, that excel in strength, that do his commandments, hearkening unto the voice of his word."

Psalm 103:20

"Are they not all ministering spirits, sent forth to minister for them who shall be heirs of salvation?"

Hebrews 1:14

"Although the Bible does not use the expression, 'guardian angels,' we believe angels are sent to guard God's children." – M. R. DeHaan

Anger

Anger is, "a violent passion of the mind excited by a real or supposed injury; usually accompanied with a propensity to take vengeance, or to obtain satisfaction from the offending party."[1] The word 'wrath' is often used in Scripture and is interchangeable with anger. Anger is an emotion that is not illegal, but when uncontrolled is a catalyst that leads to an array of other sins that are very harmful to others and are punishable by law. This includes things such as domestic violence, assault and battery, shootings, and murder. Even though anger is not a crime, it is still sin. As displayed in Proverbs 19:11, a wise man will learn to control his emotions and to overlook transgressions, obeying the Lord's command to *put off...anger.* (Colossians 3:8)

There are several biblical examples that show what can happen if anger is not dealt with properly. The first example is seen in Genesis 4:1-8 with the first siblings – Cain and Abel. Cain's jealousy toward his brother because of God's acceptance of Abel's sacrifice and not his own made him so wroth that he murdered his brother. Another example is found in Numbers 20:7-12 with Moses and the Israelites. God was providing in a miraculous way for the Israelites, but they still were not happy and began to murmur and complain. This behavior angered Moses, and in his anger, he disobeyed God's command to speak to the rock to receive water from it. Instead he struck the rock. In both cases, both men allowed their anger to overcome them and suffered greatly for it. Cain committed murder and had to go into exile for the safety of his own life; Moses struck the rock instead of speaking to it, and was therefore not allowed to enter into the promised land. Uncontrolled anger can, and usually will, lead to grave consequences.

Anger is one of the things that God commands the Christian to *put off* in Colossians 3:8. God goes even further in Proverbs 22:24-25 to say that we are not to even be friends with a person who is an *angry man.* It is more likely that a negative influence will pull down a positive one to its level than vice versa. The Christian is to display a forgiving spirit, just as Christ has forgiven us. After all, God tells us in Matthew 5:39, "But I say unto you, That ye resist not evil: but whosoever shall smite thee on thy right cheek, turn to him the other also." If the Christian is filled with the Spirit and has a forgiving spirit, it will be impossible to harbor anger. When one does not *put off* their anger bitterness takes root. Bitterness in a Christian is a poor testimony and can cause many to stumble spiritually. (Hebrews 12:15)

That said, there is such a thing as righteous anger. We see over and over again in the Bible where God or Jesus displayed anger. This anger was toward sin. God wants us to have anger toward sin as well. As sinful humans, however, we display this anger in a wrong manner, toward the person committing the sin. I'm sure you have heard the popular phrase, 'Hate the sin not the sinner;' we must heed this advice. Ephesians 4:26 supports righteous anger very well. The latter part of the verse is often lifted out and used out of context to couples, encouraging them to not go to sleep at night without having conflicts resolved. Although that is a good practice, that is not the intention of the verse. One must also read the first part of the verse, *be ye angry.* This verse is telling God's people to be angry with sin, to not commit the sins that one is to be angry about, and to not let the anger diminish.

"The discretion of a man deferreth his anger; and *it is* his glory to pass over a transgression."

Proverbs 19:11

"But now ye also put off all these; anger, wrath, malice, blasphemy, filthy communication out of your mouth."

Colossians 3:8

"Make no friendship with an angry man; and with a furious man thou shalt not go: Lest thou learn his ways, and get a snare to thy soul."

Proverbs 22:24-25

"Be ye angry, and sin not: let not the sun go down upon your wrath:"

Ephesians 4:26

"Wherefore, my beloved brethren, let every man be swift to hear, slow to speak, slow to wrath: For the wrath of man worketh not the righteousness of God."

James 1:19-20

"Anger does a man more hurt than that which made him angry." – Charles Spurgeon

Assurance

Assurance is also referred to as eternal security and is the Scriptural confidence that each person can know that they are saved because of their trust in Jesus Christ and His sacrifice on the cross and that nothing can take away that salvation. Every believer's name is written into the book of life and remains there for eternity; God doesn't have an eraser. (Revelation 3:5) He knows who is saved and who will join Him in heaven one day. This assurance of eternal salvation is only for the believer and God makes it evident throughout His Word.

God's Word assures the believer of their eternity in several places. One of the strongest is John 10:27-29 which says that nothing or no one can *pluck them out of my hand*. We see that we are sealed in verses like II Corinthians 1:22 and Ephesians 1:13; 4:30. We are told that we have eternal or everlasting life in numerous passages such as I John 5:13 and John 3:16; 6:27; 6:47. Jesus teaches assurance in the passage with the Samaritan woman at Jacob's well saying that He gives the believer living water so that they will *never thirst* again. Then there is the promise we see in John 14:2-3 that tells the saved souls that He is preparing a mansion for them in heaven and promises *I will come again, and receive you unto myself*. We believe that God cannot lie; so we must also believe in what He promises us in verses like these as well.

Thinking that a person can lose his salvation is placing works in the equation and not trusting in Christ's work on the cross. It actually does much worse; it makes Christ's suffering on the cross in vain. There are many verses in the Bible that tell us that our salvation is not of works like Ephesians 2:9 which says it is *not of works* and Isaiah 64:6 that says *all our righteousnesses are as filthy rags*. Consider Dr. John R. Rice's response to a woman that struggled with feeling that one lost their salvation if they fell into sin. He said:

> Well, that depends on how you got saved in the first place. If a Christian got saved by his good deeds, his righteousness, his faithfulness, then of course, he will have to stay saved the same way. If he got saved by his good works, then when his good works fail, he is lost. On the other hand, if one gets saved wholly by God's grace and on the merits of the crucified Saviour who promised to save those who trust in Him, then when Jesus fails, one who trusts in Him is irretrievably lost. If you save yourself, then you must do the keeping. If Christ does the saving, then He must do the keeping.[3]

It is Christ alone that saves a person; therefore, it is Christ alone who can and will secure that person's salvation for eternity.

Just as one is physically born into a family, one is spiritually born into God's family the moment they are saved. John 1:12 tells us that whoever believes on Him becomes His child and Romans 8:17 tells us that as His children we are His heirs. Our child may do something very wrong that angers us, but they are still our child. The same goes with our heavenly father; no one can be unborn out of His family. We may fall out of fellowship with God just as we lose fellowship at times with our earthly children, but we remain His children just the same. We must not base the assurance of our salvation on our feelings, but rather in our faith, in the Savior that saved us, and the things He has written in His Word so that *that ye may know that ye have eternal life*. (I John 5:13)

"My sheep hear my voice, and I know them, and they follow me: And I give unto them eternal life; and they shall never perish, neither shall any *man* pluck them out of my hand. My Father, which gave *them* me, is greater than all; and no *man* is able to pluck *them* out of my Father's hand."

John 10:27-29

"In whom ye also *trusted*, after that ye heard the word of truth, the gospel of your salvation: in whom also after that ye believed, ye were sealed with that holy Spirit of promise,"

Ephesians 1:13

"These things have I written unto you that believe on the name of the Son of God; that ye may know that ye have eternal life, and that ye may believe on the name of the Son of God."

I John 5:13

"Blessed be the God and Father of our Lord Jesus Christ, which according to his abundant mercy hath begotten us again unto a lively hope by the resurrection of Jesus Christ from the dead, To an inheritance incorruptible, and undefiled, and that fadeth not away, reserved in heaven for you, Who are kept by the power of God through faith unto salvation ready to be revealed in the last time."

I Peter 1:3-5

"Being confident of this very thing, that he which hath begun a good work in you will perform *it* until the day of Jesus Christ:"

Philippians 1:6

"How do I know I am saved? Because the Bible tells me I'm saved. You can know that you are saved and that you are a child of God." – Tom Malone

Backsliding

Backsliding is the act of renouncing one's faith and the practices of that faith; it is one falling away from one's Christian beliefs into sin and/or idolatry. One may think that backsliding is an extreme removal from the faith but that is not so. There are varying degrees, but each are dangerous. Some things may seem small and insignificant, but they will eventually lead to greater degrees until one is so far backslidden that restoration seems impossible. Finding oneself entrenched in sin is a gradual digression. A person doesn't wake up one day and decide that they are going to be an alcoholic or drug addict; it begins with one sip of an alcoholic beverage and one hit of a drug. We must recognize when we've started on that slippery slope and take actions to prevent it. As Christians we are to be Christ-like, everyday a little more like Christ. There should be a forward progression and maturity in our Christian walk. Backsliding is the opposite of this continual personal revival. When one gives in to sin and allows the flesh to win out in their lives that forward progression stops; they begin to fall back away from their current healthy state. They fall into an unhealthy state that requires God's healing to return. (Jeremiah 3:22, Hosea 14:4)

There are several things that can cause one to backslide. The first is Satan himself. I Peter 5:8 tells us that he *walketh about seeking whom he may devour*. The devil began his pursuit on the human race in the Garden of Eden disguising himself as a serpent and deceiving Eve. From this act *sin entered into the world* and we are all born with a sin nature. (Romans 5:12) We war with this sin nature daily as described in Galatians 16:17. A very big factor in this is one's friendships. Every friend we allow in our lives will have a certain influence on us. If they are the type of friend that is a negative influence, chances are they are going to cause you to backslide. If they are not at the same point as oneself in their Christian walk, then one must be cautious.

So what does one do when they find themself in a backslidden state? How does one get back on track? First and foremost, a daily devotional life must be reestablished. This involves both Bible reading (not merely reading but meditating on His Word) and a distinct prayer time. If we are not in God's Word and our prayer life is not what it should be, we cannot effectively move forward as Christians. God has given us the armor we need so that we *may be able to stand against the wiles of the devil*; but we cannot put it on if we are not in His Word and communing with Him daily in prayer. (Ephesians 6:11-18) Another important key is faithful attendance to church services. We all must be in God's house regularly to be spiritually fed and encouraged; it takes three to thrive!

The Lord's desire is always for His wayward children to return to Him. He is not only willing to welcome them back with open arms, but He rejoices in doing so. The parable of the prodigal son in Luke 15 is a perfect example; in fact, it is a picture of how Christ welcomes home His children just as the prodigal's father did of him. If one has backslidden away from God, they must simply repent and return to the Lord who WILL take them back into fellowship with Him and will do so *freely*, without hesitation. (Hosea 14:4)

"Return, ye backsliding children, *and* I will heal your backslidings. Behold, we come unto thee; for thou *art* the LORD our God."

Jeremiah 3:22

"I will heal their backsliding, I will love them freely: for mine anger is turned away from him."

Hosea 14:4

"And my people are bent to backsliding from me: though they called them to the most High, none at all would exalt *him*."

Hosea 11:7

"The backslider in heart shall be filled with his own ways: and a good man *shall be satisfied* from himself."

Proverbs 14:14

"Thine own wickedness shall correct thee, and thy backslidings shall reprove thee: know therefore and see that *it is* an evil *thing* and bitter, that thou hast forsaken the LORD thy God, and that my fear *is* not in thee, saith the Lord GOD of hosts."

Jeremiah 2:19

"Well, poor backslider, I wouldn't stay away any longer. I would come home today for it is a sad, bitter business when you have known the joy of salvation, the presence of God, the sweetness of the Bible and of answered prayer, then to lose all that joy and not be able to see the face of the God whom you love." – John R. Rice

Baptism

Baptism, practiced as one of two church ordinances, is the immersion of a believer into water as a picture of Christ's death, burial, and resurrection. (Romans 6:3-5) It is an outward expression of an inward decision. It is a public profession of one's faith. When a person is baptized, they are identifying themselves with Christ as one of His followers.

So why should a Christian be baptized? To begin, God commanded it. In the great commission, He tells us to go and tell others the Gospel, and then to baptize those who receive it. (Matthew 28:19) Christ held baptism in such high regard and considered it so important that He did it Himself as our example to follow. (Matthew 3:13) Baptism is also a first step to church membership. We see in Acts 2:41 that their salvation came first, then baptism, then church membership. They were not added unto the church before baptism.

The next question to be answered about baptism is when should baptism take place? Baptism must follow salvation. Acts 8:37 is one of several Scripture references that show this. This verse is Philip's response to the eunuch's question of what hindered him from being baptized. Philip was very clear that only if he believed could he be scripturally baptized. Although it often does not immediately follow one's decision to be saved, Scripture plainly supports baptism as soon as possible. (Acts 2:41; 9:18; 16:33) Following the Lord's command of baptism is the Christians' first step in obedience to Christ.

How baptism is to be performed can also be understood from studying Scripture. Baptism should be performed by immersion in water one time. Jesus' baptism in Mark 1:9-10 supports baptism by immersion; it says that after Jesus was baptized He came *up out of the water*. He had to be submerged in the water in order to come up out of it. Again in Acts 8:38 when Philip was performing the baptism of the eunuch it says that *they went down both into the water*. They would not have needed to go *into* the water to perform a baptism merely by sprinkling. As mentioned above, baptism is a picture of Christ's death, burial, and resurrection. The death is seen as the believer is guided back into the water, the burial is seen while the believer is beneath the water, and the resurrection is seen as the believer comes up out of the water. This picture is impossible to be seen in sprinkling. Additionally, Christ died only once so the believer should only be dipped once; to be dipped three times would be to picture Christ being put to death three times.

Perhaps one of the biggest misconceptions about baptism is that it is required for salvation. Ephesians 2:8-9 is one of many verses that tell us that we are saved only through our faith in Christ. It is not of works and although baptism is a good work, it does not save us. We touched on this earlier here as well when explaining that baptism is to come only after one is saved. We also see proof of this at the crucifixion. The one thief accepted Christ while hanging on the cross. That thief did not have time to be baptized, yet Jesus told him *to day shalt thou be with me in paradise*. (Luke 23:49) This truth is why infant baptism is unbiblical. Baptism does not save a person and comes only after salvation.

"Know ye not, that so many of us as were baptized into Jesus Christ were baptized into his death? Therefore we are buried with him by baptism into death: that like as Christ was raised up from the dead by the glory of the Father, even so we also should walk in newness of life. For if we have been planted together in the likeness of his death, we shall be also *in the likeness* of *his* resurrection."

Romans 6:3-5

"Go ye therefore, and teach all nations, baptizing them in the name of the Father, and of the Son, and of the Holy Ghost:"

Matthew 28:19

"Then cometh Jesus from Galilee to Jordan unto John, to be baptized of him."

Matthew 3:13

"Then they that gladly received his word were baptized: and the same day there were added *unto them* about three thousand souls."

Acts 2:41

"And Philip said, If thou believest with all thine heart, thou mayest. And he answered and said, I believe that Jesus Christ is the Son of God."

Acts 8:37

"Now, in baptism we have a picture of the greatest experience that can come to man – eternal salvation through faith in Christ." – Lee Roberson

Baptists

The earliest and simplest definition associated with Baptists was one who administers baptism. Today, Baptists are known as a group of Christians who trace their origin and doctrines back to the first Century church and the teachings of Jesus Christ. They believe in the literal interpretation of the Bible, which is the foundation of their faith and practice in every area of life. They deny the doctrine of infant baptism, maintaining that baptism is only to be administered after salvation by immersion in water, and hold to a set of Baptist distinctives.

The BAPTISTS title is often used as an acrostic to describe these distinctives. The 'B' represents biblical authority. (II Timothy 3:15-17) The Bible is the final authority in all matters of life. Baptists believe in a literal interpretation of the Bible and accept what it teaches as truth that is to be adhered to. The 'A' represents autonomy of the local church. (Colossians 1:18) Christ is the head of the church and the one to whom they are accountable. There is not a larger, outside, hierarchial system that determines the beliefs and/or practices of individual churches. The 'P' represents priesthood of all believers. (I Peter 2:5) Every believer has direct access to God and does not need a priest, bishop, etc. to intercede for them and/or interpret Scripture. The first 'T' represents two church offices – pastor and deacons. (I Timothy 3:1-13) The terms 'elder' and 'bishop' in the Bible all refer to the same office. Pastors and deacons are covered in more detail later in the book. The 'I' represents individual soul liberty. (Romans 14:12) God has commanded us in the great commission to go and tell of the good news of the Gospel, not to force anyone into compliance. God wants us to serve Him joyfully and has given us our own free will to choose our paths. Along with this freedom, however, comes the accountability of each person for their own soul. The 'S' represents saved and baptized church membership. (Acts 2:41, 47) Scripture shows us that people were added to the church only after they were baptized and a person cannot be scripturally baptized until after salvation, thus church members are saved and baptized. We are told in Philippians 1:27, "Only let your conversation be as it becometh the gospel of Christ: …that ye stand fast in one spirit, with one mind striving together for the faith of the gospel;" The church cannot do this if they have unsaved people in their membership (please note that we are speaking here of membership, not attendance). The second 'T' represents two ordinances observed – baptism and the Lord's Supper. (Acts 2:41; I Corinthians 11:26) These are two symbolic ordinances followed by believers in identification with and in remembrance of Christ's death on the cross. Baptism and the Lord's Supper, like pastors and deacons, are covered in more detail elsewhere in the book. The second 'S' represents separation of church and state. (Matthew 22:21; Romans 13:1-13) God established both with unique purposes and roles that are specifically separate from one another. Although we as Christians are to influence government, *no* religious group is to control the government and likewise the government is not to control the church.

Churches that hold strictly to these principles are known as independent fundamental Baptists. They have a very rich heritage throughout the ages of those who suffered persecution and martyrdom for the cause of Christ. The greatest mission of the Baptists is to evangelize the world in obedience to the Great Commission given by Christ.

"All scripture *is* given by inspiration of God, and *is* profitable for doctrine, for reproof, for correction, for instruction in righteousness:" – II Timothy 3:16

"And he is the head of the body, the church: who is the beginning, the firstborn from the dead; that in all *things* he might have the preeminence." – Colossians 1:18

"Ye also, as lively stones, are built up a spiritual house, an holy priesthood, to offer up spiritual sacrifices, acceptable to God by Jesus Christ." – I Peter 2:5

"This *is* a true saying, If a man desire the office of a bishop, he desireth a good work. …For they that have used the office of a deacon well purchase to themselves a good degree, and great boldness in the faith which is in Christ Jesus." – I Timothy 3:1, 13

"So then every one of us shall give account of himself to God." – Romans 14:12

"Then they that gladly received his word were baptized: and the same day there were added *unto them* about three thousand souls." – Acts 2:41

"For as often as ye eat this bread, and drink this cup, ye do shew the Lord's death till he come." – I Corinthians 11:26

"…Render therefore unto Caesar the things which are Caesar's; and unto God the things that are God's." – Matthew 22:21b

"We believe that the Baptists are the original Christians. We did not commence our existence at the reformation, we were reformers before Luther and Calvin were born; we never came from the Church of Rome, for we were never in it, but we have an unbroken line up to the apostles themselves." – Charles Spurgeon

Bible

The Bible is the sacred book given by inspiration of God to men by way of 66 individual books in two parts – the Old and New Testaments. It is God's revelation of Himself to man and is the guidebook for faith and practice of the Christian life.

As noted in the definition, all Scripture was given by inspiration of God. This is a very key element to understand and accept before any other principles of the Bible can be taught, understood, and accepted. We cannot put confidence in and base our faith and practice on the words of mere men. Knowing that the Bible is indeed the words of God is how we can trust verses like II Timothy 3:16 and II Peter 1:21 that tells us, "For the prophecy came not in old time by the will of man: but holy men of God spake *as they were* moved by the Holy Ghost." Believing in the inspiration of Scripture is absolutely essential to everything else we believe as Christians; it is a foundational truth.

The truth of the inspiration of Scripture necessitates its preservation and we see this written many places throughout the Bible. God preserved His word by means of man and the working of the Holy Spirit as seen in II Peter 1:21, as well as Isaiah 59:20-21 that tells us that it *shall not depart out of thy mouth, nor out of the mouth of thy seed, nor out of the mouth of thy seed's seed, saith the LORD, from henceforth and for ever.* We also see from Scripture that He will preserve His 'word' as a whole as well as His actual 'words.' Take note to the use of both 'word' and 'words' in different passages. It is not just His general thoughts or ideas that will be preserved but so will the individual parts, judgments, and words be preserved. Furthermore, just before He concluded His great work of revelation we now have through the Bible, He warns man not to add to or take away from His 'words.' It is very evident that God preserved more than just generalities.

That leads us to the question, "What is God's preserved Word for the English Speaking people today?" There are basically two families of manuscripts that all Bible translations originate from, the Textus Receptus or Received text and the Wescott-Hort. The Textus Receptus is a family of over 5,300 manuscripts (some complete, some partial) that all agree and have been in circulation and continuous use since the early church period. The Wescott-Hort is a family of only 2 nearly-complete manuscripts that do not agree and 30 partials. They do date about 150-200 years older but were 'lost' and out of circulation for 1400 years from the 5th to 19th centuries. Two primary reasons conclude that the King James Version is the preserved Word for the English Speaking people today: 1) it is the only translation that comes from the Textus-Receptus family and 2) verses such as Psalm 33:11 and 100:5 tell us that His Word would be available for all generations and the Wescott-Hort was unavailable for 1400 years (this is the family of manuscripts that all other modern versions originate from).

We can confidently believe the entire Bible, because it stands the test of history and archeology, science, unity, prophecy, and time. Satan and man have tried to destroy it, yet after 2,000 years, it still stands strong as the best-selling and most read book in the world.

"All scripture *is* given by inspiration of God, and *is* profitable for doctrine, for reproof, for correction, for instruction in righteousness:."

II Timothy 3:16

"The grass withereth, the flower fadeth: but the word of our God shall stand for ever."

Isaiah 40:8

"The words of the LORD *are* pure words: *as* silver tried in a furnace of earth, purified seven times. Thou shalt keep them, O LORD, thou shalt preserve them from this generation for ever."

Psalm 12:6-7

"For ever, O LORD, thy word is settled in heaven."

Psalm 119:89

"Heaven and earth shall pass away, by my words shall not pass away."

Matthew 24:35

"For I testify unto every man that heareth the words of the prophecy of this book, If any man shall add unto these things, God shall add unto him the plagues that are written in this book: And if any man shall take away from the words of the book of this prophecy, God shall take away his part out of the book of life, and out of the holy city, and *from* the things which are written in this book."

Revelation 22:18-19

"Although we can not point to one particular Hebrew or Greek manuscript and say that it is an exact copy of the original, we can say that God has preserved His word for every generation because He said that He would." – Bruce Lackey

Calvinism

Calvinism is a belief system in five distinct doctrines as taught by a man named John Calvin. The five points are often referred to as the TULIP. The term Calvinism is used rather loosely today and has a wide range of following such as those that will say they are a one-point, three-point, or so on Calvinist. The Bible, however, does not agree with *any* of the five points.

The 'T' in the TULIP stands for Total Depravity meaning that man is unable to choose whether or not they will be saved. The Bible, however, teaches that salvation is *only* by choice. We see in several verses that it is up to the individual to choose or receive Christ, such as in Joshua 24:15 that says we must *choose* whom we will serve. Choosing to serve the Lord is the same as choosing salvation. The 'U' represents Unconditional Election which means that God selects (or elects) those who will be saved and those who will not. Scripture once again refutes the Calvinists' teaching. II Peter 3:9 shows us that it is God's desire that *everyone* would accept Him as their Savior. It is foolishness to believe that God would predestinate anyone to hell. As explained in the first point, it comes down to our own free will to choose; if one chooses to believe, they will be saved and if one chooses not to believe, they will not be saved. (John 3:36) 'L' in the TULIP stands for Limited Atonement meaning that Christ died only for those He elected to be saved. It is easy to see a common theme throughout Scripture as to the use of all, whosoever, world, etc.. We see it in Isaiah 53:6 which disproves the 'L.' Both 'alls' in this verse refer to the same group of people. We have all sinned and gone astray; therefore, Christ died and took the iniquity of all those sinners. If what the Calvinists teach is correct, only those God elected to be saved have gone astray. We also see this theme in the most well known and recited verse of the Bible – John 3:16, "For God so loved the world…" It does not say that He loved and gave His Son for His elect. The 'I' represents Irresistible Grace teaching that if a person is elected by God to be saved, they are unable to refuse or resist their salvation. The five points found in the TULIP are so intertwined that it is difficult to separate them or for any of them to stand alone. Such is the case with the 'I'. We have established that our salvation depends on our choosing to accept God's gift. Therefore, it is more than possible for someone to refuse God's gift. Passages such as Proverbs 1:24-26 clearly show that many men are hard-hearted and simply refuse God's love and salvation. 'P' stands for Perseverance of the Saints which leads one to believe that the believer does something and is responsible for their eternal security. There is a big difference between perseverance and preservation. We are saved only by the grace of God, not by any merit or works of our own (Ephesians 2:8-9) and therefore it is God only who preserves us until death or "…the coming of our Lord Jesus Christ." (I Thessalonians 5:23)

Mark 16:15 is one of several places that we see the Great Commission given to all Christians by Christ. Here again, we see that 'all' theme; we are to spread the gospel to all people. The Calvinist mentality and lack of a soul-winning emphasis goes against this command. According to their teachings, there is no need to witness to people if God has already elected those who will be saved and those people are unable to refuse that election. Although very sincere about their beliefs, they are very much misled!

"And if it seem evil unto you to serve the LORD, choose you this day whom ye will serve; whether the gods which your fathers served that *were* on the other side of the flood, or the gods of the Amorites, in whose land ye dwell: but as for me and my house, we will serve the LORD."

Joshua 24:15

"The Lord is not slack concerning his promise, as some men count slackness; but is longsuffering to us-ward, not willing that any should perish, but that all should come to repentance."

II Peter 3:9

"All we like sheep have gone astray; we have turned every one to his own way; and the LORD hath laid on him the iniquity of us all."

Isaiah 53:6

"Because I have called, and ye refused; I have stretched out my hand, and no man regarded; But ye have set at nought all my counsel, and would none of my reproof: I also will laugh at your calamity; I will mock when your fear cometh;"

Proverbs 1:24-26

"And the very God of peace sanctify you wholly; and *I pray God* your whole spirit and soul and body be preserved blameless unto the coming of our Lord Jesus Christ."

I Thessalonians 5:23

"The elect are the whosoever wills and the non-elect are the whosoever won'ts!"
– D.L. Moody

Capital Punishment

Capital Punishment is a death penalty in which a murderer is executed for the crimes they committed against fellow mankind. The taking of life during war will be handled in greater detail later in the book. We know that God is a God of love. Jesus tells us on the Sermon on the Mount in Matthew 5:39 to turn the other cheek, but these principles are meant for our interpersonal relationships and are not applicable to law and government. God gives separate, specific instructions for how government should handle certain offences.

Old Testament Scripture is full of the clear command to put to death anyone who murders another person. (Genesis 9:6; Exodus 21:12; Leviticus 21:12; Numbers 35:16-19) They clearly call a person who ends the life of another a murderer and demand that they be handed over to the avenger of blood and/or be put to death. The 'avenger of blood' was a relative (or sometimes a friend) of the victim that was to find the murderer and kill him. This was not only allowed by God, but instituted by Him. He is a God of justice just as much as He is a God of love. As part of His plan, God set up cities of refuge for those who killed a person accidentally. Those guilty of causing an accidental death could flee to these cities for safety from the avenger of blood, but they would have to remain there until the avenger died themselves. God's death penalty was and is meant for those who murder others with malicious intent.

There are those that would argue that these commands were given under the law and are no longer applicable. Although there are parts of the law which we are no longer bound to, those parts pertaining to moral requirements are still in effect because the things that they represent have always been considered wrong. The laws regarding moral issues have never been negated; laws pertaining to things such as lying, stealing, adultery, murder, etc. Only those laws that dealt with cleansing, sanctification, and one's place in eternity were done away with. Once Christ died on the cross for our sins making a way for salvation, those parts of the law were no longer needed. Therefore, those parts of the law related to murder have not changed; murder is a moral issue.

While most of the references to the right would have been given under the law, the death penalty was still carried into the dispensation of grace by way of civil government. Government was instituted by God. Anyone in power is only given that power by God and is ordained of Him. Romans 13:1-4 is a New Testament passage that shows this truth and also shows us what our responsibility as citizens is to that government. Today, the responsibility of carrying out the death penalty lies on rulers and government.

God instituted a death penalty because He knows His creation. Without justice, the sinful flesh of mankind would run wild. Deuteronomy 17:8-13 shows us that we must follow through with due judgment even if it is difficult to do, placing a good fear in people so that they don't continue to do evil. We see this also in the Romans passage which tells us that government is to be a terror to the evil, and those who do evil should fear the government. Harsh judgment on such a gross crime as murder is necessary in order to maintain civility.

"Whoso sheddeth man's blood, by man shall his blood be shed: for in the image of God made he man."

Genesis 9:6

"He that smiteth a man, so that he die, shall be surely put to death."

Exodus 21:12

"And he that killeth any man shall surely be put to death."

Leviticus 24:17

"And if he smite him with an instrument of iron, so that he die, he *is* a murderer: the murderer shall surely be put to death. And if he smite him with throwing a stone, wherewith he may die, and he die, he *is* a murderer: the murderer shall surely be put to death. Or *if* he smite him with an hand weapon of wood, wherewith he may die, and he die, he *is* a murderer: the murderer shall surely be put to death. The revenger of blood himself shall slay the murderer: when he meeteth him, he shall slay him."

Numbers 35:16-19

"Let every soul be subject unto the higher powers. For there is no power but of God: the powers that be are ordained of God. Whosoever therefore resisteth the power, resisteth the ordinance of God: and they that resist shall receive to themselves damnation. For rulers are not a terror to good works, but to the evil. Wilt thou then not be afraid of the power? do that which is good, and thou shalt have praise of the same: For he is the minister of God to thee for good. But if thou do that which is evil, be afraid; for he beareth not the sword in vain: for he is the minister of God, a revenger to *execute* wrath upon him that doeth evil."

Romans 13:1-4

"Gross crimes deserve and demand stiff sentences. Those who commit murder forfeit their right to live themselves." – Shelton Smith

Christian Education

Christian education is an educational ministry of a local church for the purpose of assisting parents in training their children, giving them an education based on a Christ-centered philosophy that strives for spiritual, social, and mental growth. Psalm 127:3 tells us, "Lo, children *are* an heritage of the LORD: *and* the fruit of the womb *is his* reward." They are not *our* children but God's. We are entrusted with the awesome responsibility to raise them for Him, to grow to know, love, and serve Christ. We must carefully weigh our decisions regarding those children because every decision will have consequences, good or bad. Deciding how to educate them is a very weighty decision, because it greatly shapes and influences the men or women that they will become.

The Bible is clear that God has given the primary responsibility of training children to the parents. We see this in verses such as Proverbs 22:6 and Deuteronomy 6:6-7. You will notice, however, that God instructed parents to teach their children about the things of God, not emphasizing academics such as reading, writing, and arithmetic. Surely academics are important as well, but the things of God must be and are top priority. God has given the church the responsibility to teach His Word. In instituting Christian schools, the church and family become partners in working together to train the younger generations in God's ways. Christian education is not a necessity or commanded by scripture, but those children blessed with a godly home, a godly church, AND a Christian education have a tremendous advantage. The three entities are working together to teach those things God would have them learn. Those who send their children to public schools have to constantly counterbalance the opposite philosophies that their children are being taught in school.

The risk of public education is an indoctrination of worldly philosophies. Colossians 2:8 warns us against being spoiled by such philosophies. The basic philosophy of the world and its public schools is Humanism, which goes completely against our belief system as Christians. Paul Chappell quoted Charles Frances Potter, former president of the National Educators Association as saying, "Every American public school is a school of Humanism."[4] Then I Timothy 6:3-5 tells us that if someone teaches contrary to God's Word (as do the majority of public school teachers) they know nothing and are destitute of the truth and that we are to withdraw from them. So why would we let them teach our children? Finally, Psalm 1:1 instructs us not to walk in the counsel of the ungodly. By putting children in public schools, the ungodly are exactly who are counseling them.

Secular colleges pose an even higher risk and require heightened caution. The worldly philosophies within them are very prominent and are strongly pushed. It is especially sad to see a promising young person whose parents have sacrificed to send them to Christian school in order to build that biblical foundation only to have it all torn down in four short years at a secular college. God's Word clearly instructs us to be very careful and selective of those whom we allow to influence our life and our children's lives, and we take a huge risk when we let the world educate our children.

"Train up a child in the way he should go: and when he is old, he will not depart from it."

Proverbs 22:6

"And these words, which I command thee this day, shall be in thine heart: And thou shalt teach them diligently unto thy children, and shalt talk of them when thou sittest in thine house, and when thou walkest by the way, and when thou liest down, and when thou risest up."

Deuteronomy 6:6-7

"Beware lest any man spoil you, through philosophy and vain deceit, after the tradition of men, after the rudiments of the world, and not after Christ."

Colossians 2:8

"If any man teach otherwise, and consent not to wholesome words, *even* the words of our Lord Jesus Christ, and to the doctrine which is according to godliness; He is proud, knowing nothing, but doting about questions and strifes of words, whereof cometh envy, strife, railings, evil surmisings, Perverse disputings of men of corrupt minds, and destitute of the truth, supposing that gain is godliness: from such withdraw thyself."

I Timothy 6:3-5

"Blessed *is* the man that walketh not in the counsel of the ungodly, nor standeth in the way of sinners, nor sitteth in the seat of the scornful."

Psalm 1:1

"In a Christian school we look at all subjects through the bifocals of the Word of God. Just as bifocals enable the reader to see more clearly; viewing all subjects through the spiritual bifocals of the Bible will give our children a proper Christian worldview of life and living."
– Roger Salomon

Christian Service

Christian service is the things believers, being called servants, do to further God's kingdom as unto Jesus Christ. Such people are called laymen, those who are not pastors or part of a pastoral staff. A Pastor or someone else in full-time ministry is called by God to their respective ministry and to serve accordingly. This topic is directed to the laymen, every other saved Christian who works a secular job but is also to be serving Christ. Ephesians 2:10 shows us that we are created to serve Christ once we are saved; we are to do *good works*.

There is a difference, however, between community service and Christian service. Community service focuses on the temporal physical needs, whereas Christian service focuses on the eternal spiritual needs. Everything done in Christian service is for the ultimate purpose of seeing souls saved. Nursery workers watch children to allow unsaved parents to listen to the service and to allow church members to serve elsewhere in order to teach God's Word. Bus workers and drivers serve so that unchurched children can come to church to learn about Jesus. Ushers serve to collect offerings that help keep the church functioning and to send missionaries worldwide to spread the Gospel. Every job in the church can be brought back to that one main objective, to get people saved.

There may be only one main goal, but there are a wide variety of jobs that need done in a church to see that goal accomplished. It is impossible for the pastor and his pastoral staff to do them all on their own. No one job is more or less important than another either. This concept is seen in I Corinthians 12:12-25. It teaches that although we are *one* body with one unified goal, each person performing a job is a member of that body no matter how small it may seem. The body cannot function properly without all its parts.

Consider the fact that even Christ, our creator and Savior, served others during His earthly ministry. Christ served others to display humility and as an example for us to follow. Matthew 20:27-28 tells us, "And whosoever will be chief among you, let him be your servant: Even as the Son of man came not to be ministered unto, but to minister, and to give his life a ransom for many." Christ is the highest chief of all, yet He came to earth to serve us. Jesus is the example of humble service in John 13:4-16. The passage begins with Jesus washing the feet of His disciples at what came to be known as the Last Supper and ends in an exhortation by Jesus that we should follow His example. Throughout His earthly ministry, He healed people, provided food by means of several miracles, and taught His father's Word. Most assuredly, however, His greatest service to us was the sacrifice He made for us on the cross of Calvary, providing a way of salvation for all mankind.

God saves us for a purpose – to serve Him by leading others to Christ. It is our job and responsibility to further God's kingdom by serving in our local church and getting the Gospel in the hands of the unsaved. Only what we've done for Christ will matter in eternity. Our Christian service is the gold, silver, and precious stones we see in I Corinthians 3:12-15. We should all be able to sing from the heart, *We'll work 'til Jesus comes*!

"Who then is Paul, and who *is* Apollos, but ministers by whom ye believed, even as the Lord gave to every man? I have planted, Apollos watered; but God gave the increase. So then neither is he that planteth any thing, neither he that watereth; but God that giveth the increase. Now he that planteth and he that watereth are one: and every man shall receive his own reward according to his own labour. For we are labourers together with God: ye are God's husbandry, *ye are* God's building."

I Corinthians 3:5-9

"Ye call me Master and Lord: and ye say well; for *so* I am. If I then, *your* Lord and Master, have washed your feet; ye also ought to wash one another's feet. For I have given you as example, that ye should do as I have done to you. Verily, verily, I say unto you, The servant is not greater than his lord; neither he that is sent greater than he that sent him. If ye know these things, happy are ye if ye do them."

John 13:12-17

"As every man hath received the gift, *even so* minister the same one to another, as good stewards of the manifold grace of God."

I Peter 4:10

"As we have therefore opportunity, let us do good unto all *men*, especially unto them who are of the household of faith."

Galatians 6:10

"I have shewed you all things, how that so laboring ye ought to support the weak, and to remember the words of the Lord Jesus, how he said, It is more blessed to give than to receive."

Acts 20:35

"We should always look upon ourselves as God's servants, placed in God's world, to do his work; and accordingly labour faithfully for him; not with a design to grow rich and great, but to glorify God, and do all the good we possibly can." – David Brainerd

Church Discipline

Church discipline is the Bible-given process used by individuals and the local church body to confront and correct church members who have committed open and/or gross sin. God has clearly defined and laid out this process in His Word for us to follow. Our unspoken witness to the community around us often speaks more than our words. This is one reason why church discipline is needed. We must ensure that the church maintains a good testimony. Church discipline is also a means of edification of its members. The goal is not condemnation but rather restoration of the member with Christ and the church. Additionally, church discipline is necessary in order to maintain a pure doctrine free from the whims of false teachings.

We sin daily but we are not subject to church discipline on a daily basis. There are certain offences that warrant church discipline. The first would be unresolved conflict between church members as seen in Matthew 18:15. God's work can only move forward if we have unity and are of one mind. The persistence of spreading false doctrines (especially if they are teachers and/or leaders) is another. We see this from the Titus 3 passage and this is very important to keep under control in order to maintain a biblical stance that does not compromise. A third reason would be persistent and unrepented immoral and disorderly behavior as seen in I Corinthians 5:11. If such things are ignored by the church, it reflects badly on them, giving the enemy a foothold to blaspheme the name of Christ (II Samuel 12:14). All of these offences are things that can hinder or even destroy a church if left unaddressed.

The Bible gives four basic steps to be followed in church discipline and the order in which they are to be taken in Matthew 18:15-17. The first step is for the church members to attempt reconciliation privately and alone. If the problem is an offense against a member, the offended member should confront the offender to try to restore fellowship. Sometimes the offended is not aware of an offense made against them. In this instance, it is up to the offender to seek out the offended to ask forgiveness. (Matthew 5:23-24) If the problem is a case of gross sin committed by a member, the member witnessing the behavior and wishing to restore their fellow brother/sister should approach the sinning party in like manner. If this first attempt is unsuccessful, the one is then to take one or two more with them for a second attempt. It would be good if one of these additional persons be a deacon or the pastor. If resolution is still not accomplished, it then goes to the church. This is usually by means of the deacon board and pastor who will have a meeting with all parties involved in an effort to correct the problem. Finally, if the problem is not corrected and the sinning party refuses to repent they must be dismissed from church fellowship according to this passage as well as Titus 3:9-11. God's plan is one that cultivates restoration, either member to member, or a member to Christ.

When carrying out this process of church discipline it is vital that it be done with the right attitude. Those involved in the process should be spiritual and knowledgeable, living godly lives, and able to discern wisely. (Romans 15:14) Additionally, one must keep to the task at hand and not allow conversation to go towards discussing foolish questions and vain arguments because that will not get anything accomplished other than more strife. (II Timothy 2:23-26)

"Moreover if thy brother shall trespass against thee, go and tell him his fault between thee and him alone: if he shall hear thee, thou hast gained thy brother. But if he will not hear *thee, then* take with thee one or two more, that in the mouth of two or three witnesses every word may be established. And if he shall neglect to hear them, tell *it* unto the church: but if he neglect to hear the church, let him be unto thee as an heathen man and a publican." – Matthew 18:15-17

"But avoid foolish questions, and genealogies, and contentions, and strivings about the law; for they are unprofitable and vain. A man that is an heretick after the first and second admonition reject; Knowing that he that is such is subverted, and sinneth, being condemned of himself."
– Titus 3:9-11

"Take heed to yourselves: If thy brother trespass against thee, rebuke him; and if he repent, forgive him." – Luke 17:3

"Against an elder receive not an accusation, but before two or three witnesses. Them that sin rebuke before all, that others also may fear." – I Timothy 5:19-20

"But foolish and unlearned questions avoid, knowing that they do gender strifes. And the servant of the Lord must not strive; but be gentle unto all *men*, apt to teach, patient, In meekness instructing those that oppose themselves; if God peradventure will give them repentance to the acknowledging of the truth; And *that* they may recover themselves out of the snare of the devil, who are taken captive by him at his will." – II Timothy 2:23-26

"We must face the fact that many today are notoriously careless in their living. This attitude finds its way into the church. We have liberty, we have money, we live in comparative luxury. As a result, discipline practically has disappeared. What would a violin solo sound like if the strings on the musician's instrument were all hanging loose, not stretched tight, not "disciplined"?" – A. W. Tozer

Church Offices: Deacon

Deacons are men of high moral and biblical character that are chosen (and voted on by the congregation) to serve the pastor in any capacity they can so that the pastor can better perform his primary duties. The Bible only speaks of two offices within the church. Deacon is one of those offices, the other being the pastor.

The first deacons were appointed in Acts 6:1-5 by the church's congregation (referred to here as *disciples*). The ministry was growing to numbers that were hard for the apostles to handle on their own – widows were being neglected and people needed fed. Godly men were sought out who could tend to this business, and they became the first deacons. The deacon's purpose was to serve the apostles, their pastors. This remains the purpose of deacons today.

The qualifications for a deacon are very similar to that of a pastor but there are not quite as many. I Timothy Chapter 3 gives them in detail. The list for character traits to be found in deacons begins with saying they are to be *grave* or mature, take spiritual matters seriously, and have dignity. Deacons are to be honest (*not doubletongued*) and content with what the Lord provides them, not seeking after worldly gain (*not greedy of filthy lucre*). God's Word clearly speaks against the use of alcohol and a deacon will have no parts of it (*not given to much wine*). A deacon is not a hypocrite; he is strong in his faith and lives his life accordingly (*holding the mystery of the faith in a pure conscience*). Although they are unable to be perfect, their life is a testimony to others of their faith (*blameless*). Being a *husband of one wife* indicates that they must be male and rules out polygamy and any that have been divorced. According to Acts 6:3, deacons are also to be esteemed highly by those who know them as having great character. This verse also says that they should be *full of the Holy Ghost* and have the wisdom required to lead and discern issues and matters of the church. A deacon's family members are to be examined as well. Their children are to be under control (*ruling their children and their own houses*) and his wife must be spiritually mature as she will have great influence on her husband and his ministry (*even so must their wives*).

The duties of a deacon can vary widely, pretty much serving in any capacity the pastor assigns them. Acts 6:1-4 sums this up well. To serve tables was referring to tasks that are not directly ministry related (ie. finances, building projects, grounds and maintenance, etc.). They are to serve the members of the church by attending to their physical needs in order to allow the pastor the time and energy to attend to their spiritual needs. Often times deacons are assigned a portion of the church members to pray for and help in their times of need. They also assist with serving communion, teaching Sunday School classes, and supporting the church's visitation program.

A deacon is a servant just like any other Christian but with some added responsibility and accountability. They have been entrusted to one of two offices of the church to serve Christ, the church, and the pastor. Deacons are to help the pastor by lightening his load so that he can concentrate on the most important part of his job, prayer and preaching God's Word.

"Likewise *must* the deacons *be* grave, not doubletongued, not given to much wine, not greedy of filthy lucre; Holding the mystery of the faith in a pure conscience. And let these also first be proved; then let them use the office of a deacon, being *found* blameless. Even so *must their* wives *be* grave, not slanderers, sober, faithful in all things. Let the deacons be the husbands of one wife, ruling their children and their own houses well. For they that have used the office of a deacon well purchase to themselves a good degree, and great boldness in the faith which is in Christ Jesus."

I Timothy 3:8-13

"And in those days, when the number of the disciples was multiplied, there arose a murmuring of the Grecians against the Hebrews, because their widows were neglected in the daily ministration. Then the twelve called the multitude of the disciples *unto them*, and said, It is not reason that we should leave the word of God, and serve tables. Wherefore, brethren, look ye out among you seven men of honest report, full of the Holy Ghost and wisdom, whom we may appoint over this business. But we will give ourselves continually to prayer, and to the ministry of the word."

Acts 6:1-4

"Is any sick among you? let him call for the elders of the church; and let them pray over him, anointing him with oil in the name of the Lord:"

James 5:14

"It is the scriptural role of the deacon to be a helper to the pastor and move with all vigor to accomplish what God has told him to accomplish." – W. A. Criswell

Church Offices: Pastor

A pastor is a, "minister of the Gospel who has the charge of a church and congregation, whose duty is to watch over the people of his charge, and instruct them in the sacred doctrines of the Christian religion."[1] The pastor is referred to by several different titles in God's Word – bishop, elder, and pastor. These all refer to this same office of pastor. Mr. David Cloud explains, "The terms 'pastor,' 'elder,' and bishop' are used interchangeably in the N.T. and refer to the office of the same man. The different words are used to describe the three aspects of his office – shepherding, instructing, and leading."[5] A look at a passage in Titus 1 confirms this. It is giving the qualifications for a pastor (a parallel passage to I Timothy) and uses the title elder in verse 5 but then refers to him as a bishop in verse 7. The pastor plays many different roles in his ministry – counselor, teacher, friend, fund raiser, administrator, investigator, etc. – thus the use of different titles.

The office of pastor is a divine calling; it is not a career *choice*. Pastoring a church is an unusually difficult undertaking and can only be performed successfully with God's help and blessing. A man must be careful to be sure that he is indeed called of God to that position or else he is asking for heartache and trouble. Jeremiah 3:15 tells us that *God* will give us pastors and in II Timothy 1:11 Paul told Timothy that he was appointed to his position. We see the results of a ministry led by an uncalled man in Jeremiah 23:32b which reads, "...I sent them not, nor commanded them: therefore they shall not profit this people at all, saith the LORD." Desiring the office of a pastor is a good thing, but only if one is truly called of God to that office.

As was already mentioned in the first paragraph, a pastor serves many roles within his ministry. All these roles, however, basically fall under one of three categories: teaching, shepherding, and leading. The pastor acts as a teacher when he preaches the Scriptures to his people. He is instructing them in the doctrines of God, the proper way to live the Christian life, and edifying the saints through the spoken Word. (II Timothy 3:16) The pastor also usually serves as a Sunday School teacher where he can dig deeper into the Word of God with his class. The pastor is shepherding his flock when he counsels them, gently leading and guiding them through the obstacles of life. At times, the pastor must use the staff of the Word to pull a straying sheep back to the fold (rebuke, correction and church discipline). That leaves the leader category. Here we find administrative duties such as hiring, managing the budget, conducting staff meetings, etc. The pastor also leads his church in visions for the ministry. He leads in building projects, outreach campaigns, starting other ministries, and so on. The pastor does whatever is necessary in order to fulfill his main goal, leading souls to Christ and teaching them the commandments of God. (I Corinthians 9:22b)

The pastor is God's man, divinely appointed, and is given sole authority over the church God has placed in his care. With this authority, however, comes a higher accountability. The pastor will be held accountable for how he has led the people of his church. (Hebrews 13:17) The pastor is a servant of God who gives of himself sacrificially for the work of the Lord and the furthering of His kingdom.

"And I will give you pastors according to mine heart, which shall feed you with knowledge and understanding." – Jeremiah 3:15

"And he gave some, apostles; and some, prophets; and some, evangelists; and some, pastors and teachers; For the perfecting of the saints, for the work of the ministry, for the edifying of the body of Christ:" – Ephesians 4:11-12

"This *is* true saying, If a man desire the office of a bishop, he desireth a good work. A bishop then must be blameless, the husband of one wife, vigilant, sober, of good behaviour, given to hospitality, apt to teach; Not given to wine, no striker, not greedy of filthy lucre; but patient, not a brawler, not covetous; One that ruleth well his own house, having his children in subjection with all gravity; (For if a man know not how to rule his own house, how shall he take care of the church of God?) Not a novice, lest being lifted up with pride he fall into the condemnation of the devil. Moreover he must have a good report of them which are without; lest he fall into reproach and the snare of the devil." – I Timothy 3:1-7

"...I am made all things to all *men*, that I might by all means save some." – I Corinthians 9:22b

"Holding fast the faithful word as he hath been taught, that he may be able by sound doctrine both to exhort and to convince the gainsayers. For there are many unruly and vain talkers and deceivers, specially they of the circumcision: Whose mouths must be stopped, who subvert whole houses, teaching things which they ought not, for filthy lucre's sake." – Titus 1:9-11

"Take heed therefore unto yourselves, and to all the flock, over the which the Holy Ghost hath made you overseers, to feed the church of God, which he hath purchased with his own blood."
– Acts 20:28

"The preacher is a man, a mere human being, who, by virtue of his salvation and his calling, is a man of God. His lifework is thus invested in the ministry of the Gospel and the Word of God."
– Raymond W. Barber

Comfort

Comfort is the act of strengthening, cheering, and consoling another person in order to give them a relief from the distresses of the mind. We live in a sin cursed world and there are going to be trials, sickness, heartache, death, and the like in our lives. Being a born again believer does not render one immune from troubles. This is why comfort is necessary and something that we will all be in need of at some point in our lives. We should also be ready to be the one to offer comfort to another when it is needed.

Comfort begins with God; therefore, only the Christian can truly have real comfort. The Christian who is walking with the Lord and has an intimate relationship with Him will experience the comfort of God that no other can supply. II Corinthians 1:3 tells us that God is the *God of all comfort* and Psalm 9:9 tells us that we have a refuge in Him. Jesus is our comfort. Jesus left His home in heaven and humbled Himself to the lowly position of becoming flesh to walk on this earth for thirty some years so that He could say that He experienced anything we are struggling with. (Hebrews 4:15) Because of this, He can relate to us in our time of need and be an example of how we are to conduct ourselves in those situations. The Holy Spirit is the comforter that abides in us once we are saved. Jesus promised in John 16:7 and 14:15-26 that He would send us *another comforter* after He left the earth. The Holy Spirit is a constant reminder to the Christian that they are a child of God and that they are promised a home in heaven with the Father some day. This promise is above all the best comfort of all. No matter how bad things can get on this earth, it is only temporary and brief compared to the eternal splendor that awaits the saved soul in heaven.

This promise is also the best way we can comfort one another. I Thessalonians 4:18 instructs us to *comfort one another with these words.* We are not to be selfish with the comfort God gives to us. He comforts us so that we can in turn give comfort to our fellow man. (II Corinthians 1:3-4) When trying to comfort a friend, we should first try to lead the person to Christ if they are not yet saved. We do this for two reasons: 1-there is no better comfort than the promise of eternal salvation and a home in heaven, 2-as John 14:17 explains, those without Christ *cannot receive* the comfort of the Holy Spirit. One should always try to use God's Word as much as possible when giving comfort as well. There is nothing more sure than the Bible in life, and we can boldly claim the promises therein. The following are several verses that are very good in giving comfort to others: Deuteronomy 31:8; Psalm 9:9; Psalm 23:4; Psalm 55:22; Matthew 11:28-29; John 14:27; John 16:33; Philippians 4:7. Above all, one should just be a friend. They can be a listening ear which is often times all someone is looking for.

When a person finds himself in need of comfort the church family is the best place to go. God established the church for many reasons; one is to provide support and comfort. One way God provides us comfort is through His faithful people. One can look to their pastor, his wife, the deacons, or just another faithful servant for a listening ear and mature godly advice through their trials. Always remember, however, no matter who we do or do not have to speak to, the Christian always has God, the ultimate comforter, to go to in our times of need.

"Blessed *be* God, even the Father of our Lord Jesus Christ, the Father of mercies, and the God of all comfort; Who comforteth us in all our tribulation, that we may be able to comfort them which are in any trouble, by the comfort wherewith we ourselves are comforted of God."

II Corinthians 1:3-4

"The LORD also will be a refuge for the oppressed, a refuge in times of trouble."

Psalm 9:9

"Yea, though I walk through the valley of the shadow of death, I will fear no evil: for thou *art* with me; thy rod and they staff they comfort me."

Psalm 23:4

"These things I have spoken unto you, that in me ye might have peace. In the world ye shall have tribulation: but be of good cheer; I have overcome the world."

John 16:33

"But I would not have you to be ignorant, brethren, concerning them which are asleep, that ye sorrow not, even as others which have no hope. For if we believe that Jesus died and rose again, even so them also which sleep in Jesus will God bring with him. For this we say unto you by the word of the Lord, that we which are alive *and* remain unto the coming of the Lord shall not prevent them which are asleep. For the Lord himself shall descend from heaven with a shout, with the voice of the archangel, and with the trump of God: and the dead in Christ shall rise first: Then we which are alive *and* remain shall be caught up together with them in the clouds, to meet the Lord in the air: and so shall we ever be with the Lord. Wherefore comfort one another with these words."

I Thessalonians 4:13-18

"Thanks be to God, not only for 'rivers of endless joys above, but for 'rills of comfort here below."
– Adoniram Judson

Contentment

Contentment is a resting or satisfaction of mind without disquiet.[1] It is the acceptance of one's possessions and/or circumstances in life. Americans are some of the most fortunate people on this earth in more ways than one. We have so much and are among the richest people, yet many covet more and more things. Materialism has escalated to alarming proportions. We have some of the best medical care and living conditions, yet many whine at the smallest ache and at having a home that is not as good as so and so. We are blessed in abundance to the extent that many have become desensitized to what true value is. True value is not in things. One will only have contentment once they come to the point in their lives that they realize this and live by the commandment of God to be content.

Contentment with possessions is the first area one needs to master. The Bible is often misquoted to say that money is the root of all evil but I Timothy 6:10 actually says that the *love of money* is the root. It is not being blessed with financial wealth but rather the strong desire to have money that leads to evil. So what is the result of discontentment with one's possessions? For starters, the desire to gain more things will often lead a person to work longer hours and/or pursue jobs that are not best for a family because of the salary it pays. Perhaps the most common result of discontentment in this area is credit card debt. Credit card companies have made quite a lucrative business on our inability to live within our means. Once debt has begun to build, it can be very difficult and frustrating to dig oneself out. These things lead to disagreements between spouses on money spenditures and financial situations; in fact, financial stressors is one of the leading causes of divorce. Consider the life of Solomon; he was the richest man to ever live and had everything he could ever desire yet at the end of his life he said that it was all vanity. (Solomon 1:2) Trust the promise of I Timothy 6:6-8 and be content with the Lord's provisions.

Another area that is common for discontentment is in the area of circumstances. Circumstances could be your health, career, social status (rich vs. poor), and relationship status (single or unhappy with spouse) to name a few. One can learn a lot about being content with their circumstances by studying the life of Paul. Paul was persecuted greatly for the name of Christ yet still he was content. Paul wrote the great book of Philippians whose theme is the joy of the Christian life and expression of gratitude while in prison. Take special note to Philippians 4:11; he came to the place in his Christian walk that he learned to be content in *whatsoever state* he found himself in. If one cannot find contentment in the circumstances of their life, they will live a life of depression and defeat and will rob themselves of the joy God desires for His children.

Many people understand the commandment of God to be content, but don't know how to achieve it. The answer is simple – realize that all one needs is Jesus. Strive to gain the approval of God and not man. God is not impressed with one's possessions or circumstances, only what they are doing with their life to further His kingdom. When one not only realizes, but lives like Christ is all they need, only then will they truly be content.

"But godliness with contentment is great gain. For we brought nothing into *this* world, *and it is* certain we can carry nothing out. And having food and raiment let us be therewith content."

I Timothy 6:6-8

"*Let your* conversation *be* without covetousness; *and be* content with such things as ye have: for he hath said, I will never leave thee, nor forsake thee."

Hebrews 13:5

"Not that I speak in respect of want: for I have learned, in whatsoever state I am, *therewith* to be content."

Philippians 4:11

"Let us not be desirous of vain glory, provoking one another, envying one another."

Galatians 5:26

"But as God hath distributed to every man, as the Lord hath called every one, so let him walk. And so ordain I in all churches."

I Corinthians 7:17

"Better *is* a little with righteousness than great revenues without right."

Proverbs 16:8

"You don't have to have something to be somebody." – Bob Vallier

Counseling

Counseling is giving advice, an opinion, or instruction, given upon request or otherwise, for directing the judgment or conduct of another.[1] It is essential that this counsel be Biblical. God gave us His Word to be a help and instruction in our lives. (II Timothy 3:16-17) There is no better advice we can get than the ways of God.

There are many reasons to seek counsel. Counsel should always be sought before making any life changing decisions. Some examples of such decisions would include: choosing a college, getting married, purchasing a home, and making a career change. Proverbs 15:22 tells us that *without counsel purposes are disappointed*. The Hebrew word for purposes has the idea of plans, thoughts, and intentions. So God is telling us that our best thought out plans and intentions, without first seeking counsel, will often be a disappointment. Earlier in Proverbs 11:14, God tells us that those who have not received counsel will fall. One should not sabotage themselves, but seek godly counsel in those major decisions and trying times of their lives.

Counsel will only benefit a person, however, if it comes from the right person. Our ultimate counselor is God, but there are often times when we need a person in the flesh to help mediate that counsel to us. Only a Christian counselor is going to be able to do that; so when seeking a counselor, the Christian should seek a Christian counselor not a secular one. As I stated at the onset, all counsel must be based on the Bible and God's perfect plan; a secular counselor's advice will be a result of the thoughts of sinful man. Psalm 1:1-2 exhorts us to not walk *in the counsel of the ungodly,* but to delight in *the law of the LORD.* Besides professional counselors, there are many people within one's church that are able, and most often times willing and pleased, to give them counsel. The first and most logical person to consult is one's pastor; God has placed him over the church for just such purposes. The deacons of the church are also a good place to turn. Never underestimate the value of every other lay person in the church. There is a very large assembly of believers within one's church that have fought the fight and have many years of experience that has increased their wisdom in certain matters. Only make sure that those chosen to seek counsel from are mature, godly Christians; one does not want to seek advice from those peers that are at or below their maturity level in their Christian walk. Don't be foolish as Rehoboam was in I Kings 12:6-20 whose kingdom was divided because he failed to take the advice of the *old men,* but instead hearkened to the counsel of the *young men.* Take advantage of the support group God has created within His institution of the church.

One's church has the *multitude of counselors* the Bible speaks of in Proverbs 11:14 and 15:22; if one seeks them, they will save themselves from falling and disappointment. Whether it is making an important decision or working through a trial of life, it is important to get advice and counsel from several people in order to get a larger perspective and picture of the situation. II Corinthians 1:2-4 tells us that God helps us so that we can reciprocate that and help others. One should take advantage of the help made available to them and be sure to give help to others when the opportunity presents itself.

"Counsel in the heart of man *is like* deep water; but a man of understanding will draw it out."

Proverbs 20:5

"Where no counsel *is*, the people fall: but in the multitude of counselors *there is* safety."

Proverbs 11:14

"Without counsel purposes are disappointed: but in the multitude of counselors they are established."

Proverbs 15:22

"Blessed *be* God, even the Father of our Lord Jesus Christ, the Father of mercies, and the God of all comfort; Who comforteth us in all our tribulation, that we may be able to comfort them which are in any trouble, by the comfort wherewith we ourselves are comforted of God."

II Corinthians 1:3-4

"All scripture *is* given by inspiration of God, and *is* profitable for doctrine, for reproof, for correction, for instruction in righteousness: That the man of God may be perfect, throughly furnished unto all good works."

II Timothy 3:16-17

"A ruler who does not have a wise counselor to guide him in his decisions is like a ship at sea with no one at the helm." – John Phillips

Creation

Creation is the act of causing to exist, and especially, the act of bringing this world into existence.[1] Creation consists of two things: the Creator and His creation. Through the years, people have attempted to discredit creation because they want to discredit the Creator. Accepting the creation account as recorded for us in the Bible means that one must acknowledge God the Creator and therefore submit to His authority found in the rest of the Bible. As has always been the cycle, there are an increasing number of people who do not want that authority over their lives. If the beginnings of the Bible are refuted/discredited, it destroys everything that follows and the entire foundation of Christianity.

God records the creation account in the first chapter of the Bible. Genesis, meaning origin, is the book of beginnings. Not only did God create the universe, but He did it in six literal days. The morning and evening phrase seen in Genesis 1:5 was used by God at the end of each day of creation to clearly communicate the fact of a literal day. Furthermore, the week and Sabbath day kept by the Israelites was compared to the week of creation in Exodus 20:8-11, "Remember the Sabbath day, to keep it holy. Six days shalt thou labour, and do all thy work: But the seventh day *is* the sabbath of the LORD thy God: ...For *in* six days the LORD made heaven and earth, the sea, and all that in them *is*, and rested the seventh day: wherefore the LORD blessed the sabbath day, and hallowed it." This clearly disproves that the use of the word 'day' in Genesis could be a period of time like is used in 2 Peter 3:8. If that were true, the Israelites would have been expected to work for 6,000 years or more before having a 1,000 year rest. The Bible must always be kept in context. There is no language (i.e. as, as if, like, like unto, even so, etc.) in Genesis to suggest that we should not take God's words here literally.

Besides the Biblical proof, science proves what God has already told us about creation. The supporting laws of science are too numerous to give an exhaustive list here, but one example is the laws of thermodynamics. The laws of thermodynamics state: 1) no matter or energy is being created or destroyed and 2) all existing matter and energy is in an irreversible path of cessation. In other words, everything is either in a state of conservation or decay but the theories of evolution are the complete opposite. Another supportive law of science is the law of causality stating that no effect can be greater than its cause. Science has proved over and over through the history of time that things do not become organized and complex from something that is unorganized and simple. So why then can someone sensibly support that our very complex and intricate world was the result of a chaotic explosion of simple matter? The accepted laws of science validate creation.

Creation places its foundation on an eternal God versus eternal matter. The first sentence of God's Word states simply, "In the beginning God created..." God does not attempt to explain how, when, or where He began because there is no beginning. Isaiah 40:28 and Revelation 1:8 speak of this eternal characteristic of God. There is a measure of faith required here, but for the Christian who believes the Bible is God's Word this is simple and natural. Which would you rather put your faith in: an eternal God or eternal matter?

"In the beginning God created the heaven and the earth."

Genesis 1:1

"In the beginning was the Word, and the Word was with God, and the Word was God. The same was in the beginning with God. All things were made by him; and without him was not any thing made that was made."

John 1:1-3

"The heavens *are* thine, the earth also *is* thine: *as for* the world and the fulness therof, thou hast founded them. The north and the south thou hast created them:"

Psalm 89:11-12a

"For by him were all things created, that are in heaven, and that are in earth, visible and invisible, whether *they be* thrones, or dominions, or principalities, or powers: all things were created by him, and for him: And he is before all things, and by him all things consist."

Colossians 1:16-17

"And God called the light Day, and the darkness he called Night. And the evening and the morning were the first day."

Genesis 1:5

"No other cosmogony, whether in ancient paganism or modern naturalism, even mentions the absolute origin of the universe. All begin with the space/time/matter universe, already existing in a primeval state of chaos, then attempt to speculate how it might have 'evolved' into its present form. ...But, very significantly, the concept of the special creation of the universe of space and time itself is found nowhere in all religion or philosophy, ancient or modern, except here in Genesis 1:1." – Henry Morris

Cremation

Cremation is a funeral rite choice in which the dead body is burned by fire and reduced to ashes. We must remember that as Christians, our bodies are not our own; our bodies are the temple of the Holy Ghost and belong to God. (I Corinthians 9:16) The burning of human bodies in the Bible is always seen in a negative light (i.e. human sacrifices of heathen and idolatrous religions or to show contempt and disgrace), whereas burial is seen as a sacred and honorable event. We strive to live lives pleasing to God while we are alive and should want to please God in this final decision as well.

The burning of human bodies, dead or alive, is never portrayed in a positive light anywhere in the Scriptures. Cremation is actually punished by God as seen in Amos 2:1, after Moab cremated King Edom's body. Bodies were burned by godly people in the Bible only to show contempt. (II Samuel 23:7) Cremation's origin is that of heathen religions and practices. Religions like Hinduism and Buddhism cremate out of their belief in reincarnation and often times as a belief that doing so releases the soul from the body. Any way you look at it, cremation is not an honorable choice.

Burial, on the other hand, was the ordinary and honorable way to treat the dead all throughout the Bible. God's chosen people, the Jews, had very particular procedures that they followed for treating the dead. Christ Himself buried Moses in Deuteronomy 34:5-6 and Jesus' followers afforded Him the same decency after His cruel crucifixion in John 19:38-42. As Christ is our example in all things, one should follow His example in how to treat the body at death. Furthermore, receiving a proper burial was held in such a high regard that not getting one was considered a disgrace. This is demonstrated in Ecclesiastes 6:3 which says that it would have been better to have never lived or died at birth than to not have had a proper burial. You see this again in II Kings 9:10 where Jezebel was deprived of a proper burial as punishment for part in Naboth's murder. Burial was clearly the godly choice exhibited in the Bible.

So many things in the Bible either looked forward to Christ's first coming or look forward to His second coming. The act of burying is one such thing – one that looks forward to His second coming. The physical body is the seed that is buried in order that it will one day bring forth new life when those who are saved will be resurrected from the grave with new bodies. Paul speaks of this physical seed that brings forth a spiritual body in I Cor. 15:38, 42-44, 49, "But God giveth it a body as it hath pleased him, and to every seed his own body. ...So also *is* the resurrection of the dead. It is sown in corruption; it is raised in incorruption; It is sown in dishonour; it is raised in glory: it is sown in weakness; it is raised in power: It is sown a natural body; it is raised a spiritual body. There is a natural body, and there is a spiritual body. ...And as we have borne the image of the earthy, we shall also bear the image of the heavenly." This is not to say that burial is a requirement for a resurrected body at the Lord's second coming, however. God can make a glorified body for the one who does cremate or dies a death that destroys their physical bodies, but our goal should always be to follow God's plan and design whenever possible. Leave this earth in a manner that looks forward to His coming.

"And Joshua said, Why hast though troubled us? the LORD shall trouble thee this day. And all Israel stoned him with stones, and burned them with fire, after they had stoned them with stones."

Joshua 7:25

"Thus saith the LORD, *For* three transgressions of Moab, and for four, I will not turn away *the punishment* therof; because he burned the bones of the king of Edom into lime:"

Amos 2:1

"If a man beget an hundred *children*, and live many years, so that the days of his years be many, and his soul be not filled with good, and also *that* he have no burial; I say, *that* and untimely birth *is* better than he."

Ecclesiastes 6:3

"Then took they the body of Jesus, and wound it in linen clothes with the spices, as the manner of the Jews is to bury."

John 19:40

"For I delivered unto you first of all that which I also received, how that Christ died for our sins according to the scriptures; And that he was buried, and that he rose again the third day according to the scriptures:"

I Corinthians 15:3-4

"There is nothing Christian about cremation." – David W. Cloud

Cults/False Prophets

A cult is a religious group, often characterized by extreme devotion to its leader and his/her teachings, whose faith and practices seriously deviate from the Bible. A false prophet is anyone who teaches something contrary to the Word of God, thus why the two are a closely interchangeable. Some commonly known cults include: Jehovah's Witness, Christian Science, Scientology, Islam, Mormonism, Buddhism, Gnosticism, and Spiritism. A very common organization that is not always viewed as a cult because it is not an organized religious group, but is very cultish in the way it conducts itself is Freemasonry. The Freemasons are a secret, fraternal society that creates a unity of its members in that they are loyal to fellow masons above those who are not. Several things easily identify them as a cult. First is the secrecy involved in many aspects of their organization (initiation ceremonies, secret handshakes, symbols, passwords, and signs). Secrecy is a form of deceit and Paul very clearly renounces this conduct in II Corinthians 4:2. Secondly, they swear blood oaths that are taken very seriously, but God fulfilled the last blood covenant or oath on the cross. Third, their prayers are said to a generic god because there are fellow craft members of varied religions; multiple gods, books, and ways to heaven must be accepted. A true Christian, however, knows that there is only one God, one Bible, and one way to heaven. No Christian should be involved in such an organization as the Masons or any other cult.

A look at their origin reveals the truth that every cult is heresy and the works of man. Christianity traces its origins and doctrines back to the first century and Jesus Christ Himself. Cults, on the other hand, can be traced back to a person(s) who deviated and misinterpreted the Bible. For example: Jehovah's Witness = Charles T. Russell and J. F. Rutherford, Christian Science = Mary Baker Eddy, Scientology = L. Ron Hubbard, Islam = Muhammad, and Mormonism = Joseph Smith and Brigham Young. These people have deviated so much in so many areas, major areas, yet they still claim to be Christian which is simply false. God tells us in His Word that we are to follow Him rather than man (Psalm 118:8), so why put any trust in the religions of men?

How do so many get deceived into believing the lies of cults? They begin by communicating love and acceptance to appeal to people's natural emotional needs. Language is confused by using common terminology found in Christianity but not revealing that those terms imply completely different meanings up front. They are careful to avoid direct usage of terminology that would elicit a response of rejection. Once a person starts to accept their twisted teachings, the process of psychological reconditioning begins in order to train its members to believe and respond a particular way. It is not long before the love they first saw is turned into antagonism and intolerance for other beliefs. God warns us as early as Genesis 3:1 of the subtilness of Satan; he is the king of deceit. God also gives strong warnings in His Word about false prophets and how we are to handle them. They will come in abundance and one must be in His Word in order to recognize them and *mark them*. (Romans 16:17) God commands us to *avoid them* lest we be accused of being *partaker of his evil deeds*. (Romans 16:17, II John 1:11)

"Beloved, believe not every spirit, but try the spirits whether they are of God: because many false prophets are gone out into the world."

I John 4:1

"But there were false prophets also among the people, even as there shall be false teachers among you, who privily shall bring in damnable heresies, even denying the Lord that bought them, and bring upon themselves swift destruction:"

II Peter 2:1

"Beware of false prophets, which come to you in sheep's clothing, but inwardly they are ravening wolves."

Matthew 7:15

"Now I beseech you, brethren, mark them which cause divisions and offences contrary to the doctrine which ye have learned; and avoid them."

Romans 16:17

"For many deceivers are entered into the world, who confess not that Jesus Christ is come in the flesh. This is a deceiver and an antichrist. Look to yourselves, that we lose not those things which we have wrought, but that we receive a full reward. Whosoever transgresseth, and abideth not in the doctrine of Christ, hath not God. He that abideth in the doctrine of Christ, he hath both the Father and the Son. If there come any unto you, and bring not this doctrine, receive him not into *your* house, neither bid him God speed: for he that biddeth him God speed is partaker of his evil deeds."

II John 1:7-11

"...false teaching damns many souls and causes strife and division and unrest among God's people..." – John R. Rice

Daily Walk

One's daily walk is the things one does each day that help to bring them into a closer companionship and communion with Jesus Christ consisting primarily of daily prayer and devotions. There are so many things in our lives that we refuse to go without, such as sleep, eating, and personal hygiene. What about God? Is He a daily part of your life?

Jesus Christ is our example in all things and in His earthly ministry, the area of prayer was not neglected. Jesus prayed often and gave the model prayer in Matthew 6:9-13 which asks for *our daily bread*, implying going daily to the Lord in prayer. He also told us in I Thessalonians 5:17 to *pray without ceasing*; this implies praying not only daily, but many times throughout the day. Prayer is how we communicate with God, our personal line that is never busy. One will never see the Lord's blessings and working in their life until they have talked with Him in prayer. One's day is doomed for trouble if they do not start their day by inviting Him into it and yielding their daily activities to His will and leading. The topic of prayer will be covered in greater detail later in the book.

Christ was also our example in making the Scriptures a priority in His daily walk. Just as He taught daily in the temple (Luke 19:47a), one needs to be in His Word studying it daily. Psalm 119:105 tells us, "Thy word *is* a lamp unto my feet, and a light unto my path." A person must make daily personal devotions a priority in their life if they want God's guidance in life. Don't try to walk in the dark. Note that I said 'personal' devotions. Family devotions and group Bible studies are edifying, however, they cannot replace a personal time alone with God. There is no prescribed way to go about one's daily personal devotions, but there are some things that may be of help. First, be sure to begin daily devotions in prayer. It does not have to be a lengthy prayer, just a prayer to ask God for direction and understanding. Seek God as the Psalmist did in Psalm 119:18 when he said, "Open thou mine eyes, that I may behold wondrous things out of thy law." Secondly, although it is not necessary, it is best to do one's personal devotions in the morning, to begin their day with the Lord. (Proverbs 8:17) What's most important, however, is that a time is set aside that one does not have to be rushed, a time that can be used to meditate on His Word rather than just reading through Scripture for the sake of checking off a to-do list. (Joshua 1:8) Thirdly, read the Scriptures slowly. Don't worry about making lots of ground by way of number of verses. It is so much better to read only a couple or even one verse and completely digest and internalize what the Lord is speaking to the reader through it than to read 20 verses and come away unchanged. Lastly, consider using a journal. This will provide a place to keep track of what has been studied as well as to write down observations and insights that have been discovered and the application in applying it to one's own life. The Bible is a gold mine, but just like with the precious stones, one has to mine and dig to find the gold.

We always expect God to be there for us when we *need* Him, yet so many do not invest the time into a daily walk with Him that will cultivate a personal relationship with Him. What if God took a day off? One should strive to let it be said of them as it was of Enoch – that they *walked with God.* (Genesis 5:24)

"And he said to *them* all, If any *man* will come after me, let him deny himself, and take up his cross daily, and follow me."

Luke 9:23

"Give us this day our daily bread."

Matthew 6:11

"Now when Daniel knew that the writing was signed, he went into his house; and his windows being open in his chamber toward Jerusalem, he kneeled upon his knees three times a day, and prayed, and gave thanks before his God, as he did aforetime."

Daniel 6:10

"This book of the law shall not depart out of thy mouth; but thou shalt meditate therein day and night, that thou mayest observe to do according to all that is written therein: for them thou shalt make thy way prosperous, and then thou shalt have good success."

Joshua 1:8

"These were more noble than those in Thessalonica, in that they received the word with all readiness of mind, and searched the scriptures daily, whether those things were so."

Acts 17:11

"And daily in the temple, and in every house, they ceased not to teach and preach Jesus Christ."

Acts 5:42

"Watch the morning watch. Do not see the face of man until you have seen the face of God. Before you enter on the day with its temptations, look up into His face and hide His Word in your heart." – F. B. Meyer

Dance

Dance, as is often thought of today, is a form of worldly entertainment in which men and women move rhythmically to music, most often making close physical contact with one another. This behavior is most often practiced in nightclubs, school dances, and weddings. It is an activity that blurs the lines of proper Christian conduct and often leads to immorality.

The popular argument is, 'There's nothing wrong with dancing because it is in the Bible.' The problem is, however, the dancing spoke of in the Bible is not the same kind of dancing that people are participating in today. Examples of biblical or spiritual dancing are seen in references such as Exodus 15:20, Judges 21:21, Psalm 149:3, and II Samuel 6:13-14. In all of these passages, dancing could be defined as jumping for joy in celebration; it was an expression of worship to the Lord. Biblical dance was done primarily by women and never by couples. It was done before the Lord in praise and worship, never as a social entertainment. Most importantly, the dances were not characterized by sexual or sensual body movements but rather a jumping, marching, or moving in a circle while holding hands. The one exception is found in Matthew 14:1-11 when Herodias' daughter, Salome, danced before Herod. Salome, however, was a wicked woman who when Herod was pleased with her dancing and offered her anything she wanted, followed her mother's instruction and asked for John the Baptist's head on a platter which was so given. Although she danced alone, her dance was immoral, being for man's pleasure and not the same as those godly examples given above. Biblical dance is not seen in the New Testament or practiced today. David Cloud explains, "The reason no dancing is mentioned in the N.T. is probably because this is the period of Christ's rejection and exile. The Bridegroom is away in a far country. Contrast this with Rev. 19:7, the marriage of the Lamb. Then will come the time to 'be glad and rejoice,' and the joyful dancing referred to in Psalm 149 and 150 and Jeremiah 31 will begin."[6]

It is easy to see the sinfulness in modern dance. The terms 'revellings' and 'rioting' are better understood as wanton dancing or lewd and lustful dancing. God strictly forbids such behavior and even lumps it together with murder. (I Peter 4:3, Romans 13:13, Galatians 5:21) Also take note in these three verses that this 'dancing' is mentioned in conjunction with drunkenness which is also against God's Word (see alcohol). Modern dance is rooted in sexuality, and the physical contact made during such dancing is unbiblical, being reserved only for those bound in matrimony. Consider the atmosphere of most modern dance, in darkened rooms and often in nightclubs where sin abounds. A Christian is to be a child of light; Satan is the god of darkness. Perhaps the most evident reason is the ungodly music that is associated with modern dance (music is covered later in the book). Can one possibly need any more reasons to abstain from modern worldly dancing?

If one is going to obey the command given in I Thessalonians 5:22, they will not participate in dancing. Modern dance is the entertainment of the world, a world that we are not to love. (I John 2:15) We must live a Christian life of gravity and sobriety that will be worthy of reverence, respect and honor. (Titus 2:7)

"Let us walk honestly, as in the day; not in rioting and drunkenness, not in chambering and wantonness, not in strife and envying."

Romans 13:13

"Envyings, murders, drunkenness, revellings, and such like: of the which I tell you before, as I have also told *you* in time past, that they which do such things shall not inherit the kingdom of God."

Galatians 5:21

"In all things shewing thyself a pattern of good works: in doctrine *shewing* uncorruptness, gravity, sincerity,"

I Thessalonians 2:7

"Abstain from all appearance of evil."

I Thessalonians 5:22

"Love not the world, neither the things *that are* in the world. If any man love the world, the love of the Father is not in him."

I John 2:15

"Dancing is based on sex and awakens sex passions; dancing is opposed to Scripture teaching; dancing is inconsistent with the Christian life." – H. F. Gilbert

Dating

Dating is a relationship that is formed before marriage between a man and a woman for the purpose of finding the right spouse. Although the Bible does not specifically talk about dating, it does give clearly understood principles that, as in every area of life, should be applied and followed throughout the dating relationship. The purpose of dating, however, is often misunderstood. Contrary to contemporary belief, dating is not a social recreation purely for one's pleasure. God said in Genesis 2:18 that, "...*It is* not good that the man should be alone; I will make him an help meet for him." Thus the dating relationship is for the purpose of finding a life-long mate, the one that completes the other. If one is not ready to be married, one should not be dating (which is one of several reasons why teenagers should not be dating). Dating is a time for the couple to get to know one another on a deeper level than the casual acquaintance or even friend. During this time they share their likes and dislikes, dreams and goals, and most importantly their faith.

This area of faith is the most important area of discussion between a couple. II Corinthians 6:14 is one of several verses that tells us believers should not enter into a close relationship with an unbeliever. There is more involved in the concept of not being unequally yoked than just salvation, however. God puts much importance on doctrine in His word. (Proverbs 4:2; Isaiah 28:9, 29:24; Mark 4:2; John 7:17; Acts 2:42; Romans 16:17; Ephesians 4:14; I Timothy 4:13 &16, 6:3; II Timothy 3:16, 4:2; Titus 2:1; II John 1:9-10) Sure, even the closest couples are bound to disagree on something, but a strong couple will agree on the major, foundational doctrines. Each other's spiritual maturity should also be considered. One that is on fire for the Lord and serving fervently must use caution in getting seriously involved with someone that is very immature in their spirituality. If one is serving the Lord with their whole life and the other is a 'Sunday morning Christian' conflict is bound to arise. It is absolutely vital that the couple are on the same page in regards to their faith, or heartache is sure to follow.

Another area that is often a trap for sin is the area of physical displays of affection. Specific guidelines have to be decided on by the couple (and parents when still living at home) that will ensure that things do not go too far. Sexual desires are instinctual and remarkably strong, stronger perhaps than any other instinct other than self-preservation. They are so strong that they can easily overpower even the most devout Christian into acting against his predetermined will to stay pure. Physical displays of affection arouse these sexual desires, desires that were designed by God to lead to sexual relations, relations that are primarily intended for the purpose of procreation and are to be enjoyed *only* in the confines of marriage. (I Corinthians 7:1-2) Setting strict physical boundaries for the dating relationship will help the couple remain pure until marriage.

Second to one's salvation, deciding who one will marry is one of life's biggest decisions. Although the length of the dating relationship can vary greatly from one couple to the next, it is equally important in every couple's journey to finding the spouse God would have them marry. Seek God's face in prayer and allow Him to lead through this very important decision.

"And the LORD God said, *It is* not good that the man should be alone; I will make him an help meet for him."

Genesis 2:18

"Be ye not unequally yoked together with unbelievers: for what fellowship hath righteousness with unrighteousness? and what communion hath light with darkness?"

II Corinthians 6:14

"Now concerning the things whereof ye wrote unto me: *It is* good for a man not to touch a woman. Nevertheless, *to avoid* fornication, let every man have his own wife, and let every woman have her own husband."

I Corinthians 7:1-2

"In all thy ways acknowledge him, and he shall direct thy paths."

Proverbs 3:6

"It is very important that we choose carefully the people with whom we develop close emotional relationships. This practice will prepare us for choosing the right spouse."
– Don Woodard

Demons

Demons make up the third of the angels that fell along with Satan in his rebellion against God. (Revelation 12:3, 4, 9) The Bible does not refer to them as 'demons,' however, it uses the term 'devil(s)' and 'unclean spirit(s).' They are also referred to as Satan's angels, being under his rule and control. (Matthew 12:24) Although they are followers of Satan, demons know that God is real and recognize and admit to God's power and authority over even them and Satan. (Matthew 8:29-31; Mark 1:23-24, 3:11, 5:7; Luke 8:28; Acts 19:15, James 2:19)

The Bible has much to say about demons and their heinous work. Demons are very clever and intelligent spirit beings that have no bodies. (Mark 5:8-12) In this passage, they knew that they needed a physical body to occupy and bargained with Jesus to let them enter the swine. This is the trait that most people tend to associate with demons – possession. Demons wreaked havoc on the bodies of those they possessed. They made their victims dumb (Matthew 9:32-33, 12:22), blind (Matthew 12:22), suicidal (Mark 9:22), insane (Luke 8:26-36), supernaturally strong (Luke 8:29), and physically deformed (Luke 13:11-17). Jesus and His disciples cast them out of many suffering people. (Matthew 8:16; Mark 5:1-20; Luke 10:17; Acts 5:16, 8:7, 16:16-18, 19:12) Demons did their best to destroy people's lives.

Demons still exist today, but their work differs somewhat from that which we see recorded in the Bible. Zechariah 13:1 speaks of a day when a fountain will be opened up, which was fulfilled when Jesus died on the cross. Zechariah continues in verse 2 to say that in that day (a time after Jesus died for our sins) these demons (*unclean spirit*) will be no more. So the next question is, 'When exactly after Jesus died did demon possession cease?' The same time all other miraculous gifts ceased, when *that which is perfect has come* – the complete Word of God. (I Corinthians 13:8-10) Casting out demons was one of these gifts. God allowed for demon possession for a time in order to show forth His power when they were cast out.[7] God has ceased to allow this action by demons, but has not bound Satan and his demons entirely as a look around our world reveals. But Satan is not omnipresent as God is and needs his demons to roam about helping in his *spiritual wickedness in high places*. (Ephesians 6:12)

Rest assured, however, that the judgment and fate of Satan and his demons will come and they are fully aware of it. God has prepared a place of *everlasting fire* for them. (Matthew 25:41) Just before Jesus was about to cast some demons out of two people, the demons ask Jesus why He is tormenting them *before the time*, the time of judgment that they know is yet to come. (Matthew 8:29) The powers of evil may be very real and strong but they are still under subjection to the power of our Lord.

Satan has deceived many into the worship of evil. God has strictly forbidden the worship and even fellowship with spirits of evil. Idol worship and dark magic such as astrology and witchcraft are all forms of demon worship, and all are strictly forbidden by God. (Leviticus 17:7; I Corinthians 10:20; Deuteronomy 18:9-12; II Chronicles 33:6) A true Christian will stay as far away from Satan's dark world as possible!

"And there appeared another wonder in heaven; and behold a great red dragon, having seven heads and ten horns, and seven crowns upon his heads. And his tail drew the third part of the starts of heaven, and did cast them to the earth: ...And the great dragon was cast out, that old serpent, called the Devil, and Satan, which deceiveth the whole world: he was cast out into the earth, and his angels were cast out with him."

Revelation 12:3,4,9

"Thou believest that there is one God; thou doest well: the devils also believe, and tremble."

James 2:19

"Then shall he say also unto them on the left hand, Depart from me, ye cursed, into everlasting fire, prepared for the devil and his angels:"

Matthew 25:41

"And they shall no more offer their sacrifices unto devils, after whom they have gone a whoring. This shall be a statute for ever unto them throughout their generations."

Leviticus 17:7

"But I *say*, that the things which the Gentiles sacrifice, they sacrifice to devils, and not to God: and I would not that ye should have fellowship with devils."

I Corinthians 10:20

"The 'Demons' belong to the 'Powers of Darkness.' They are not few in number, but are a great 'Martialed Host,' veterans in the service of Satan. Their central camp or abode is the "Bottomless Pit' from which they 'sally forth' at the command of their leader."
– Clarence Larkin

Depression

Depression is a sinking of the spirits or state of sadness that is want of courage and animation.[1] The Bible does not use the word depression but rather uses language including: downcast, sad, forlorn, discouraged, downhearted, mourning, troubled, miserable, despairing, and brokenhearted. Worldly philosophy views it as a disease or psychological disorder that often times requires medication and lengthy counseling sessions. Although there are times when a legitimate underlying medical condition is present that does cause depression, more often than not it is a result of one's sin or circumstances in life.

One's behavior will determine one's feelings. We see this demonstrated in the Bible as early as Genesis chapter four after God rejects Cain's sacrifice. God tells Cain that if he does right, he will be accepted and therefore feel good, his countenance will not fall. (Genesis 4:6-7) There are several biblical examples of those who suffered with depression. Besides Cain, there was David. The guilt he had over his sin of adultery with Bathsheba and the murder of her husband Uriah led him to a place of despair, saying *day and night thy* [God's] *hand was heavy upon me*. (Psalm 32:4) Then there is Naomi, who became so depressed that she changed her name to Mara to match the bitterness she felt in her heart. Naomi's plight was a result of her and her husband's compromise to enter into a heathen country when times got tough. There are times, however, when depression is simply a result of life's trials, as was the case with Job. He was probably dealt the worst hand any human has ever been dealt, and understandably had some periods of depression, so much so that he cursed the day he was conceived. (Job 3:3) Before one can make any progress out of a state of depression, they must ask, 'Is sin involved in my depression?'

So what does one do when feeling depressed? First and foremost, seek the Lord. If sin is the source of depression, confess it to the Lord and ask for forgiveness – He will give it. Confession of sin brings relief and happiness. Psalm 32 and 51 are confessions of David to the Lord after his sin with Bathsheba. Verse 5 of Psalm 32 shows how David first acknowledged his sin, then confessed it to the Lord, and finally received forgiveness. He ends the Psalm telling us to *be glad in the LORD, and rejoice*. He had cured his depression by seeking the Lord and confessing his sin. If depression is a result of life's trials, seek comfort in God's Word realizing that Jesus experienced many undeserved trials during His earthly ministry and that He understands how we feel. Claim and accept Romans 8:28, God is in control and has a master plan that our short term vision cannot always understand. If unable to get clarity of mind and spirit after much sincere prayer and study of God's Word, one should seek godly counsel. See the counseling topic earlier in the book for more detail on counseling.

When trying to explain and help a person with depression, the world focuses on the end result instead of the root; the world tries to pass blame rather than accept responsibility. The Christian will realize that more often than not depression is a result of sin. And regardless of whether sin is the root or not, God is the ultimate comforter, and we can have an intimate relationship with Him through study of His Word and regular time in prayer.

"Why are though cast down, O my soul? and why art thou disquieted within me? hope in God: for I shall yet praise him, *who is* the health of my countenance, and my God."

Psalm 43:5

"Casting all your care upon him; for he careth for you."

I Peter 5:7

"For his anger *endureth but* a moment; in his favour *is* life: weeping may endure for a night, but joy *cometh* in the morning."

Psalm 30:5

"And the LORD said unto Cain, Why art thou wroth? and why is thy countenance fallen? If thou doest well, shalt thou not be accepted: and if thou doest not well, sin lieth at the door. And unto thee *shall be* his desire, and thou shalt rule over him."

Genesis 4:6-7

"Now we exhort you, brethren, warn them that are unruly, comfort the feebleminded, support the weak, be patient toward all *men*."

I Thessalonians 5:14

"I find myself frequently depressed - perhaps more so than any other person here. And I find no better cure for that depression than to trust in the Lord with all my heart, and seek to realize afresh the power of the peace-speaking blood of Jesus, and His infinite love in dying upon the cross to put away all my transgressions." – Charles Spurgeon

Discipleship and Mentoring

A disciple is one who receives instruction from another, an adherent to the doctrines and precepts of another. To disciple someone means to teach, train, or convert others to particular doctrines and/or principles.[1] Discipleship is something one needs to give to a baby Christian whether they ask for it or not. It centers a lot on teaching doctrine and the fundamentals of the faith. Mentoring comes after discipleship. It is when a wiser, more experienced person counsels and guides a less experienced, often younger, person to help them get to the next level in any area of life – most often in a career or one's spiritual walk. Mentorship can only be successful when there is a mutual agreement by both parties in the process. Both discipleship and mentorship require an investment of time.

Discipleship and mentorship is not an idea made up by man; it is a command of God. It is seen even in the Great Commission. In Matthew 28:20, we are told to be *teaching them to observe all things whatsoever I have commanded you*. I Peter 5:1-5 is rich in these concepts. It exhorts the elders of the church to take the lead of the church in a graceful manner (*not by constraint*) in order to bring up the next generation while also exhorting the young to take heed to how the older are trying to guide them. The Bible also showcases several examples of this process taking place. We see it in Paul and Timothy (I & II Timothy), Elijah and Elisha (II Kings 2), and the ultimate example seen in Christ and His disciples. This is not reserved for just men, however. The older women are exhorted in Titus 2:3-5 to be disciples and mentors to the younger women. God's plan is for discipleship and mentorship to be a continuous cycle: one teaches the next in order that they can in turn teach the same thing to those who will follow behind them. (II Timothy 2:2)

The older, more seasoned followers should always be seeking out those whom they can mentor along life's journey. A mentor has to find someone, however, who is willing to allow them to invest in their lives. On the other hand, a mentee looking for a mentor must find someone that is willing to invest in them. The mentee must be selective in the one they choose, they want to find one that will sharpen their countenance, not dull it. (Proverbs 27:17) There is danger in looking to one's peers for this kind of guidance. More often than not, one's peers are not going to be wiser, more experienced, or more mature in their Christian walk. The mentee must also be careful to find someone who will lead them in the right paths. Luke 6:40 says, "The disciple is not above his master: but every one that is perfect shall be as his master." This verse is used in a negative light here, a blind spiritual leader leading someone into the same pit he is in (just as apostate college professors often do). The truth still remains that the mentee will become like or at least believe the same as the mentor; finding a good mentor that is doctrinally sound is important.

We must all have the heart and yearning that the Psalmist of Psalm 71:18 had, one that pleads with God to not take us home until we can share those things that we have learned of Him with the next generation. It should be our desire to invest in the next generation. They are the future of the church. Their success is our success!

"The elders which are among you I exhort, who am also an elder, and a witness of the sufferings of Christ, and also a partaker of the glory that shall be revealed: Feed the flock of God which is among you, taking the oversight *thereof*, not by constraint, but willingly; not for filthy lucre, but of a ready mind; Neither as being lords over *God's* heritage, but being ensamples to the flock. And when the chief Shepherd shall appear, ye shall receive a crown of glory that fadeth not away. Likewise, ye younger, submit yourselves unto the elder. Yea, all *of you* be subject one to another, and be clothed with humility: for God resisteth the proud, and giveth grace to the humble."

I Peter 5:1-5

"The aged women likewise, that *they be* in behaviour as becometh holiness, not false accusers, not given to much wine, teachers of good things; That they may teach the young women to be sober, to love their husbands, to love their children, *To be* discreet, chaste, keepers at home, good, obedient to their own husbands, that the word of God be not blasphemed."

Titus 2:3-5

"And the things that thou hast heard of me among many witnesses, the same commit thou to faithful men, who shall be able to teach others also."

II Timothy 2:2

"Iron sharpeneth iron; so a man sharpeneth the countenance of his friend."

Proverbs 27:17

"Now also when I am old and grayheaded, O God, forsake me not; until I have shewed thy strength unto *this* generation, *and* thy power to every one *that* is to come."

Psalm 71:18

"Everyone should have a Paul and everyone should have a Timothy." – Clarence Sexton

Disciplining Children

To discipline is to correct, to chastise, to punish.[1] The training and discipline of children is the responsibility of parents. Consider Eli and his two sons in I Samuel 3:12-14. Verse 13 says that Eli and his entire house was judged because *his sons made themselves vile, and he restrained them not*. Eli was being held accountable for his lack of discipline towards his sons. God uses parents as tools to punish sin.

The plan of salvation begins by helping one acknowledge their sin nature. We are naturally wicked, children included. Verses like Romans 5:12 explain this (Sin is covered in greater detail later in the book). A child does not have to be taught how to lie, be selfish, bite, steal, disobey, etc.; they have the sin nature in their blood at conception. It is the job of the parents to mold and shape young lives into adults with biblical morals, principles, habits, and character who love Christ and want to serve Him.

This process of guiding and training a child into an adult is done through proper chastening. We chasten our children just as God chastens His. (Hebrews 12:7) Many times in His Word, God relates His relationship with His children to earthly fathers with theirs. (Psalm 103:13; Matthew 7:11) Part of this chastening process is corporal punishment. Corporal punishment is simply spanking a child, a biblical form of punishment. In Ephesians 6:4, nurture is the greek word *paideia* meaning chastening. This is very similar to the Greek work *paideuo* used in Luke 23:16 & 23:22 which speaks of the scourging of Jesus. There are several verses in Scripture that refer to using a rod for correction, admonishing parents that not using one will lead to disobedience and shame and using the rod will save your child from hell. (Proverbs 29:15, 13:24, 23:13-14.) Of course common sense needs to be exercised here. This does not give parents the authority to abuse their children. A newborn baby that cannot willfully disobey should not be spanked, and a baby should never be shaken out of frustration. Spanking of a toddler or older child should be done only to the bottom and never in anger. Punishment performed in a biblical manner with a godly spirit will yield favorable results. (Proverbs 22:6)

Proverbs 22:6 also says that we are to *train up a child*. This involves more than chastening. Love, praise, and encouragement of good behavior are also a part of discipline. Parents must commit to family time together in God's Word and prayer in order to teach their children the right things to do. Perhaps most importantly, children must be able to see a good godly example in their own parents, an earthly example of Christ that they can emulate.

The earlier a biblical manner of disciplining your children is begun, the easier it will be on all parties, and the better results will be achieved. Proverbs 13:24 ends by saying that the parent that loves their child will chasten them *betimes* which in Hebrew means to seek early. Once parents have dedicated themselves to raising their children for the Lord, they must not give up, but remain consistent and faithful throughout the child's life. Training up a child for the Lord is an awesome responsibility that is difficult and often times wearisome, but the stakes are high and worth all the effort.

"Train up a child in the way he should go: and when he is old, he will not depart from it."
— Proverbs 22:6

"And, *ye* fathers, provoke not your children to wrath: but bring them up in the nurture and admonition of the Lord." — Ephesians 6:4

"If ye endure chastening, God dealeth with you as with sons; for what son is he whom the father chasteneth not?" — Hebrews 12:7

"Chasten thy son while there is hope, and let not thy soul spare for his crying." — Proverbs 19:18

"The rod and reproof give wisdom: but a child left to *himself* bringeth his mother to shame."
— Proverbs 29:15

"He that spareth his rod hateth his son: but he that loveth him chasteneth him betimes."
— Proverbs 13:24

"Withhold not correction from the child: for *if* thou beatest him with the rod, he shall not die. Thou shalt beat him with the rod, and shalt deliver his soul from hell." — Proverbs 23:13-14

"All through life discipline pays off! In school, at work or in the armed services it will always be proven true that the young person who has been properly disciplined at home will get along far better." — Hugh Pyle

Divorce and Remarriage

A divorce is a legal dissolution of the bonds of matrimony, or the separation of husband and wife by a judicial sentence.[1] Biblical language for divorce is usually seen as being referred to as 'putting away.' For our discussion here, remarriage will be considered the marriage of a man or woman after one or both of them have been divorced. Marriage was instituted by God way back in the garden of Eden. God created man and woman for the purpose of companionship and to be a help to one another through life. Marriage is also a picture of our relationship to Christ, and just as we are secure in Him for life once we accept Him as our Savior, so did He intend on marriage being a lifelong covenant.

Divorce is *never* God's plan, He hates it. We see this clearly set forth in passages such as those referenced. It cannot get much clearer than *he hateth putting away* as seen in Malachi 2:16. Because of sin, however, God's perfect plan has been tainted, and He made an allowance for divorce on two biblical grounds only. The first is fornication or adultery. Matthew 19:5 says that when a couple marries they become one flesh, but the sin of fornication/adultery breaks that one flesh relationship. This does not mean, however, that an adulterous act is an automatic reason or requirement for divorce. Reconciliation would be God's perfect plan even in this situation. Yet, if a spouse continues in this sin and cannot be reclaimed to a life of purity, then the other spouse has scriptural grounds for divorce. The second biblical grounds for divorce is an unbeliever leaving a believer as understood in I Corinthians 7:15. Earlier in this passage in verses 12-13, however, we see that a believer should never put away the unbeliever. The godly testimony of the believer, even if it is a silent one, can easily be the very thing that leads the unsaved spouse to the Lord.

This then raises the question of remarriage. I Corinthians 7:11 commands the woman to *remain unmarried* because God's will would be for the couple to be *reconciled* which is always possible so long as neither spouse has remarried. As with divorce, however, the exception would be when fornication has occurred. If a divorced man marries another woman he has then committed adultery (Matthew 5:32, 19:9) creating a biblical grounds for the divorce. The divorced wife would no longer have a biblical obligation to that marriage and could remarry.

The best remedy for divorce is taking an active role in preventing it. The first thing to be sure of is that both parties are saved; a marriage will not be blessed of God otherwise. Secondly, the couple must recognize and accept that marriage is for life. The world views marriage as a contract between two people that can be broken, but Christians should view marriage as what it truly is – a covenant between a man, a woman, and God that cannot be broken. Another important concept to grasp is that marriage should not be built around feelings. True love is a *choice* not a feeling. Our feelings are so fickle and should not be the guiding force behind such important decisions. Dr. Curtis Hutson wrote, "The secret of staying together is not never having a cross word or bad feelings. It is deciding that you are not going to allow your feelings to determine your decisions. We must do right whether or not we feel like it."[8] Anyone wishing to please God and follow His plan will never view divorce as an option.

"...Is it lawful for a man to put away his wife for every cause? And he answered and said unto them, Have ye not read, that he which made *them* at the beginning made them male and female, And said, For this cause shall a man leave father and mother, and shall cleave to his wife: and they twain shall be one flesh? Wherefore they are no more twain, but one flesh. What therefore God hath joined together, let not man put asunder. They say unto him, Why did Moses then command to give a writing of divorcement, and to put her away? He saith unto them, Moses because of the hardness of your hearts suffered you to put away your wives: but from the beginning it was not so. And I say unto you, Whosoever shall put away his wife, except *it be* for fornication, and shall marry another, committeth adultery: and whoso marrieth her which is put away doth commit adultery."

Matthew 19:3b-9

"For the LORD, the God of Israel, saith that he hateth putting away:..."

Malachi 2:16a

"And unto the married I command, *yet* not I, but the Lord, Let not the wife depart from *her* husband: But and if she depart, let her remain unmarried, or be reconciled to *her* husband: and let not the husband put away *his* wife. But to the rest speak I, not the Lord: If any brother hath a wife that believeth not, and she be pleased to dwell with him, let him not put her away. And the woman which hath an husband that believeth not, and if he be pleased to dwell with her, let her not leave him. For the unbelieving husband is sanctified by the wife, and the unbelieving wife is sanctified by the husband: else were your children unclean; but now are they holy. But if the unbelieving depart, let him depart. A brother or a sister is not under bondage in such *cases*: but God hath called us to peace. For what knowest thou, O wife, whether thou shalt save *thy* husband? or how knowest thou, O man, whether thou shalt save *thy* wife."

I Corinthians 7:10-16

"Divorce has terrible consequences for families and for our society. God is not in favor of it. But we should not be against divorced people. When God forgives someone, they are completely forgiven." – R. B. Ouellette

62

Drug Use/Abuse

Drug abuse can be defined as the habitual use of addictive and/or illegal drugs. At first glance, it does not seem that the Bible speaks specifically on the evils of drug use, but a closer study of the original Greek in Revelation 18:23 shows that it indeed does. The word sorceries here is the Greek work *pharmakeia* meaning the use or administering of drugs and poisoning. This verse is speaking of future events, a time when the nations of the world will be deceived by those who sell (*merchants*) drugs (*thy sorceries*). Satan is the king of deceit, and drugs are just one of the tools he uses to deceive the world.

Satan deceives people into believing that drugs will solve their problems. People don't want to deal with and think about the problems of their life, and mistakenly believe that drugs will somehow relieve or at least drown out these stressors. They may seem to give temporary relief, but it is short lived; the original problems still remain and new ones have been created. Some become involved in drug use as a social and/or recreational activity thinking it will help them fit in with a desired group of people. They will soon find, however, that those people are not real friends and are just a tool of the devil to keep them from those people that will draw them closer to the Lord. The true answer lies in the Lord (Philippians 4:6, 13) and surrounding ourselves with people that Love God (Psalm 119:63).

Besides these truths, we must remember that the body of the saved person is the temple of God and does not belong to the Christian. (I Corinthians 6:19-20) Drug use destroys this temple. Drugs have a wide range of adverse effects on the body. The Centers for Disease Control and Prevention (CDC) give a general overview of the effects of both prescription and illegal substance abuse. These can range from damage to the brain, liver, kidneys, respiratory system, circulatory system, and immune system. The CDC also explains that drug abuse can cause depression, exhaustion, pain, and irritability.[9] If one would not dare destroy the interior of their church, then why willingly destroy the body, the home of the Holy Spirit?

Prescription drugs are not excluded from drug abuse. Many prescription drugs, particularly those used for severe pain, can be very addictive. Supposed 'mental illness' is another area where prescription drugs are over prescribed and often abused. More often than not, depression and 'mental' problems are sin problems that need corrected from the root (the sin) rather than merely treating symptoms with drugs. Our culture is one that has become soft to life's trials, not willing to withstand any discomfort or inconvenience. They want a quick fix and find it easier to pop a pill instead of dealing with problems in a biblical fashion. The use of prescription drugs should be approached as only being used when absolutely necessary and only for as long as absolutely necessary. Pray to the Great Physician for His healing, but be willing to accept that He may ask you to live with a 'thorn in the flesh.' When dealing with prescription drugs one needs to keep I Corinthians 6:12 in mind.

One must run as far away as possible from illegal drugs and approach prescription drugs with extreme caution.

"And the light of a candle shall shine no more at all in thee; and the voice of the bridegroom and of the bride shall be heard no more at all in thee: for thy merchants were the great men of the earth; for by thy sorceries were all nations deceived."

Revelation 18:23

"I *am* a companion of all *them* that fear thee, and of them that keep thy precepts."

Psalm 119:63

"What? know ye not that your body is the temple of the Holy Ghost [which is] in you, which ye have of God, and ye are not your own? For ye are bought with a price: therefore glorify God in your body, and in your spirit; which are God's."

I Corinthians 6:19-20

"All things are lawful unto me, but all things are not expedient: all things are lawful for me, but I will not be brought under the power of any."

I Corinthians 6:12

"There are many people…that have more confidence in the family doctor and in the dope they take and the pills they take than they do in the Lord Jesus Christ." – Lester Roloff

End Times

The End Times consists of a series of events that will take place beginning with the rapture of the saints (those who have accepted Christ as their Savior), both dead and alive. This will be followed by the judgment seat of Christ and the 7-year tribulation coming to an end with the battle of Armageddon. This is when the 'Second Coming' of the Lord happens. This term brings much confusion as to exactly what and when it is. The 'Second Coming' is when the Lord returns to this earth to begin His 1,000-year millennial reign during which time Satan will be bound in a pit/abyss. At the close of this period, Satan will be loosed for a season. He will rally his troops from among the unsaved descendants of those who lived through the millennium to go up against the city of Jerusalem. God will then call down fire from heaven to destroy them and the earth. It is at this point that Satan is cast into the lake of fire for the rest of eternity. This is followed by the white throne judgment at which anyone not found in the book of life will be cast into the lake of fire with Satan. Finally, a new heaven and earth will begin. (Revelation 20:7 – 21:1)

There are three things about the end times that are often misunderstood and/or disputed. The first is that no one knows when they will begin. Although there are many people who have tried and are still trying to predict it, the Bible clearly tells us that such attempts are futile because no one knows the exact time. We see this truth in Matthew 24 which tells us that even the angels do not know the time; only the Father of heaven knows. A second area often argued is that there are those that don't believe these to be literal events and try to spiritualize them, saying that the Lord will not physically return to this earth one day. Again, the Bible refutes this claim. Consider Acts 1:10-11 that tells us that He will *come in like manner as ye have seen him go into heaven*. This was being told to those who had just witnessed the living Jesus' resurrected body ascend into heaven. A third area of disagreement is in the timing of the rapture. Some believe that the rapture will be after the tribulation. The Bible, however, supports a pretribulation rapture. Study verses such as Jeremiah 30:7, Luke 21:25-36, I Thessalonians 1:10, and Revelation 3:10. God's Word is plain when it states: *keep them from the hour of temptation*. It is as simple as believing what you read in God's Word.

The Matthew 24 passage also urges us to be ready and prepared for this time. We are to watch for His coming. The first and most important area in which to be prepared is salvation. Only those who have accepted Christ as their Savior will be raptured with the church; after this point it will be too late. Anyone who has not received Christ will enter into the tribulation and eventually spend an eternity in hell. This terrible fate is why we must tell others about Christ's free gift of salvation. We should also be 'watching' by living a Christ-honoring life in order to be prepared for the judgment seat of Christ that will immediately follow the rapture. This judgment is not to determine who will gain access into heaven to live with God for eternity, but rather to judge the works of the saved to determine the gifts and crowns they will receive, crowns that will be placed at the feet of Christ. (I Corinthians 3:13; Revelation 4:10-11) One must do all that can be done to prepare themselves for an eternity with Christ and take as many as they can with them.

"Heaven and earth shall pass away, but my words shall not pass away. But of that day and hour knoweth no *man*, no, not the angels of heaven, but my Father only. But as the days of Noe *were*, so shall also the coming of the Son of man be....Watch therefore: for ye know not what hour your Lord doth come. But know this, that if the goodman of the house had known in what watch the thief would come, he would have watched, and would not have suffered his house to be broken up. Therefore be ye also ready: for in such an hour as ye think not the Son of man cometh."

Matthew 24:35-37, 42-44

"And while they looked stedfastly toward heaven as he went up, behold, two men stood by them in white apparel; Which also said, Ye men of Galilee, why stand ye gazing up into heaven? this same Jesus, which is taken up from you into heaven, shall so come in like manner as ye have seen him go into heaven."

Acts 1:10-11

"And if I go and prepare a place for you, I will come again, and receive you unto myself; that where I am, *there* ye may be also."

John 14:3

"For if we believe that Jesus died and rose again, even so them also which sleep in Jesus will God bring with him. For this we say unto you by the word of the Lord, that we which are alive *and* remain unto the coming of the Lord shall not prevent them which are asleep. For the Lord himself shall descend from heaven with a shout, with the voice of the archangel, and with the trump of God: and the dead in Christ shall rise first: Then we which are alive *and* remain shall be caught up together with them in the clouds, to meet the Lord in the air: and so shall we ever be with the Lord."

I Thessalonians 4:14-17

"If the presence of one righteous man prevented the outpouring of deserved judgment on the city of Sodom, how much more will the presence of the church on earth prevent the outpouring of divine wrath until after her removal." – J. Dwight Pentecost

66

Entertainment

Entertainment is the amusement or pleasure which the mind receives from anything interesting, and which holds or arrests the attention.[1] There is a wide range of entertainment choices including tv/movies, sporting events, Amusement parks, outdoor activities, bowling, etc.. While none of these things are sinful and can be a source of good, clean, wholesome enjoyment, we were not created for the sole purpose of entertaining ourselves. The problem lies when these things are not kept in moderation and begin to take over our lives, robbing us of precious time to win others to Christ. Winning souls to Christ is the one job and purpose that Christ commanded for every Christian. We need to be *redeeming the time* for our God-called purpose. (Ephesians 5:16)

Viewing of television programs and movies is probably one of the biggest forms of entertainment today. Our society has become enamored with Hollywood and what it puts out. Hollywood stars have been elevated to a place of becoming idols. Our God is a jealous God and tells us in Exodus 20:3 that we are to have no other gods before Him. These gods can be anything that take His place in our lives. In addition to this, Hollywood portrays, and even goes so far as to promote, activities and lifestyles that are contrary to how the Bible tells us we ought to live. Hollywood films are full of the works of the flesh seen listed in Galatians 5:19-21, mocking sin and God Himself. If one can clearly see the wickedness displayed in film, then why would one allow it to pass through their eye gate? (Psalm 101:3) Another area that is high on the entertainment list is partying and the bar room/night club scene. There are so many activities that go hand-and-hand with these choices that make it evident that these are not appropriate sources of entertainment. These areas are saturated with alcohol, drugs, ungodly music, immodesty, and fornication; not to mention that they are almost always masked in darkness. I Thessalonians 5:22 tells us to *abstain from all appearances of evil* which is most assuredly represented in places like these.

Society has become so addicted to the world's entertainment that it has become a society that feels they need to be entertained at all times and in every aspect of life. This mentality has allowed entertainment to creep into the church as well. Many churches have compromised their beliefs and the sanctity of the church by using the world's entertainment in efforts to draw a crowd. They have introduced the world's music, used strobe lights and smoke machines, and adopted a lackadaisical and casual atmosphere. Church services have become rock concerts all supposedly in the name of God. We are to be in church to worship God and focusing the entire church service on Him, but these types of church services put the focus on the 'performances' rather than God. God deserves and demands our reverence (Psalm 89:7; Hebrews 12:28) and His house is a holy place (Leviticus 19:30, 26:2) that should not be desecrated with such activities!

Philippians 4:8 tells us those things that we are to think on and allow into our minds. We must also remember the very important lesson in I Corinthians 6:12, to discern what is good for us and not allow ourselves to become controlled by anything but God.

"I will set no wicked thing before mine eyes: I hate the work of them that turn aside; *it* shall not cleave to me."

Psalm 101:3

"Now the works of the flesh are manifest, which are *these*; Adultery, fornication, uncleanness, lasciviousness, Idolatry, witchcraft, hatred, variance, emulations, wrath, strife, seditions, heresies, Envyings, murders, drunkenness, revellings, and such like: of the which I tell you before, as I have also told *you* in time past, that they which do such things shall not inherit the kingdom of God."

Galatians 5:19-21

"Finally, brethren, whatsoever things are true, whatsoever things *are* honest, whatsoever things *are* just, whatsoever things *are* pure, whatsoever things *are* lovely, whatsoever things *are* of good report; if *there be* any virtue, and if *there be* any praise, think on these things."

Philippians 4:8

"All things are lawful unto me, but all things are not expedient: all things are lawful for me, but I will not be brought under the power of any."

I Corinthians 6:12

"Thou shalt have no other gods before me."

Exodus 20:3

"The filthiest movies that ever invaded the homes are in the homes today. You wonder what's wrong with the American home; I'm mopping up after a bunch of worldly mothers and daddys that left Hollywood come in and take the place of the family altar..." – Lester Roloff

Family – Children's Role

A family can be considered one's course of descent, genealogy, or line of ancestors, but in the scope of our discussion the family is the collective body of persons who live in one house and under one head or manager including father, mother, and children.[1] Satan desires to destroy the family because with its destruction, comes the fall of so many other areas of society. Children are a blessing from God, *an heritage of the Lord.* (Psalm 127:3-5) They bring life and excitement to the home. Children are also the next generation of parents and leaders. This is why children must recognize their importance and the potential that is in them, and strive to learn and do what is necessary to ensure they grow to become good, godly parents and leaders.

Obedience and honor to the parents is the primary role and responsibility of the child. This is taught in several verses in Scripture including Colossians 3:20 and Proverbs 6:20. Hebrews 12:9 speaks of the reverence that is to be shown to the parents. God has created an order to His creation, and when it is followed the outcome is much sweeter. As we see in Ephesians 6:3, those who obey, honor, and respect their parents pave an easier and happier path before them. Children who do not are much more likely to have a life scarred from their poor choices and sinful lifestyles. It is also important to note that this honoring and revering of your parents continues into adulthood. Proverbs 23:22 says, "Hearken unto the father that begat thee, and despise not thy mother when she is old." The dynamic of the child's life changes when they leave the home and become an adult; outright obedience is no longer required. However, the child must forever give their parent's advice sincere consideration and hold them in high regard with honor and reverence.

Another role of the child is to learn the things of God and serve Him. The child is to listen to the instruction of their parents for the purpose of gaining understanding. (Proverbs 4:1) We see in Luke 2:41-52 that Jesus, at the age of twelve, was found in the temple among the great men of Jerusalem listening to them and asking them questions. As a side note here, even He, God of the universe, placed Himself under the subjection of His earthly parents – what an example! This passage also tells us that He increased in wisdom. We see another example in I Samuel chapter 1. Samuel was taken to serve the priest Eli as a very young boy fulfilling a promise Hannah made to God. (I Samuel 1:27-28) God calls for the youth to serve Him as well. (Psalm 34:11; 119:9-11) Those that learn to serve God and make a habit out of it in their youth will be more likely to serve Him into adulthood.

Fulfilling these roles prepares the young person for living the Christian life as an adult. The child who learns to honor, obey, and reverence their parents is preparing themselves for the proper attitudes and responses they should have toward God. Everyone in life has authority (wife/husband, employee/employer, citizen/law enforcement, student/teacher). Hebrews 12:9 speaks of the correlation between serving our earthly father and our heavenly Father. Learning to be in subjection to all these other authorities prepares the child for the ultimate authority in their life – God.

"Lo, children *are* an heritage of the LORD: *and* the fruit of the womb *is his* reward. As arrows *are* in the hand of a mighty man; so *are* children of the youth. Happy *is* the man that hath his quiver full of them: they shall not be ashamed, but they shall speak with the enemies in the gate."

Psalm 127:3-5

"Children, obey *your* parents in all things: for this is well pleasing unto the Lord."

Colossians 3:20

"Honour thy father and mother; (which is the first commandment with promise;) That it may be well with thee, and thou mayest live long on the earth."

Ephesians 6:2-3

"Hear, ye children, the instruction of a father, and attend to know understanding."

Proverbs 4:1

"Furthermore we have had fathers of our flesh which corrected *us,* and we gave *them* reverence: shall we not much rather be in subjection unto the Father of spirits, and live?"

Hebrews 12:9

"Oh, the potential that is in those boys and girls! Great men of God, like D. L. Moody, used to be children. … I am sure there were thousands who saw no potential in him, but there were those in Heaven who did. Every great man, every great woman of God one day was a little child. And all the potential they had and all they did was there when they were little boys and girls just like it was when they were grown men and women!" – Jimmy Ervin

Family – Father's Role

A family can be considered one's course of descent, genealogy, or line of ancestors, but in the scope of our discussion the family is the collective body of persons who live in one house and under one head or manager including father, mother, and children.[1] Satan desires to destroy the family because with its destruction, comes the fall of so many other areas of society. Fathers play a very important and vital role in the family. God's plan is that a father be the head of the household, responsible for providing for his family and being the spiritual leader of the home. (I Corinthians 11:3) Without fathers, there cannot be the unity in the family that is spoken of in Malachi 4:6, and without this unity, it is impossible to have a happy home.

Parents are given the responsibility to train up God's children that He has placed on loan to them for a time; they are to give them guidance and direction in order that they may be able to make wise, godly decisions on their own some day. (Proverbs 22:6) Although fathers and mothers work together on this, being the spiritual leader in the home makes the father the one ultimately responsible for fulfilling this duty. The father must take the lead in family devotions and prayer as well as establish a pattern and love for regular worship in God's house. Part of this training is administering discipline, without which will result in a rebellious child. The Bible has much to say about the methods of discipline and the spirit in which it should be performed to ensure a positive outcome. (Proverbs 13:24; Ephesians 6:4; discipline is also covered in greater detail earlier in the book) Although the pastor, Sunday School teachers, and Christian school teachers are a wonderful asset to parents, they can never replace the training a child must receive in the home from their fathers.

Along with the father's role of 'head of household' comes the burden of providing financially for his family. Situations may necessitate some assistance from the mother in this area, but as will be discussed in the next topic, the mother's primary responsibility is in the home. God speaks very strongly about this in I Timothy 5:8, saying that any man who does not provide for his family is worse than an infidel. The father is also to provide physical protection for his family. John 15:13 says, "Greater love hath no man than this, that a man lay down his life for his friends." If for a friend, how much more should a father take this verse to heart for his family? Additionally, the father is a picture of Christ. The earthly father is to imitate the heavenly Father before his family and our Father laid down His life in order to save ours.

Fathers will leave something for their children, good or bad. The decisions fathers make today will affect their children in the future. Those decisions will shape the way they think and view life. Poor choices can lead to trials and heartache. (Lamentations 5:7) An inheritance is admirable and right as is encouraged in Proverbs 13:22, but this verse is concerned more with *who* an inheritance should be left to when there is one to be had rather than the *importance* that one be left. A wise man will ask himself what *legacy* he is leaving his children. Solomon speaks of the vanity of money and material wealth in Ecclesiastes 5:14-17. How much more a father should want to leave his loved ones with memories and lessons learned rather than just material things.

"And he shall turn the heart of the fathers to the children, and the heart of the children to their fathers, lest I come and smite the earth with a curse."

Malachi 4:6

"Train up a child in the way he should go: and when he is old, he will not depart from it."

Proverbs 22:6

"He that spareth his rod hateth his son: but he that loveth him chasteneth him betimes."

Proverbs 13:24

"And, ye fathers, provoke not your children to wrath: but bring them up in the nurture and admonition of the Lord."

Ephesians 6:4

"But if any provide not for his own, and specially for those of his own house, he hath denied the faith, and is worse than an infidel."

I Timothy 5:8

"Our fathers have sinned, *and are* not; and we have borne their iniquities."

Lamentations 5:7

"It is a sacred place and a sacred responsibility that He has placed upon the fathers of the world that the man is to be the head of his home, that he should be in the place of absolute authority." – Joe Henry Hankins

Family – Mother's Role

A family can be considered one's course of descent, genealogy, or line of ancestors, but in the scope of our discussion the family is the collective body of persons who live in one house and under one head or manager including father, mother, and children.[1] Satan desires to destroy the family because with its destruction, comes the fall of so many other areas of society. Genesis 2:18 reveals the purpose of the woman, to be *an help meet* for her husband. As a mother, this means taking on the principal care and responsibility for the children. Motherhood is a high calling of God for women and should not be belittled or taken lightly. I Timothy 2:15 says that *she shall be saved in childbearing*. This was meant to be an encouragement after being instructed of her transgression in the garden and her duty to submit herself to her husband. The catch, however, is that only those who *continue in faith and charity and holiness* will recognize the sweetness and honor that motherhood is.

Perhaps the biggest, or at least most time consuming, role of motherhood would be providing for the physical needs of the children. This includes, but is surely not limited to, buying/making/cleaning their clothes, preparing their meals, feeding babies and toddlers, helping with homework, and being chauffer. Even Hannah, although she had given her son back to God by means of service to the priest Eli, found a small way to provide for the physical needs of her son by making and delivering a new coat to him each year. (I Samuel 2:19) A mother must sacrifice herself and her time to the high demands required of children. A mother also provides for the emotional needs of her children. It is nearly impossible for a mother to ignore or forget her child, for she has such compassion for her children that she usually hurts alongside them. (Isaiah 49:15a) A mother takes a special interest in everything her child does (ie., every play, musical, craft, etc.) making her child feel extra special. She is the ultimate comforter to a hurt, sad, or discouraged child; no one else seems adequate in such moments. There is simply an atmosphere of comfort when mother is around. Christ compares the comfort He gives to that of a mother's in Isaiah 66:13. A godly mother is an earthly example of the compassion, comfort, and unconditional love we receive from God.

Although the husband/father is to be the spiritual leader in the home, mothers should never underestimate the great impact and influence they have on their children's spiritual condition. A very big part of this is lifting up the children's father and treating him in such a way that she turns the hearts of her children to their father. Their father is to be an earthly example of Christ to them, so the mother must lead them to love and respect their father if they are ever to do the same for Christ. Since the mother's role is such that she usually has more interaction with the children, she has many opportunities to teach the children about God. A mother should read Bible stories to younger children and Bible studies/devotionals with older children as much as she can, finding ways in everyday situations to teach them how a Christian should respond to the world around them. Most importantly, be a godly example that they can observe and emulate. Being a *godly* mother is a tough job, but those who take it seriously and genuinely do the best they can, will have a family that will *arise up and call her blessed.* (Proverbs 31:28)

"And the LORD God said, *It is* not good that the man should be alone; I will make him an help meet for him."

Genesis 2:18

"Notwithstanding she shall be saved in childbearing, if they continue in faith and charity and holiness with sobriety."

I Timothy 2:15

"Can a woman forget her sucking child, that she should not have compassion on the son of her womb? ..."

Isaiah 49:15a

"As one whom his mother comforteth, so will I comfort you; and ye shall be comforted in Jerusalem."

Isaiah 66:13

"Her children arise up, and call her blessed; her husband *also*, and he praiseth her."

Proverbs 31:28

"The Bible places a great emphasis on the importance of godly mothers and the tremendous spiritual contribution which they can render in both the home and life of a nation." – Bob Gray

Fasting

Fasting is the voluntary abstinence from something in order to focus more time in prayer and an expression of inner devotion toward God and His leading. Although fasting is usually associated with giving up food, either completely or a meal a day, for a certain period of time, it could also be giving up anything that takes up one's time and that they enjoy and replacing it with time spent in prayer and meditation on God's Word. Daniel 6:18, for example, says that the king went without food and his beloved *'musick.'* Fasting could be giving up a daily trip to the coffee shop, just a favorite food (Daniel 10:2-3), television programs, going to the gym, sleep, or marital intimacy (I Corinthians 7:3-5) to name a few possibilities. The point of fasting is to deny the flesh and humble oneself before God in order to get closer with Him, thus being more apt to hear His leading and prepared to yield to His will.

So much emphasis is put on the physical needs and nourishment of our bodies, but very little emphasis is given to our spiritual needs. Almost every American regularly (makes it a necessity actually) eats three meals a day, but how many are skipping their spiritual meals. Matthew 4:4 very clearly states that, "...Man shall not live by bread alone, but by every word that proceedeth out of the mouth of God." One needs to feed himself with the Word of God as well, to chew on it and digest what it has to say! Matthew continues in chapter 5, verse 6 to tell us what we need to hunger after more than food – *'righteousness.'* This verse ends with a promise that *they shall be filled*. Just so, there is promise of reward and answer to the Christian who disciplines himself to fast. (Matthew 6:18; Ezra 8:23)

When it comes to fasting, there are some rights and wrongs that accompany it. First and foremost, it is not to be done for show or to be seen of men. (Matthew 6:16-18) As with anything done in the Christian life, motive is very important to God; He will not reward those with self-serving motives for they have their reward already. There are many reasons to fast such as when being tempted, for protection, in mourning, for victory over impossible circumstances, repentance, or when earnestly seeking wisdom as Daniel did in Daniel 9:3. Fasting is always accompanied by something else, such as confession of sin, meditation on God's Word, service to God, and *always* with prayer.

Fasting was a rather regular observance in the Bible. A few examples include Moses in Exodus 34:28, Elijah in I Kings 19:8, Paul in II Corinthians 6:5 and 11:27, and the disciples and Pharisees in Mark 2:18. Jesus found benefit in fasting as well, as we see demonstrated in verses like Matthew 4:1-2, Mark 1:12-13, and Luke 4:1-2. Fasting is not a command or ordinance, but Joel 2:12 does show us that Christ compelled His own to do so. He felt it is important enough that He observed it Himself as an example for us to follow. Fasting is an observance that has sadly been largely abandoned today. Too many Christians are Sunday only Christians, doing what they feel they are obligated to do and/or doing enough to look good to those around them. Fasting is above and beyond what we should already be doing in church attendance, devotions, prayer, service to God, etc. in order to receive that very special blessing from the Lord.

"Therefore also now, saith the LORD, turn ye *even* to me with all your heart, and with fasting, and with weeping, and with mourning:"

Joel 2:12

"So we fasted and besought our God for this: and he was intreated of us."

Ezra 8:23

"Moreover when ye fast, be not, as the hypocrites, of a sad countenance: for they disfigure their faces, that they may appear unto men to fast. Verily I say unto you, They have their reward. But thou, when thou fastest, anoint thine head, and wash thy face; That thou appear not unto men to fast, but unto the Father which is in secret: and thy Father, which seeth in secret, shall reward thee openly."

Matthew 6:16-18

"And I set my face unto the Lord God, to seek by prayer and supplications, with fasting, and sackcloth, and ashes:"

Daniel 9:3

"And it came to pass, when I heard these words, that I sat down and wept, and mourned *certain* days, and fasted, and prayed before the God of heaven."

Nehemiah 1:4

"What Jesus meant is that when we fast, when we abstain from food, it should be done as expressing deep humility and sorrow of heart…He will go into his secret place alone with God, and his fasting will be an expression of feeling toward God, an earnestness in his relationship with God. Therefore God will approve such stewardship and will reward that man's fasting and prayer." – Oliver B. Greene

Fellowship

Fellowship is a state of being together, companionship; it is the mutual association of persons on equal and friendly terms.[1] Fellowship among believers is necessary for encouragement and reproof throughout the Christian life. Hebrews 10:25 instructs us to gather together. Although this verse is often associated with structured church services (which is a form of fellowship), that is not the only application of this verse. Fellowship, when kept within biblical guidelines, will be of great value to the believer.

The first and most important biblical guideline is that fellowship should be among believers of Christ. God's Word is filled with verses that attest to this. Take special note to I John 1:3. We see here that we can have fellowship one with another because of our mutual faith in Christ (*truly our fellowship is with the Father*). It demonstrates that we witness to others in order to bring them to Christ and *only then* can we have fellowship. In Psalm 119:63, David speaks of his close relationship (*companion*) with those who know God. I John 1:7 says *we have fellowship one with another* only *if we walk in the light*. God warns against associations with unbelievers in verses like Ephesians 5:11 and II Corinthians 6:14. Saved and unsaved (*righteousness* and *unrighteousness*, *light* and *darkness*) people do not have harmony one with another. Although salvation is the first and ultimate guideline, it is important to realize that fellowship should also only be enjoyed among those of *like faith*. Doctrinal differences, although not necessarily a deciding factor in salvation, are important to God and should be important to us. 'Doctrine' is found 51 times in God's Word saying that it is *pure*, it is *good*, and that we should *learn* and *understand* it. (Job 11:4; Proverbs 4:2; Isaiah 29:24, 28:9) The Bible also tells us that we are to be wary of *any other thing that is contrary to sound doctrine*, we are to *teach no other doctrine*, and we are to be grounded in what we believe so as not to be *carried about with every wind of doctrine*. (I Timothy 1:10, 1:3; Ephesians 4:14) I Timothy 4:13 tells us that we are to *give* attendance to *doctrine*; to give attendance has the idea of being mindful of, attentive to, and holding or cleaving to something. It is difficult to find common ground and move forward in a positive direction when those involved do not agree on the particulars of God's Word. (Amos 3:3)

The guidelines for fellowship carry over into the next level of choosing our friendships. A Christian must choose friends that will uplift them and help them do right. (Proverbs 27:17) Close friendships with unbelievers, or even those on a different level of their Christian walk, will more likely pull us down. Close friendships are a blessing, but compromise cannot be made in this area in an attempt to gain them. For the Christian that does not have many friends, he must remember that he always has a friend in Jesus, because He *is a friend that sticketh closer than a brother*. (Proverbs 18:24)

Fellowship is an important aspect of church and the Christian life, but not the only one. Many churches put so much of an emphasis on fellowship that they change their name to such. God instituted church to encourage believers, but also to exhort them in proper Christian living and training them to go out and reach others for God's Kingdom.

"Not forsaking the assembling of ourselves together, as the manner of some *is*; but exhorting *one another*: and so much the more, as ye see the day approaching."

Hebrews 10:25

"That which we have seen and heard declare we unto you, that ye also may have fellowship with us: and truly our fellowship *is* with the Father, and with the Son Jesus Christ."

I John 1:3

"I *am* a companion of all *them* that fear thee, and of them that keep thy precepts."

Psalm 119:63

"And have no fellowship with the unfruitful works of darkness, but rather reprove *them*."

Ephesians 5:11

"Be ye not unequally yoked together with unbelievers: for what fellowship hath righteousness with unrighteousness? and what communion hath light with darkness?"

II Corinthians 6:14

"Iron sharpeneth iron; so a man sharpeneth the countenance of his friend."

Proverbs 27:17

"Our love to God is measured by our everyday fellowship with others and the love it displays."
– Andrew Murray

Forgiveness

Forgiveness is the act of pardoning an offender, by which the offender is then considered and treated as not guilty.[1] God offers us the ultimate forgiveness and in turn commands us to forgive others. Acceptance of forgiveness is necessary in order for the complete reconciliation which Christ desires to occur. One cannot control the attitude and response of the person they are offering forgiveness to or requesting forgiveness from, therefore, God does not hold us responsible for their response. God only holds one responsible to do whatever they possibly can to foster forgiveness among all parties.

First we'll consider God's forgiveness toward us. We can claim the promises of the Bible such as I John 1:9 that He *will* offer us forgiveness if we would only seek it and ask for it. God promises it to us, but we must ask for it, and ask for it on a continual basis. We not only seek His ultimate forgiveness of our sins for salvation, but we must daily ask His forgiveness for known sins in order to remain in continuous fellowship with the Lord keeping the lines of communication open between us and God. Once God offers forgiveness, He FORGETS those trespasses that we commit against Him. Psalm 103:12 says He forgets them a*s far as the east is from the west*; they never meet just as God *never* remembers those things He forgives us for. We see a perfect picture of how God forgives us in the story of the prodigal son. Christ (the father) willingly forgives and welcomes us (the prodigal) back to His fold with rejoicing when we ask Him. (Luke 15:11-32)

Next, we need to consider the forgiveness that we are to give to others. As in everything, Christ is our example, and we are to forgive others as He forgave us. (Colossians 3:13) A big key to forgiveness is letting those who have offended you know that they have (in a kind, Christ-like Spirit of course). Often times, others are not even aware that they have done anything that hurt us and will usually be remorseful and apologetic once they realize how they have hurt someone. If they do respond in such a manner, we are commanded to forgive them as seen in Luke 17:3. That said, Matthew 5:44 tells us we are to *love your enemies* and *bless them that curse you*. This command constitutes we forgive even the unrepentant. We are also to forgive time and time again; Matthew 18:21-22 says *seventy times seven*. Of course this is not intended to mean that you count 490 offences and on the 491st forgiveness is no longer given. God meant here that we are to be patient with people and forgive them indefinitely. Once forgiveness has been offered, the offence must not be 'remembered.' Of course our human brains are incapable of 'forgetting' the offence, but to not 'remember' it means that it should not be held against the person. We should not be historians that log every offense and then bring things back up the next time a quarrel erupts. God's command is simple, *be ye kind* and be *forgiving*. (Ephesians 4:32)

One should not expect to receive God's forgiveness for their sins if they are not willing to forgive those that sin against them. (Matthew 6:14) If Christ can call out, "...Father, forgive them, for they know not what they do..." to God about those who crucified Him on the cross, can we not so much the more offer forgiveness to those who wrong us? (Luke 23:34)

"If we confess our sins, he is faithful and just to forgive us *our* sins, and to cleanse us from all unrighteousness."

I John 1:9

"Forbearing one another, and forgiving one another, if any man have a quarrel against any: even as Christ forgave you, so also *do* ye."

Colossians 3:13

"Take heed to yourselves: If thy brother trespass against thee, rebuke him; and if he repent, forgive him."

Luke 17:3

"Then came Peter to him, and said, Lord, how oft shall my brother sin against me, and I forgive him? till seven times? Jesus saith unto him, I say not unto thee, Until seven times: but, Until seventy times seven."

Matthew 18:21-22

"And be ye kind one to another, tender-hearted, forgiving one another, even as God for Christ's sake hath forgiven you."

Ephesians 4:32

"For if ye forgive men their trespasses, your heavenly Father will also forgive you:"

Matthew 6:14

"If God can forgive you, surely you can do the far lesser work of forgiving others who have done you wrong. Mankind has done more wrong to Christ than any man has ever done to any other man." – John G. Butler

Gambling

Gambling, "is taking an artificial risk for hope of excessive gain far beyond what the investment of time, money or skill would justify."[10] It is paying money (usually by means of a 'game') in hopes of winning larger sums of money or valuable material items. Gambling encompasses much more than that which is done in casinos. It includes the lottery, Bingo, 50/50 raffles, gun raffles, football pools, and so on. It is not often that you find a God-fearing Christian in the casino, but there are many that involve themselves in these types of gambling. These types of gambling are minimized and not thought of as such, but any time you are putting out money in hopes of winning a prize from it you are gambling.

The Bible speaks very clearly about easy and dishonest gain, hard work, and contentment. Gambling is exploiting the losses of others for one's personal gain. God warns that wealth gotten by these means will not last long. (Proverbs 13:11; 28:8) On the contrary, God blesses and looks very highly on those who work hard and labor for their income. Proverbs 13:11 says that those who *gathereth by labour shall increase*. In II Thessalonians 3:10, God rebukes the slothful or lazy saying that if one does not work they do not get the privilege of eating. God exhorts every Christian to be content throughout His Word, including Hebrews 13:5. He promises to provide everything we 'need.' The problem is that too many equivalate their wants for 'needs', and when they do not see God supplying all their 'needs,' they lose faith. The underlying reason for gambling is discontentment with what God has provided – the 'love' of money (not the money itself). (I Timothy 6:10) Gambling begins to look like an easy way to provide those things that God is not giving. The one who gambles puts their trust in a game of chance and demonstrates a lack of faith in God and His promises.

God's Word also warns about the destruction that results from gambling. Proverbs 28:22 says that poverty will come to those who seek quick money, and I Timothy 6:9 says he will *fall into temptation and a snare* and *drown...in destruction and perdition*. Besides the Bible warnings, statistics prove a path of ruined lives will result from gambling. Families, being a prime target of Satan, suffer tragically from gambling. Paychecks that should be going to groceries and bills are spent as soon as it comes in on chances that do not deliver. Spouses are torn apart from arguments about the spending. States and cities that have legalized gambling suffer from increased crime rates, rampant prostitution, excessive alcohol use, elevated selling and using of drugs, etc. The internet is not lacking for examples of horror stories of those who won the lottery only to squander it away in a very short time and end up poorer than they were before they won. The stories continue about families ripped apart in fights and lawsuits over the winnings and even those who were murdered for their money. Gambling is an addictive, sinful, and flesh driven activity that leads to nothing but destruction.

One must remember that all the money in our possession belongs to God; it is He who provides it for us. (James 1:17) When one gambles, he takes grave chances with God's wealth. God expects us to be good stewards of what He has provided, to make wise choices in what we spend it on and invest it in. Those who are wise stewards God blesses. (Luke 12:42-44).

"Wealth *gotten* by vanity shall be diminished: but he that gathereth by labour shall increase."

Proverbs 13:11

"He that by usury and unjust gain increaseth his substance, he shall gather it for him that will pity the poor."

Proverbs 28:8

"For even when we were with you, this we commanded you, that if any would not work, neither should he eat."

II Thessalonians 3:10

"*Let your* conversation *be* without covetousness; *and be* content with such things as ye have: for he hath said, I will never leave thee, nor forsake thee."

Hebrews 13:5

"He that hasteth to be rich *hath* an evil eye, and considereth not that poverty shall come upon him."

Proverbs 28:22

"But they that will be rich fall into temptation and a snare, and *into* many foolish and hurtful lusts, which drown men in destruction and perdition. For the love of money is the root of all evil: which while some coveted after, they have erred from the faith, and pierced themselves through with many sorrows."

I Timothy 6:9-10

"There is no institution in which His name is more often blasphemed and in which the sightless goddess of chance reigns supreme than in the room given over to gambling." – W. B. Riley

God – Mercy/Grace/Justice

God is an awesome being, and we will never know or understand everything there is to know about Him. There are some attributes that His Word reveals about Him that we can study in order to learn and understand as much as we can. An attribute is a characteristic or inherent part of someone, with God they are those characteristics that help us understand who He is. Three of these attributes relate directly to our salvation, those that best describe who He is to us as individuals and what He does for us personally; they are Mercy, Grace, and Justice. He offers salvation to all who would accept it through His mercy and grace; He shows justice to those who reject His gift by refusing to allow them into Heaven and judges those who are saved for their works and the rewards they will receive in Heaven because of them.

Mercy is God *withholding* from us what we deserve. (Ephesians 2:4-6; Titus 3:5) We have been sinful creatures since the fall of Adam and Eve in the Garden of Eden and deserve God's wrath. Romans 3:23 tells us, "For all have sinned, and come short of the glory of God;" We fall short! There is nothing we can do to merit God's favor or entrance into heaven; all our 'works' are as filthy rags. (Ephesians 2:9; Isaiah 64:6) Every good thing we enjoy in life is because of His mercy. We deserve pain and punishment for our sinful desires and actions, but He withholds those things because of His mercy.

Grace is God *giving* us what we do not deserve. (Romans 3:24; Ephesians 4:7) I have heard it said before that grace is **G**od's **R**iches **A**t **C**hrist's **E**xpense. Because of our sin, we all deserve to go to hell, but because He loves us and because of His grace, He sent His Son to take our penalty on the cross so that whosoever believes can have eternal life with Him in Heaven. (John 3:16) God also extends His grace to us on a daily basis by way of the non-eternal blessings he bestows on us. Saved and unsaved alike enjoy these blessings everyday (ie., a warm home, a job, vehicles, a beautiful sunny day, relationships, etc.) Every good thing we enjoy in life is because of His Grace; we deserve nothing but death. (Genesis 2:17, 3:6; Romans 6:23)

Justice is what God exhibits over all mankind; He is the ultimate judge. (Genesis 18:25) Many people like to talk about God's mercy and grace, but few linger long on His justice. People often reference God's love and say that God wouldn't send anyone to hell. God is a God of love and shows us His mercy and grace, but He is also a just God. God is a fair judge that looks at all people no matter their station in life and judges them according to His Word. (I Peter 1:17) The saved will be rewarded for the things we've done for the cause of Christ with the right attitude and for the right reasons, but we'll also be judged for what we did that we should not have and what we did not do that we should have. God is so pure that He cannot even look upon sin (Habakkuk 1:13) and will not let sin go unpunished (Proverbs 11:21; Nahum 1:3; Romans 12:19).

God provides mercy, grace, and judgment in salvation, but also throughout all of life. He gives us grace and mercy in our times of need (Hebrews 4:16) and judges individuals and nations for their disobedience to His commands. One can enjoy the blessings of mercy and grace but also live in such a manner that testifies of their reverential fear of the Lord.

"But God, who is rich in mercy, for his great love wherewith he loved us, Even when we were dead in sins, hath quickened us together with Christ, (by grace ye are saved;) And hath raised *us* up together, and made *us* sit together in heavenly *places* in Christ Jesus:"

Ephesians 2:4-6

"Not by works of righteousness which we have done, but according to his mercy he saved us, by the washing of regeneration, and renewing of the Holy Ghost;"

Titus 3:5

"Being justified freely by his grace through the redemption that is in Christ Jesus: "

Romans 3:24

"But unto every one of us is given grace according to the measure of the gift of Christ."

Ephesians 4:7

"And if ye call on the Father, who without respect of persons judgeth according to every man's work, pass the time of your sojourning *here* in fear:"

I Peter 1:17

"That be far from thee to do after this manner, to slay the righteous with the wicked: and that the righteous should be as the wicked, that be far from thee: Shall not the Judge of all the earth do right?"

Genesis 18:25

"So the certainty of the judgment day out yonder before you is true. Why? Because God said He hath appointed, He has fixed a day in the which He is going to judge this world in righteousness." — B. R. Lakin

God the Father

God is three persons acting simultaneously under one Godhead – God the Father, God the Son, and God the Holy Spirit. These three make up what is known as the Trinity. (I John 5:7) The closest example to help explain the trinity is the states of water. Water can exist in three forms – ice, liquid, and gas. Each state is different yet still the same chemical compound of H_2O. The difference between this example and God is that water can only be one state at a time; God is all three at all times. God is eternal, having always existed and will exist for eternity to come. (Revelation 1:8) He is omniscient/all knowing (Proverbs 15:2; Acts 15:18), omnipresent/everywhere at one time (Psalm 139:7-10), and omnipotent/all powerful (Luke 1:37; Revelation 21:22). All three persons of the Godhead are equal, but God the Father would be the leader and the One whose will is fulfilled by God the Son and God the Holy Spirit.

God the Father is the creator of all. His Word begins saying *God created the heavens and the earth*. (Genesis 1:1) Verse 26 reveals that this creation was the will and plan of God the Father when it says *And God Said, Let us make man in our image*. We see again in Matthew 26:39 that it is the Father's will that is to be done in all things. God the Son said just before His crucifixion, *nevertheless not as I will, but as thou wilt*. When God finished His creation He said it was *very good*. (Genesis 1:31) Unfortunately, man disobeyed God's one rule to them in the Garden of Eden and the sinful nature of mankind was birthed. Because God is a just God that cannot look upon sin He had to punish that sin, but also made a provision through His only Son so that fellowship between God and man could be restored. God made a provision for the problem of sin, but also created in man a free will which enables him to choose or deny that provision. The Father is greater than all and it is He who holds secure the salvation of those who choose to accept that provision. (John 10:29)

The Father created our physical bodies (Psalm 139:14), but He also works to create in us our character. He molds the saved Christian as much as they allow Him to do so. (Isaiah 64:8) It is the Father to whom we are to pray and the Father who answers our prayers. (Matthew 6:6, 8-9) God the Son and God the Holy Spirit have been manifested in such forms that the human eye could see them, but the Father has been seen or heard of no one. (John 1:18, 5:37) And no one will ever see or hear Him until we go to be with Him in His house (heaven) to dwell in the mansion that has been prepared for each born again believer.

The Father is always on His throne! Psalm 47:8 says, "God reigneth over the heathen: God sitteth upon the throne of his holiness." The word 'heathen' here simply means people or nations. Often times people will ask, 'Where was God' when a tragedy or major natural disaster happens. First, God never promised the Christian that bad things would never happen to them, actually the contrary. God does promise, however, to be there with us *when* they happen. Second, it is only because of God's protection that we do not suffer more. As we, personally or as a nation, turn our backs on Him, He sometimes withholds His hand of protection in order to turn us back to Him. We can be assured that *all things work together for good to them that love God*. (Romans 8:28)

"And he went a little further, and fell on his face, and prayed, saying, O my Father, if it be possible, let this cup pass from me: nevertheless not as I will, but as thou *wilt*."

Matthew 26:39

"My Father, which gave *them* me, is greater than all; and no *man* is able to pluck *them* out of my Father's hand."

John 10:29

"But now, O LORD, thou *art* our father; we *are* the clay, and thou our potter; and we all *are* the work of thy hand."

Isaiah 64:8

"But thou, when thou prayest, enter into thy closet, and when thou hast shut thy door, pray to thy Father which is in secret; and thy Father which seeth in secret shall reward thee openly."

Matthew 6:6

"And the father himself, which hath sent me, hath borne witness of me. Ye have neither heard his voice at any time, nor seen his shape."

John 5:37

"In my Father's house are many mansions: if *it were* not *so*, I would have told you. I go to prepare a place for you."

John 14:2

"If God is not Creator, King, and Redeemer, there is no resting place for man other than the restlessness of agnosticism." – G. Campbell Morgan

God the Holy Spirit

God is three persons acting simultaneously under one Godhead – God the Father, God the Son, and God the Holy Spirit. These three make up what is known as the Trinity. (I John 5:7) The closest example to help explain the trinity is the states of water. Water can exist in three forms – ice, liquid, and steam. Each state is different yet still the same chemical compound of H_2O. The difference between this example and God is that water can only be one state at a time; God is all three at all times. God is eternal, having always existed and will exist for eternity to come. (Revelation 1:8) He is omniscient/all knowing (Proverbs 15:2; Acts 15:18), omnipresent/everywhere at one time (Psalm 139:7-10), and omnipotent/all powerful (Luke 1:37; Revelation 21:22). The Holy Spirit was sent to man when the Son left the earth to aide as our comforter and conscience.

Although God the Holy Spirit performs distinct and specific duties from the other 'persons' of the Trinity, the Holy Spirit is still indeed God Himself. (I John 5:7; II Corinthians 3:17) Being God, The Holy Spirit has existed for eternity. We see Him and His involvement in creation as early as Genesis 1:2 which tells us that the S*pirit of God moved upon the face of the waters*. The Holy Spirit indwells every believer at the moment of salvation as is written in Acts 2:38. Some misread this verse to mean that you only receive the Holy Spirit after one is baptized because of how it is listed in the verse. A closer study of the verse, however, will show that the emphasis is on *Repent*. The verse then says *'and' be baptized ... 'and' ye shall receive the gift of the Holy Ghost*. 'And' is used because these two things are both to accompany salvation. Baptism is not required to be saved but is expected as soon as possible once a person is saved. (see baptism earlier in the book) When a person is saved, 'and' they should be baptized 'and' they receive the Holy Spirit. The Holy Spirit offers comfort to the believer in times of sorrow and fear. (John 14:16, 18, 26) During the times of despair when words seem hard to come by, it is the Holy Spirit that intercedes for us in prayer. (Romans 8:26) Another big need the Holy Spirit meets for us is in the area of instruction. He helps guide in learning the things of God and illumines the Scriptures to the Christian. (John 14:26; I Corinthians 2:14)

There will come a day when the Holy Spirit will leave the earth. I already stated that the Holy Spirit serves as the conscience of people; He instills a sense of right and wrong and personal inhibition. II Thessalonians 2:6-7 speaks of One that *withholdeth*. That One is the Holy Spirit; it is He who restrains Satan from unleashing all of his evil and the antichrist from being revealed. Once the church is raptured from the earth, the Holy Spirit will leave along with all the believers allowing all of Satan's evil to be unleashed beginning the tribulation.

This truth is that all Christians are called to be witnesses unto Jesus, to save souls from hell and the judgment of the tribulation. (Mark 16:15) It is the Holy Spirit that gives us the boldness required to fulfill that command and the power to be able to reach into the hearts of lost souls. (Acts 1:8, 4:31) The Christian that loves God and wants to serve Him to the best of their ability will desire not only to have the Holy Spirit, but be 'filled' with the Holy Spirit. And God promises that those who *hunger and thirst after righteousness* will be filled. (Matthew 5:6)

"Now the Lord is that Spirit: and where the Spirit of the Lord *is*, there *is* liberty."

II Corinthians 3:17

"Then Peter said unto them, Repent, and be baptized every one of you in the name of Jesus Christ for the remission of sins, and ye shall receive the gift of the Holy Ghost."

Acts 2:38

"But the Comforter, *which is* the Holy Ghost, whom the Father will send in my name, he shall teach you all things, and bring all things to your remembrance, whatsoever I have said unto you."

John 14:26

"Likewise the Spirit also helpeth our infirmities: for we know not what we should pray for as we ought: but the Spirit itself maketh intercession for us with groaning which cannot be uttered."

Romans 8:26

"And when they had prayed, the place was shaken where they were assembled together; and they were all filled with the Holy Ghost, and they spake the word of God with boldness."

Acts 4:31

"And now ye know what withholdeth that he might be revealed in his time. For the mystery of iniquity doth already work: only he who now letteth *will let*, until he be taken out of the way."

II Thessalonians 2:6-7

"The Holy Ghost is God – not God standing out on the rim of creation surveying His handiwork, not even God at Bethlehem or Calvary, but God moved in. He is God dwelling in men's hearts."
– R. P. Shuler

God the Son

God is three persons acting simultaneously under one Godhead – God the Father, God the Son, and God the Holy Spirit. These three make up what is known as the Trinity. (I John 5:7) The closest example to help explain the trinity is the states of water. Water can exist in three forms – ice, liquid, and gas. Each state is different yet still the same chemical compound of H_2O. The difference between this example and God is that water can only be one state at a time; God is all three at all times. God is eternal, having always existed and will exist for eternity to come. (Revelation 1:8) He is omniscient/all knowing (Proverbs 15:2; Acts 15:18), omnipresent/everywhere at one time (Psalm 139:7-10), and omnipotent/all powerful (Luke 1:37; Revelation 21:22). God the Son, Jesus Christ, was sent by the Father to pay the price for our sins on the cross of Calvary in order to offer us salvation from eternal separation from Him in hell.

God the Son was sent to earth as a babe some 2,000 years ago, but He has existed eternally as He is God. John 17:5 says, "And now, O Father, glorify thou me with thine own self with the glory which I had with thee before the world was"; this places Him before creation. It was, however, His humble birth in Bethlehem that begins what we really know of Him. His birth was a miraculous birth, by way of a virgin (Matthew 1:23) and of the Holy Spirit (Matthew 1:18, 20). The virgin birth was essential in order for Him to be the propitiation for our sins; it was required that He be sinless to be the *only* worthy sacrifice. If he was just another man, He would have been born with the same sin nature as you and I, and His sacrifice would have done no more than those of the goats and calves of the Old Testament. (Hebrews 9:12) Jesus Christ is fully God as proclaimed in John 10:30 and as demonstrated in Mark chapter 6 when he fed the 5,000 (vs. 32-44) and walked on the water (vs. 45-52). Jesus was also fully man. He experienced physical feelings of thirst in John 19:28 and hunger in Matthew 4:2, emotional feelings of sorrow in John 11:35, and spiritual temptation of the devil in Matthew 4:1. Becoming our sacrifice, He also became our intercessor between us and God the Father. It is through Jesus that we come to the Father, for salvation and for prayer and communion (I Timothy 2:5; John 14:6; Matthew 10:32-33) This is why all our prayers should be ended, 'In Jesus name, Amen.'

Jesus is in heaven now with the Father seated at His right hand (Ephesians 1:20), but He will return to this earth once more someday to set up His kingdom in which He will rule and reign. (I Corinthians 15:24) People can get weary of waiting for that day and begin to question its validity. II Peter 3:9 tells us, however, "The Lord is not slack concerning his promise, as some men count slackness; but is longsuffering to us-ward, not willing that any should perish, but that all should come to repentance." God is a loving God who does not want to see anyone go to hell or suffer the wrath of the tribulation, so therefore is delaying His return in hopes that even more would come to Him.

"Behold, a virgin shall be with child, and shall bring forth a son, and they shall call his name Emmanuel, which being interpreted is, God with us."

Matthew 1:23

"I and *my* Father are one."

John 10:30

"Neither by the blood of goats and calves, but by his own blood he entered in once into the holy place, having obtained eternal redemption *for us*."

Hebrews 9:12

"After this, Jesus knowing that all things were now accomplished, that the scripture might be fulfilled, saith, I thirst."

John 19:28

"For *there is* one God, and one mediator between God and men, the man Christ Jesus;"

I Timothy 2:5

"Which he wrought in Christ, when he raised him from the dead, and set *him* at his own right hand in the heavenly *places*,"

Ephesians 1:20

"Christ is unique because of His claims. He claimed to be the Son of God. He claimed to be coequal with God. He claimed to be God. ...but mark the unique element of this claim. He not only claimed to be God, but He proved His claim!" – John Linton

God's Chosen People

God's chosen people are the Israelites. This is revealed in Genesis 12:1-3 which is the declaration of the Abrahamic covenant. Abraham was promised blessings and divine protection and that he would be a great nation. Isaac was the promised son to Abraham and Sarah; he received the blessings of his father Abraham. Isaac had two sons, Esau and Jacob. Isaac's birthright was passed to Jacob who was renamed Israel after he wrestled with God. (Genesis 32:24-32; 35:10) All descendants of Jacob are Israelites. Jacob had twelve sons who became the twelve tribes of Israel. There is often confusion concerning the Jews; some people think the Jews alone are God's chosen people. They are indeed, but they are only 1/12 of God's chosen people being the descendants of only one of the twelve sons of Jacob. The term Jew was given to those that were descendants from the tribe of Judah. Therefore, all Jews are Israelites but not all Israelites are Jews. God's chosen people goes beyond just the Jews.

The Israelites are God's chosen people, yes, but that does not mean they get a free pass into heaven. They too must be saved by believing in the Gospel of Jesus Christ and receiving Him as their personal Savior. In Romans 1:16, Paul said that he was not ashamed of spreading this Gospel and that the Jews were on the top of his list to whom he was going to share it with. He continued in Romans 10:1 to say, "Brethren, my heart's desire and prayer to God for Israel is, that they might be saved." Paul had a clear and sincere burden for God's chosen people to be saved; they had to be reached just like everyone else. God's desire, as is with all mankind, is that they be saved.

Part of the Abrahamic covenant was a defined portion of land with which God promised to bless His chosen people. God led Abraham to this land in Genesis 12:6-7 where He made the first promise to give that land *unto thy seed*. This promise was confirmed to Isaac in Genesis 26:3 and then to Jacob in Genesis 28:13. The boundaries of this promised land are laid out in Genesis 15:18-21 and Joshua 1:2-4 which is equivalent today to the land from Lebanon to the Nile River in Egypt North to South and from the Mediterranean Sea to the Euphrates River West to East. This means that current day Israel is only occupying a small portion of the land God has promised to them.

God's Word is very clear that the Israelites are the chosen people of God. He has promised specific blessings for them and in turn has promised judgment and curses for those who do not treat them accordingly. Zechariah 2:8 tells us that when we touch this group of people we *toucheth the apple of his eye*. We are expected to treat and respond to the nation of Israel in a positive and amiable manner. As part of the Abrahamic Covenant, God gives this warning in Genesis 12:3, "And I will bless them that bless thee and curse him that curseth thee…" Psalm 105:15 says that we are to *touch not mine anointed, and do my prophets no harm*. The United States has been blessed of God because it is a Christian nation that has supported and treated the nation of Israel favorably. We must heed caution that as we fall away from God's Word and begin to turn our backs on Israel, God's blessings and hand of protection will be removed.

"For thou *art* an holy people unto the LORD thy God: the LORD thy God hath chosen thee to be a special people unto himself, above all people that *are* upon the face of the earth. The LORD did not set his love upon you, nor choose you, because ye were more in number than any people; for ye *were* fewest of all people: But because the LORD loved you, and because he would keep the oath which he had sworn unto your fathers, hath the LORD brought you out with a mighty hand, and redeemed you out of the house of bondmen, from the hand of Pharoah king of Egypt."

Deuteronomy 7:6-9

"O ye seed of Abraham his servant, ye children of Jacob his chosen. He *is* the LORD our God: his judgments *are* in all the earth. He hath rememberd his covenant for ever, the word *which* he commanded to a thousand generations. Which *covenant* he made with Abraham, and his oath unto Isaac; And confirmed the same unto Jacob for a law, *and* to Israel *for* an everlasting covenant: Saying, Unto thee will I give the land of Canaan, the lot of your inheritance: When they were *but* a few men in number; yea, very few, and strangers in it. When they went from one nation to another, from *one* kingdom to another people: He suffered no man to do them wrong: yea, he reproved kings for their sakes; *Saying*, Touch not mine anointed, and do my prophets no harm."

Psalm 105:6-15

"Sojourn in this land, and I will be with thee, and will bless thee; for unto thee, and unto thy seed, I will give all these countries, and I will perform the oath which I sware unto Abraham thy father;"

Genesis 26:3

And I will bless them that bless thee, and curse him that curseth thee: and in thee shall all families of the earth be blessed."

Genesis 12:3

"The time has come, and long past, when the United States should keep its promise and take a firm stand for law and order in that land that has given the world its Bible and Saviour."
– J. Frank Norris

God's Will for Your Life

God's will is His commands, direction, and divine determination for your life.[1] As soon as a person is saved, they should seek to find and do God's will for their life; they should ask, *Lord, what wilt thou have me to do?* (Acts 9:6) We are to seek God's will in every avenue of life, every decision, no matter how big or small. Every saved person can be assured that God has a specific will for their life. *The steps of a good man are ordered by the Lord* says Psalm 37:23. If the Lord did not have a job (or will) for the Christian to do, then why did He let them remain on this earth after they were saved? If there was nothing for the Christian to do, He would have taken them to be with Him in Heaven the moment they received Him as Savior. The saved person can also be assured that God wants us to know what His will is for our lives. (Ephesians 5:17) So if God has a will for each person's life and wants them to know what it is, how then do they find it?

The first order of business is to do the written will of God that He has given to us in His Word. God has given many direct commands concerning things like being baptized, sharing the Gospel with others, how we are to treat others, those things that we should do and not do in our daily Christian lives, etc.. God will not reveal His unwritten will for one's life until they are willingly doing those things that He has already revealed in His Word. Once God's written will is a natural part of a person's life, they can begin learning what His unwritten will for their life is. There are seven steps that will help one learn this.[11] 1) Be daily in God's Word; one cannot find their way without it. (Psalm 119:105) 2) Have a strong and regular prayer life; God will give wisdom to whomever asks for it. (James 1:5) 3) Seek Godly counsel; take advantage of the wisdom the Pastor and other seasoned Christians around have to offer. (Proverbs 11:14) 4) Consider the circumstances; God directs a Christian's steps by way of opened and closed doors. 5) Use common sense; the Christian that has close fellowship with the Lord and fills their mind with holy things will have a sound mind to think through things. (II Timothy 1:7) 6) Allow personal desires and gifts to play a part; God is the one who created those abilities for a purpose and He places godly desires in the heart of the one who delights in Him. (Psalm 37:4) 7) Listen to the leading of the Holy Spirit; He will give a peace about what God would have one do. (Colossians 3:15; Isaiah 26:3; Romans 8:14-16) Be careful not to place more emphasis on any one step (especially if others do not seem to agree); the goal is that they should all harmonize together. Besides these seven steps, be mindful of those things that will hinder a Christian from learning God's will. James 4 is a rebuke of worldliness and a study of this chapter will show those things that could make one miss God's will despite all the attempts and progress through the seven steps.

Once one knows God's will for their life and has surrendered to do it, God will provide all that is needed to follow through. He will open the doors necessary and give the ability, finances, and whatever else may be required. God will perform His will that He has called the Christian to do in his life. (I Thessalonians 5:24) Don't be afraid to follow God's leading. God's will is the best, and happiest, place for one to be; it is *good, and acceptable, and perfect.* (Romans 12:1-2) There is no more miserable place than being outside of God's will!

"The steps of a *good* man are ordered by the LORD: and he delighteth in his way."

Psalm 37:23

"Wherefore be ye not unwise, but understanding what the will of the Lord *is*."

Ephesians 5:17

"I delight to do thy will, O my God: yea, thy law *is* within my heart."

Psalm 40:8

"Faithful *is* he that calleth you, who also will do *it*."

I Thessalonians 5:24

"I beseech you therefore, brethren, by the mercies of God, that ye present your bodies a living sacrifice, holy, acceptable unto God, *which is* your reasonable service. And be not conformed to this world: but be ye transformed by the renewing of your mind, that ye may prove what *is* that good, and acceptable, and perfect, will of God."

Romans 12:1-2

"God has a purpose for your life; don't let Satan, the world, or the flesh keep you from fulfilling that purpose." – Wayne Thompson

Gossip

To gossip is to go about collecting tales and then tattling, speaking idle talk, backbiting, and telling news.[1] It is a sin that God hates. Paul was inspired to name it among a list of ungodly and unrighteous things God will judge. It is listed as *whisperers* and *backbiters* along with *wickedness*, *murder*, and *haters of God*. (Romans 1:18-19, 28-30) Gossip is an ugly use of the tongue that hurts others.

Sometimes, people are unsure of what constitutes gossip. There are some simple questions that can be asked about what is being said that will indicate whether it may be gossip. Ask, "Is what I'm going to say going to edify the person it's about," (Ephesians 4:29) "Am I sharing something told to me in confidence," (Proverbs 11:13) "Am I venting," (Philippians 2:14) and perhaps the biggest one, "What is my motive for sharing this?" Determining one's motive can be tricky because as Jeremiah 17:9 says, our *heart is deceitful* and *desperately wicked*. We are really good at justifying our motives. One must be utterly honest with themselves and if they cannot say that they have genuine love for the person involved and desperately want to help them then they are gossiping. Gossip can sometimes be subtle. For instance, gossip is often committed by means of prayer requests. Is the prayer request being given for someone genuinely loved and cared about that the prayer will benefit, or is the motive just trying to let people know what is going on without looking like a gossip? A good rule to follow when determining if it is alright to say something is to not share if we are not involved in the situation and/or we cannot do anything to change or help the situation.

The tongue is very powerful, causing just as much damage (and often times more) than the physical wounds of battle weapons. James speaks of this in Chapter 3 verses 6 and 8 saying that the tongue is *a world of iniquity...set on fire of hell* and *full of deadly poison*. Gossip is destructive. One must always remember that gossip is often times only one side of the story and it doesn't give the individual(s) involved the opportunity to defend themselves. It destroys reputations, both of the slandered party and of the one spreading the gossip as well. Reputations have great impact on one's life and are very hard to redeem once tarnished. God speaks of the value of a good reputation in Proverbs 22:1 and Ecclesiastes 7:1; defaming them should not be taken lightly. Gossip also divides. Proverbs 16:28 says that it *separateth chief friends*. God calls us to be of *one mind* and *striving together* for the cause of spreading the Gospel. (Philippians 1:27)

Those who gossip will be judged for their sin. We will give account for the things we say *in the day of judgment*; our words will either justify us or condemn us. (Matthew 12:36-37) Words that justify are those that uplift and edify fellow believers; gossip is counterproductive to that command. (Ephesians 4:29, 31-32) There are ways to help avoid being a gossip or cultivating an environment for gossip. Avoid being idle and being a busybody. Idleness leads to many a sin, including gossip. (I Timothy 5:13) Instead, keep busy doing the work of the Lord. You can stop gossip by not listening or giving ear to the gossiper. Don't add fuel to the fire and heed God's command to *meddle not* with them. (Proverbs 26:20, 20:19)

"Let no corrupt communication proceed out of your mouth, but that which is good to the use of edifying, that it may minister grace unto the hearers."

Ephesians 4:29

"A talebearer revealeth secrets: but he that is of a faithful spirit concealeth the matter."

Proverbs 11:13

"A froward man soweth strife: and a whisperer separateth chief friends."

Proverbs 16:28

"And withal they learn *to be* idle, wandering about from house to house; and not only idle, but tattlers also and busybodies, speaking things which they ought not."

I Timothy 5:13

"Where no wood is, *there* the fire goeth out: so where *there is* no talebearer, the strife ceaseth."

Proverbs 26:20

"He that goeth about *as* a talebearer revealeth secrets: therefore meddle not with him that flattereth with his lips."

Proverbs 20:19

"If there were no gratified hearers of ill reports, there would be an end of the trade of spreading them." – Charles Spurgeon

Government

Government is, "the exercise of authority; direction and restraint exercised over the actions of men in communities, societies or states. [It is] the system of polity in a state; that form of fundamental rules and principles by which a nation or state is governed, or by which individual members of a body politic are to regulate their social action."[1] God's plan was for us to be ruled by Him as was Adam and Eve in the Garden and the nation of Israel until they desired to be led by a king and the beginning of Saul's reign in 1095 B.C. Because of sin, God needed to create a system of order and instituted human government.

We are responsible to obey those authorities that God ordained and has placed over us. (Romans 13:1) Our government has organized a process of voting for those who are to be in power. We have a responsibility as Christians to exercise our right to vote so that God's way can be voiced by means of how we vote. Regardless of whether our choice is elected, however, we must obey the authority that is placed in power. We are to be *subject unto the higher powers* and *submit yourselves to every ordinance of man*. (Romans 13:1; I Peter 2:13) Those in authority are called *God's ministers* and are placed there for order and judgment. (Romans 13:1-7; I Peter 2:14) God also commands us to pray for our leaders; we cannot expect to live *a quiet and peaceable* life if we do not. (I Timothy 2:1-2)

The idea of 'separation of church and state' is a false and twisted representation of the first amendment to the U.S. Constitution. It has turned into an idea that the church is not to be involved in the affairs of the government or have any influence over how government works. This amendment is actually quite clear, however, and reads that, "Congress shall make no law respecting an establishment of religion, or prohibiting the free exercise therof." Truth be told that when this amendment was written by the forefathers of this nation, it was not meant to keep the church out of government but rather for the purpose of keeping the government out of the church. It is actually rather baffling at how there is so much confusion over something that is very plainly written. Our forefathers had immigrated to this land for refuge from a country that was forcing a state religion on the people. They formed their own new nation so that they could serve God as they felt was right without worry of the government dictating their religion. God created man with a free will and Himself gives man the choice to choose or reject to serve Him. (Joshua 24:15; Romans 10:13) So ought we and the government give man the choice of their religion. Because choosing Christ and His salvation is a choice, it is not something that can be dictated, controlled, or chosen for a person by the government. John 1:12-13 says we become the *sons of God...nor of the will of man*. God desires a relationship with His children and no forced religion from the government can produce that. (Matthew 15:7-8)

Even if our government refuses to allow Christianity to shape the way it operates and twists everything opposite to God's Word, we must remember that our hope is not in our government. Yes, we are responsible as citizens to obey the government that God has ordained, but only to the extent that they do not expect us to go against God's Word. (Mark 12:17) Our higher duty is to God!

"Let every soul be subject unto the higher powers. For there is no power but of God: the powers that be are ordained of God. Whosoever therefore resisteth the power, resisteth the ordinance of God: and they that resist shall receive to themselves damnation. For rulers are not a terror to good works, but to the evil. Wilt thou then not be afraid of the power? Do that which is good, and thou shalt have praise of the same: For he is the minister of God to thee for good. But if thou do that which is evil, be afraid; for he beareth not the sword in vain: for he is the minister of God, a revenger to *execute* wrath upon him that doeth evil. Wherefore *ye* must needs be subject, not only for wrath, but also for conscience sake. For this cause pay ye tribute also: for they are God's ministers, attending continually upon this very thing. Render therefore to all their dues: tribute to whom tribute *is due*; custom to whom custom; fear to who fear; honour to whom honour."

Romans 13:1-7

"Submit yourselves to every ordinance of man for the Lord's sake: whether it be to the king, as supreme; Or unto governors, as unto them that are sent by him for the punishment of evildoers, and for the praise of them that do well."

I Peter 2:13-14

"I exhort therefore, that, first of all, supplications, prayers, intercessions, *and* giving of thanks, be made for all men; For kings, and *for* all that are in authority; that we may lead a quiet and peaceable life in all godliness and honesty."

I Timothy 2:1-2

"And Jesus answering said unto them, Render to Ceasar the things that are Ceasar's, and to God the things that are God's. And they marvelled at him."

Mark 12:17

"It is impossible to rightly govern a nation without God and the Bible." – George Washington

Guns

Guns are the modern weapon of choice for many. Specific reference to guns is not found in the Bible having not yet been invented at that time, but the Bible is not lacking in examples of how weapons of that time were used for different purposes. The Bible is our guidebook for all things in life and the topic of guns is no exception; God's Word is timeless. I Timothy 5:8 tells us, "But if any provide not for his own, and specially for those of his own house, he hath denied the faith, and is worse than an infidel." This is most often referred to in reference to men providing financially for their family. A husband/father is to provide in other ways as well. He provides food, which he may choose to provide by hunting it on his own, and physical protection from those seeking to harm his family. In the Bible, men provided those things with swords and bows, today guns have been added to the weapon list. There are times when weapons are needed, and according to Christ, more important than your garments. (Luke 22:36)

Man uses guns to provide food for their families. Up until the flood of Noah, all men were vegetarian by God's decree. But after the flood, this order was changed and God gave us animals for food. (Genesis 9:3) Common sense tells you that the animal must be killed to be eaten. (Acts 10:13) Isaac, having wanting to savor a venison meal before he died, told his son to take up his weapons (in this case a bow) and go kill him a deer. (Genesis 27:3) Guns are the most effective and humane way to harvest animals for food today. The man of the home (or Mom in the absence of Dad) also has the obligation to protect his home and families' lives. Life is precious to God and we are to place as much value in it as He does and do whatever possible to preserve it. For this reason we should only use such drastic measures as taking someone's life when absolutely necessary. God warns, however, in Ezekiel 33:6 that a watchman (the husband/father is the watchman of their home) who sees trouble coming but does nothing about it is subject to the judgment of God. Unfortunately, guns must sometimes be used for personal protection.

War is an awful thing and everyone loves peace rather than war, but sin has determined that war is inevitable and sometimes necessary as seen in Mark 13:7. God's Word is full of wars and instances where God instructed His people to conquer and utterly destroy entire people groups. The United States of America never would have been or remained without wars and the guns that aided brave men and woman in winning them. Guns will continue to be required to protect our nation and nations abroad that need our military aid.

An armed military, law enforcement, and citizenship is necessary to maintain order and thwart crime; it strikes fear in those who do evil. (Romans 13:4) It must be understood that guns do not kill people, people kill people. Drunk driving murder statistics is a great comparison. We do not ban cars because of deaths caused by drunk drivers because it seems understood that the drunk driver is the one at fault not the car; the same goes for guns. Just as was seen in the first murder, the condition of Cain's heart was what led him to murder his brother. (Genesis 4:5, 8) Guns are not a threat, but rather a necessity for civil order.

"Then said he unto them, But now, he that hath a purse, let him take *it*, and likewise *his* scrip: and he that hath no sword, let him sell his garment, and buy one."

Luke 22:36

"And there came a voice to him, Rise, Peter; kill, and eat."

Acts 10:13

"But if the watchman see the sword come, and blow not the trumpet, and the people be not warned; if the sword come, and take *any* person from among them, he is taken away in his iniquity; but his blood will I require at the watchman's hand."

Ezekiel 33:6

"For he is the minister of God to thee for good. But if thou do that which is evil, be afraid; for he beareth not the sword in vain: for he is the minister of God, a revenger to *execute* wrath upon him that doeth evil."

Romans 13:4

"Firearms are second only to the Constitution in importance; they are the peoples' liberty's teeth." – George Washington

Heaven

There are actually three heavens spoken of in the Bible. The first is the firmament or sky which surrounds the earth and that in which the birds and planes fly and clouds form. The second starts just beyond that and goes on for as far as the eye or powerful telescope can see. It is what we usually refer to as space: the area which holds the sun, moon, and stars. The third heaven is the unseen residence of God, Jesus Christ, angels, and saved loved ones that have passed on before us. Before Christ's resurrection, saved saints that died went to a place referred to as Abraham's bosom or paradise. (Luke 16:22 & 23:43) This temporary abode was in the heart of the earth (Luke 16:23,26; Matthew 12:40) until Jesus' resurrection when paradise was opened and the dead saints made their journey to heaven. (Matthew 27:52-53)

Heaven's grandeur and size is beyond our imagination or what can be explained on paper; Revelation 21:16-25 does give us a glimpse of what we can expect however. The passage starts by giving the dimensions of this immense eternal paradise (vs. 16-17). Precious jewels of every kind that garnish the walls, foundations, and gates are described in verses 18-21. We will walk on streets of gold so purified that they are transparent (vs. 21). Verse 25 tells us that there will be no more night, but at the same time there is no sun because *the glory of God did lighten it* (vs. 23). Among all these beautiful surroundings, God's magnificent throne is found described in Revelation 4:2-5. Besides the stunning sights of heaven, we have more wonderful truths to glory in. The first great truth about heaven is that we will enjoy the absence of sin. (Revelation 21:27) Because there is no sin there will be no more pain, sickness, or tears. (Revelation 21:4) We will be reunited with our saved loved ones that went on before us, although, there will be no more marriage in heaven. (Matthew 22:30) Another great truth of heaven is the new, perfect and without blemish body we will receive at the resurrection of the church. (Philippians 3:20-21; I Thessalonians 16-17) Rest assured, however, that even though we have new bodies and do not associate with our spouses as we do here on earth, we will still know each other just as the rich man knew Abraham and Lazarus. (Luke 16:22-24) Above all, we will be in the presence of our Lord who is preparing a mansion for every believer in heaven and has promised that He will come back to take us to be with Him there. (John 14:2-3)

People often ask, "What we will do for an eternity in heaven?" God's children will glory in service to God. (Revelation 7:15) Simultaneous with service to God, heaven will be a place of rest (Revelation 14:13) and comfort (Luke 16:25). We will rejoice with God and the angels over souls saved. (Luke 15:10) Above all, heaven will be a place of glory and worship to God. Revelation 5:13 gives example of the praises that will be sung to God by all creatures. In heaven, we will receive crowns for those things we did on earth for the cause of Christ. There will be no higher honor, however, than to place those crowns at the feet of our Lord in worship and honor to Him. (Revelation 4:10-11) God revealed enough to us about heaven to understand that it is an indescribably wonderful place, even so, it will be far better than we can imagine. Jesus Christ resides there now at the right hand of His Father awaiting His second coming. (Hebrews 10:12-13) One will want to make sure this glorious place is their destination and share the good news with others so that they can bring as many as they can with them!

"And the foundations of the wall of the city *were* garnished with all manner of precious stones. The first foundation *was* jasper; the second, sapphire; the third, a chalcedony; the fourth, an emerald; The fifth, sardonyx; the sixth, sardius; the seventh, chrysolite; the eighth beryl; the ninth, a topaz; the tenth, a chrysoprasus; the eleventh, a jacinth; the twelfth, an amethyst. And the twelve gates *were* twelve pearls; every several gate was of one pearl: and the street of the city *was* pure gold, as it were transparent glass."

Revelation 21:19-21

"And God shall wipe away all tears from their eyes; and there shall be no more death, neither sorrow, nor crying, neither shall there be any more pain: for the former things are passed away."

Revelation 21:4

"For our conversation is in heaven; from whence also we look for the Saviour, the Lord Jesus Christ: Who shall change our vile body, that it may be fashioned like unto his glorious body, according to the working whereby he is able even to subdue all things unto himself."

Philippians 3:20-21

"In my Father's house are many mansions: if *it were* not *so*, I would have told you. I go to prepare a place for you."

John 14:2

"And every creature which is in heaven, and on the earth, and under the earth, and such as are in the sea, and all that are in them, heard I saying, Blessing, and honour, and glory, and power, *be* unto him that sitteth upon the throne, and unto the Lamb for ever and ever."

Revelation 5:13

"But if you want to know the length and breadth and height and depth of the love of God, go to the Celestial City and begin to measure its proportions. It has been built to house a great multitude that no one can number." – Harry J. Hager

Hell

Hell is a place of punishment and torment where those who have not received Christ as their Savior will spend eternity when they die. Matthew 25:41 explains that it was a place prepared by God for the Devil and his angels. Like Heaven, hell is a general term used to express different root words and places. In Hebrew, hell is usually translated from *sheol* and in Greek from *hades*. The current hell is the same place spoken of in Luke 16:19-31 in the heart of the earth. It is a temporary abode for the souls of the unsaved dead until the final judgment. We see this supported in II Peter 2:4 which explains that the fallen angels were sent to hell *to be reserved unto judgment*. The wicked dead in the current hell will get their bodies back before raising for this great white throne judgment that will come after the 1,000-year millennial reign of Christ (see end times). It is at this judgment that they will be cast into the lake of fire which is also known as eternal hell and/or the second death where they will spend eternity. (Revelation 20:14-15)

Eternal torment is the best way to describe hell. First, eternal; Matthew 25:46 says that it is *everlasting punishment* and Revelation 20:10 says that the torment will be *day and night for ever and ever*. The torment suffered there will go on for an eternity and there is absolutely no way to escape it once a person has been sentenced to go there. (Luke 16:26) Secondly, torment; hell will not be a party! It is a place of *fire and brimstone*. (Revelation 20:10) Brimstone is related to sulphur and being highly combustible. The fire will burn forever for Mark 9:43 says it *shall never be quenched* and the soul will never be consumed by the fire. It is a place where the soul will thirst for relief but will receive none. (Luke 16:24) Matthew 13:50 describes *wailing and gnashing of teeth* which relays lamentation and extreme anguish and utter despair. Luke 16:19-31 shows us a man that found himself in this wretched place and begging for relief. When he was offered no relief he pleaded with Abraham to send someone from the grave to warn his family so that they did not end up in the same awful place he found himself.

An interesting fact to note is that there will be different degrees of punishment in hell just as there are different levels of rewards in heaven. Revelation 20:12-13 says that those entering hell are judged *according to their works*. Luke 12:47-48 speaks of this as well with *many stripes* and *few stripes*. Verse 48 says that those who *knew not* will not receive as harsh a punishment (like those who were never reached with the Gospel) but will nonetheless still go to hell. These differences will seem minimal, however, in a place of unspeakable suffering.

Hell is a very real place and a place more awful than can be imagined. God does not wish for anyone go to hell, being longsuffering that all would receive Him and escape its torment. (II Peter 3:9) God is a holy God, however, and will not look upon sin or place Himself in the presence of sin which means sin cannot be allowed into Heaven where He resides. (Isaiah 59:2; Habakkuk 1:13) God is also a just God and this truth constrains Him to judge sin. (see God-Mercy/Grace/Justice) Knowing what we do about Hell must give us a sense of urgency and prompt us to get serious about telling others how they can escape the fires of hell.

"And whosoever was not found written in the book of life was cast into the lake of fire."

Revelation 20:15

"For if God spared not the angels that sinned, but cast *them* down to hell, and delivered *them* into chains of darkness, to be reserved unto judgment;"

II Peter 2:4

"And if thy hand offend thee, cut if off: it is better for thee to enter into life maimed, than having two hands to go into hell, into the fire that never shall be quenched:"

Mark 9:43

"And in hell he lift up his eyes, being in torments, and seeth Abraham afar off, and Lazarus in his bosom. And he cried and said, Father Abraham, have mercy on me, and send Lazarus, that he may dip the tip of his finger in water, and cool my tongue; for I am tormented in this flame."

Luke 16:23-24

"And shall cast them into the furnace of fire: there shall be wailing and gnashing of teeth."

Matthew 13:50

"Jesus preached more about Hell than He did about Heaven; more about Hell than He did about life; more about Hell than He did about death; more about Hell than He did about anything that He preached in this world. Why? ...He knew there were multitudes there screaming and crying and writhing in their pain and lost forever and forever." – Dolphus Price

Holidays - Christmas

Christmas is, "the festival of the Christian church observed annually on the 25th day of December in memory of the birth of Christ."[1] It has become customary to celebrate Christ's birth with children's pageants at churches that tell of the story of His birth, trimming of trees to symbolize the hope of everlasting life we can have in Jesus, and giving gifts to show expressions of love like God did when He gave us His Son and as the wise men did toward Jesus on the first Christmas.

The birth of Christ was necessary in order for any of us to be able to go to heaven when we die. God created a perfect and sinless human race in Adam and Eve but with their sin in the garden, sin entered the world and we were separated from fellowship and communion with God. God loves every one of us, however, and created a way for this to be remedied; that remedy is His Son Jesus Christ. (John 3:16) Isaiah prophesied of His birth some 732 years before He was born. (Isaiah 7:14) This prophecy was fulfilled and recorded in Matthew and Luke. (Matthew 1:18-21) The birth of Christ brought the God-man (Jesus Christ) to earth as flesh to dwell among His creation for 33 years for the sole purpose of dying on the cross to pay the punishment of our sins so that our fellowship could be restored and we can go to be with Him in heaven when we die. Jesus Christ's one purpose was to *seek and to save that which was lost*, and the Christmas holiday celebrates the fulfillment of that purpose. This event is so important, so monumental, that all secular history dates around His birth. It is the silent testimony of the truth of Christmas.

Perhaps the most important fact of Christmas is the truth of the virgin birth; salvation is dependent on it. First, Jesus could not be the Son of God who has existed for eternity as part of the trinity without the virgin birth. (John 1:1) If Joseph were His father, he would have been nothing but a mere human man, the son of Mary and Joseph. Second, He was sinless as was necessary for Him to be able to pay for our sins. (I Peter 2:22; I John 3:5) The sin nature would have been passed to Him if Joseph had been his father. The Bible clearly states that Christ was born of a virgin; it was the first miracle of a public ministry full of miracles. If Jesus was not virgin-born He would not have been an acceptable sacrifice for our sins.

So how did Santa Claus get into the Christmas holiday? 'Santa Claus' is traced back to a real man in history named St. Nicholas of Myra who was a Catholic priest in Turkey. He was known and remembered as a generous man toward children and, through the years, has been morphed into a mythical children's character. Satan has used the popularity of 'Santa Claus' with children to elevate him above Christ's place of preeminence in an attempt to hide the real meaning of Christmas. Likewise, Satan has done the same with gift giving. Gift giving began as a very small part of the holiday but Satan has used retailers to exploit this innocent tradition into a priority of the holiday that has gotten out of hand. No matter how commercialized the Christmas holiday has become, however, Satan has failed to completely eliminate Christ from Christmas. It is the one time of the year when the Gospel of Christ is rung through all the stores by means of Christmas carols!

"For God so loved the world, that he gave his only begotten Son, that whosoever believeth in him should not perish, but have everlasting life."

John 3:16

"Therefore the Lord himself shall give you a sign; Behold, a virgin shall conceive, and bear a son, and shall call his name Immanuel."

Isaiah 7:14

"Now the birth of Jesus Christ was on this wise: When as his mother Mary was espoused to Joseph, before they came together, she was found with child of the Holy Ghost. Then Joseph her husband, being a just *man*, and not willing to make her a publick example, was minded to put her away privily. But while he thought on these things, behold, the angle of the Lord appeared unto him in a dream, saying, Joseph, thou son of David, fear not to take unto thee Mary thy wife: for that which is conceived in her is of the Holy Ghost. And she shall bring forth a son, and thou shalt call his name JESUS: for he shall save his people from their sins."

Matthew 1:18-21

"And the Word was made flesh, and dwelt among us, (and we beheld his glory, the glory as of the only begotten of the Father,) full of grace and truth."

John 1:14

"For the Son of man is come to seek and to save that which was lost."

Luke 19:10

"It is true that Christmas has been commercialized; it is true that many will sing the Christmas carols who do not know the Lord. Yet the carols are sung! All the civilized world is constantly reminded of the Christian's Christmas." – Louis T. Talbot

Holidays - Easter

Easter is a Christian holiday observed to remember and commemorate the resurrection of Jesus Christ after His crucifixion. Most churches will make a special emphasis on their Easter Sunday services and often have Easter musicals and decorate the buildings with Lilies, a flower that symbolizes purity (the purity of Christ), hope (the hope we have in a living Christ), and life (the risen life of Christ and the eternal life He gives to the believer). Palm Sunday (the Sunday before Easter) is often part of the Easter holiday celebrations commemorating Jesus' triumphal entry into Jerusalem just five days before His crucifixion. Just as with Christmas, Satan has used commercialism to shroud the true meaning of the Easter holiday. The Easter bunny and colored eggs, although innocent traditions symbolizing new life, are mere tools of Satan to take over yet another Christ honoring holiday.

Easter is equally as vital to our salvation as is Christmas. Although the resurrection is highlighted most during the Easter holiday, Easter celebrates the entire Gospel. (I Corinthians 15:3-4) Easter is the purpose for which the babe of Christmas came. We pay tribute and express thankful hearts toward God for the price His Son paid on the cross for our sin. (Isaiah 53:5) Jesus' body was then buried in a borrowed tomb with a heavy stone placed at the entrance and guards to ensure no tampering of the body. When ladies went to the tomb to prepare the body of their Lord with spices days later, as was the custom, they were greeted with an empty tomb and angels announcing His glorious raising from the dead. (Luke 24:1-6a) Every part of Jesus' death, burial, and resurrection was carefully planned, including what Walter L. Wilson explains about John 20:7. He says, "Probably this is a picture of the separation that was to take place between Christ, the head of the Church, and His followers who constituted His body. By this means the Savior is telling that He was to leave this earth, leave the Christians behind, and ascend to His Father. The head was to be in heaven, while the Church, which is His Body, was to remain on earth."[12]

The bodily resurrection of Christ is absolutely essential to the Christian faith. (I Corinthians 15:17) First, it was necessary to fulfill prophecy, otherwise so many verses found in God's Word would be a lie. For example: Jesus said He would raise the temple in three days (speaking of His body) in John 2:19. Many places in Scripture God says He is with us which would not be possible if He were dead. (Joshua 1:9; Isaiah 4:10; Matthew 28:20) What about the blessed hope we have in John 14:2? A dead god cannot prepare us a mansion in heaven and come back to take us to be with Him. Furthermore, it is His living presence and working in us that leads us along the way, makes us what we are, and helps us to grow in our Christian walk; a dead god cannot do that. (I Corinthians 15:10) Romans 14:9 tells us that He not only rose, but *revived* so that He can be our Lord, to rule them that are living and receive those who die. God did not leave us without proof of this necessary truth either. I Corinthians 15:5-8 gives testimony of the multitudes that saw Him after His resurrection. Additionally, Romans 8:17 says that we are *joint-heirs with Christ* and only a living person can be an heir. The resurrection of Christ proves He is who He claimed to be and declares the power needed to be Lord of all. (Romans 1:4)

"For I delivered unto you first of all that which I also received, how that Christ died for our sins according to the scriptures; And that he was buried, and that he rose again the third day according to the scriptures:"

I Corinthians 15:3-4

"But he *was* wounded for our transgressions, *he was* bruised for our iniquities: the chastisement of our peace *was* upon him; and with his stripes we are healed."

Isaiah 53:5

"Now upon the first *day* of the week, very early in the morning, they came unto the sepulchre, bringing the spices which they had prepared, and certain *others* with them. And they found the stone rolled away from the sepulchre. And they entered in, and found not the body of the Lord Jesus. And it came to pass, as they were much perplexed thereabout, behold, two men stood by them in shining garments: And as they were afraid, and bowed down *their* faces to the earth, they said unto them, Why seek ye the living among the dead? He is not here, but is risen..."

Luke 24:1-6a

"And if Christ be not raised, your faith *is* vain; ye are yet in your sins."

I Corinthians 15:17

"For to this end Christ both died, and rose, and revived, that he might be Lord both of the dead and living."

Romans 14:9

"Everything depends on the resurrection of Jesus Christ. That's the cornerstone upon which the whole superstructure of Christianity rests; undermine it, and the whole business drops."
– William Edward Biederwolf

Holidays - Halloween

Halloween is a secular holiday based on pagan beliefs about the dead and powers of evil. It originated from ancient Druid beliefs that honored Samhain (or Saman), the Lord of the Dead. It was believed that on the eve of the November 1 celebrations, that the spirits of the dead were released to mingle among the human population to haunt and harm them. In an attempt to keep the evil spirits at bay, a party and bonfire was observed. Villagers went house to house asking for food for the event, many of them wearing costumes; it is this that has evolved into the trick-or-treat tradition that is observed today. Even the Jack-o-lanterns of Halloween trace back to stories of a damned soul named Jack that could not enter Heaven or Hell and was doomed to wander until Judgment Day with only a lantern. Halloween is the Devil's holiday, in fact, Halloween is to Satan and those who serve him what Christmas and Easter is to Christians. Commercialism has turned it into a high profit based holiday (second only to Christmas) focused on selling costumes, candy, greeting cards, decorations, and haunted house/tour entertainments. It may seem like innocent fun but the devil is especially good at making wrong and evil things look fun and wonderful on the outside. God admonishes us to not twist evil and good in Isaiah 5:20, which is what Satan has done with Halloween.

God's Word is filled with exhortations to stay away from evil and all the things that pertain to Satan. I Thessalonians 5:22 tells us that we are to stay away from those things that even resemble evil. A saved person is a child of God and light and we see in II Corinthians 6:14 that light and darkness have no fellowship or communion with one another – they do not mix. You cannot be a child of God and partake of His blessings while partaking in the things of Satan. (I Corinthians 10:21) We are to bear fruit for the Lord but the things of Satan are unfruitful. (Ephesians 5:11) According to this verse, we are to not only refrain from fellowship with the things of darkness, but we are to reprove them – or expose the truth. A saved person is also the temple of God. We are to cherish and honor that temple (our bodies) but according to Leviticus 19:31 regarding the things of darkness defiles a person and makes them unclean. Deuteronomy 18:10-12 gives a long list of things related to darkness, evil, and Satan which are those things that Halloween is centered around and all of which God calls an abomination.

Every holiday is observed to honor someone or something. At Christmas, we celebrate Christ's birth and at Easter, it is His resurrection. Christopher Columbus is honored on Columbus Day, and those who served in the military are remembered and shown appreciation on Veteran's Day. What/who do we honor on Halloween? – evil and Satan. Halloween is a holiday that glorifies death and celebrates evil and the things of darkness. We read in Philippians 4:8, "Finally, brethren, whatsoever things are true, whatsoever things are honest, whatsoever things *are* pure, whatsoever things *are* lovely, whatsoever things *are* of good report; if *there be* any virtue, and if *there be* any praise, think on these things." God wants us to fill our minds and time with those things that edify and lift ourselves and those around us up. Christians are to celebrate life, not death. Christ has conquered death and given us the victory over it through acceptance of Him as our Savior. (II Timothy 1:10; I Corinthians 15:55, 57; Hebrews 2:14)

"Woe unto them that call evil good, and good evil; that put darkness for light, and light for darkness; that put bitter for sweet, and sweet for bitter!"

Isaiah 5:20

"But I *say*, that the things which the Gentiles sacrifice, they sacrifice to devils, and not to God: and I would not that ye should have fellowship with devils. Ye cannot drink the cup of the Lord, and the cup of devils: ye cannot be partaker of the Lord's table, and of the table of devils."

I Corinthians 10:21

"And have no fellowship with the unfruitful works of darkness, but rather reprove *them*."

Ephesians 5:11

"Regard not them that have familiar spirits, neither seek after wizards, to be defiled by them: I *am* the LORD your God."

Leviticus 19:31

"There shall not be found among you *any one* that maketh his son or his daughter to pass through the fire, *or* that useth divination, *or* an observer of times, or an enchanter, or a witch, Or a charmer, or a consulter with familiar spirits, or a wizard, or a necromancer. For all that do these things *are* an abomination unto the LORD: and because of these abominations the LORD thy God doth drive them out from before thee."

Deuteronomy 18:10-12

"It is obvious that the elements, symbols and traditions of the Halloween observance with its emphasis on goblins and demons, witches and skeletons, ghosts and apparitions constitute a dabbling with the very things which Scripture forbids, and places Christians in the realm of demonic activity." – Lev Humphries

Holidays – New Year's

New Year's is the celebration of the advent of a New Year on the Gregorian calendar (a.k.a. Western and/or Christian Calendar). The Gregorian calendar is the internationally accepted civil calendar. The New Year holiday is a time of reflection, a time to think back over the previous year and contemplate what you did well and not so well, what was good and what was bad. Many people make New Year's resolutions regarding things that they want to change in their lives. Sadly, counting one's blessings is very often neglected and should definitely be a part of the reflection process.

New Year's is a perfect time to examine oneself in several different areas of life. We are to admit those areas in which we are not meeting God's standard and strive to serve God to the best of our ability. (Lamentations 3:40) Ask yourself if you are attending church regularly and if you are involved in your local church ministry. Are you tithing and giving to the work of the Lord through your local New Testament church? Do you have a close relationship with the Lord through a strong daily prayer and devotional life? Are there personal relationships that are tense or broken and need repaired? Are you living a separated life to God apart from the world? What about your witness, are you fulfilling God's command to tell others about the Gospel of Christ? As Romans 13:11-12 tells us, *it is high time to awake out of sleep*; we need to shake off the fleshly sinful habits and behaviors and put on works of righteousness. It is important to remember that we are a new creature in Christ once we are saved, our slate has been wiped clean, and we have a new beginning. Likewise, on New Year's God places before us a new beginning to start fresh and anew. Confess all known sin to God and be assured that He will forgive. (I John 1:9) Because of God's forgiveness we can forget past failures and have faith that God does have a *new thing* for us in the New Year. (Isaiah 43:18-19)

As with everything in life, Satan does all he can to get a foot hold and lead people in the wrong ways. The New Year's holiday is no different. Partying and drunkenness have become synonymous with the holiday. For many people, ringing in the New Year at the stroke of midnight on January 1 is a must. There is no harm in such a tradition, but sadly this is often accompanied by alcohol consumption and lewd behavior, things God speaks against (see topic on alcohol). There are also a number of myths that linger around this holiday regarding prospering in the New Year. These myths range from certain foods to eat like pork and sauerkraut or black eye peas and collard greens to rituals like wearing yellow, having money in your wallet at midnight, and sleeping with a horseshow under your pillow New Year's Eve. Although generally harmless, we know from reading Psalm 1:1-6, that it is those who *delight in the law of the Lord* and live by His precepts that prosper regardless of any superstition.

Whether it be by death or the Lord's return, we must live every year like it is our last year on earth. Ephesians 5:16 tells us that we are to be *redeeming the time because the days are evil*. We are living in an evil, sinful world that is filled with people that are dying and going to hell. God has left us here to lead others to Himself and New Year's is the perfect time to evaluate how well we are fulfilling that purpose.

"Let us search and try our ways, and turn again to the LORD."

Lamentations 3:40

"And that, knowing the time, that now *it is* high time to awake out of sleep: for now *is* our salvation nearer than when we believed. The night is far spent, the day is at hand: let us therefore cast off the works of darkness, and let us put on the armour of light."

Romans 13:11-12

"Therefore if any man *be* in Christ, *he is* a new creature: old things are passed away; behold, all things are become new."

II Corinthians 5:17

"Remember ye not the former things, neither consider the things of old. Behold, I will do a new thing; now it shall spring forth; shall ye not know it? I will even make a way in the wilderness, *and* rivers in the desert."

Isaiah 43:18-19

"Redeeming the time, because the days are evil."

Ephesians 5:16

"Now, as we close the gates of the old year and enter the portals of the new, God has given to you and me a brand new page. There is not a dirty page on the new calendar, and we can make it all it ought to be if we make up our minds and work at it." – Curtis Hutson

Holidays - Thanksgiving

Thanksgiving is a public celebration of divine goodness; it is a day set apart especially to acknowledge the goodness of God in both the remarkable deliverances from major trials as well as the everyday trivial blessings.[1] President Abraham Lincoln issued a Thanksgiving Proclamation on October 3, 1863 (in the midst of the Civil War) that set forth Thanksgiving Day as a federal holiday to be observed on the fourth Thursday of the month of November. Besides the giving of thanks, the holiday has become synonymous with the bounties of harvest time and turkey meals with all the fixings.

Most of us know the basics of the very first Thanksgiving observed by the Pilgrims. One hundred two Pilgrims traveled to America in September 1620 with bright hopes of a new beginning for religious freedom. They were gravely unprepared for the harsh winter of Plymouth which claimed forty-five of their lives. An English-speaking native named Squanto (along with some Pokanoket Indians) came to their aide by showing them how to plant corn, where to fish, and where to hunt beaver. Although the land and weather took quite a toll on the Pilgrims, the 53 remaining decided to count the blessings they had in their first harvest and give thanks unto God by celebrating with a feast from that harvest. They invited their Indian friends to join in their celebration which took place in late autumn of 1621.

The Pilgrims got the idea of giving thanks from the same Bible we use today. God's Word is filled with admonitions to be thankful and to give praise to God. A special day set aside for us as a nation to reflect on our blessings and recognize that they are from God is a great thing, however, we should not need a special day to be thankful and to give thanks unto God. According to Ephesians 5:20 we are to be *giving thanks always* and Hebrews 13:15 says *continually*. We are not only to give thanks every day, but also in everything. (Ephesians 5:20; I Thessalonians 5:18). We are to be thankful even for the trials, knowing that the Lord is working them together for our good. (Romans 8:28) Thankfulness is demonstrated when we enter into the gates of His churches and give Him praise (Psalm 100:4) and when we do for God what we promise to do as seen in Psalm 50:14 that says to *pay thy vows unto the most high*. Our thankfulness is not to be taken lightly either. Hebrews 13:15 says it is a *sacrifice of praise*. Just as the animal sacrifices were costly to those who offered them and David refused to offer the Lord anything that did not cost him anything, so will our praise cost us something. Our praise may cost us hatred from others, persecution, time, and/or energy. No matter the cost, we must continue to praise and be careful to heed the warning found in Romans 1:21 concerning the unthankful heart; it leads to *vain...imaginations* or foolish thinking and reasoning.

Sadly, we have become a generation of unthankful people that have a sense of entitlement and have turned the holiday into nothing more than a time to eat a big meal, watch football and a Macy's parade, and kick off the Christmas shopping season. We are deserving of nothing and if nothing else, can be thankful to the Lord for our salvation and His mercy and grace. He has prepared a way that we can escape the fires of hell because of His mercy and enjoy the blessings of heaven because of His grace.

"Giving thanks always for all things unto God and the Father in the name of our Lord Jesus Christ;"

Ephesians 5:20

"By him therefore let us offer the sacrifice of praise to God continually, that is, the fruit of *our* lips giving thanks to his name."

Hebrews 13:15

"In every thing give thanks: for this is the will of God in Christ Jesus concerning you."

I Thessalonians 5:18

"Enter into his gates with thanksgiving, *and* into his courts with praise: be thankful unto him, *and* bless his name."

Psalm 100:4

"Offer unto God thanksgiving; and pay thy vows unto the most High:"

Psalm 50:14

"We would worry less if we praised more. Thanksgiving is the enemy of discontent and dissatisfaction." – H. A. Ironside

Homosexuality

Homosexuality is referred to as sodomy in the Bible. Webster's 1828 Dictionary defines sodomy simply as, "a crime against nature." More specifically, however, homosexuality is a lifestyle of sexual relations among those of the same sex. God created men and women separately, differently, and with unique purposes; His creation was male and female, a distinction that is not to be blurred. (Genesis 1:27; Mark 10:6-8) God's plan and design is for sexual relations to only occur within the bounds of marriage (I Corinthians 7:1-9) and His plan for marriage is one man and one woman (Genesis 2:22-24). This leaves homosexuality a lifestyle that goes against God and His perfect creation.

We see a pattern in Genesis during the week of creation. God looked about His creation and saw *it was good*. (Genesis 1:4,10,12,18,21,25). After the creation of man and woman He saw *it was very good*, a step up from the rest. (Genesis 1:31) God's creation was perfect, without sin or blemish! As already stated, He created them distinctly male and female and they were to complete one another. God did not create that which He calls an abomination (we will explain that in a moment). In other words, no one is born homosexual. Romans 1:26-27 clearly states that these affections go against the *natural use*, the way God created things to be. Romans 1:31 and II Timothy 3:3 call it *without natural affection*. Homosexuality is a sin and those who engage in it are making the choice to sin.

God hates this sin and speaks against it very clearly in His Word. There is no question that Leviticus 18:22 is speaking about homosexual behaviors; in this verse, God calls it an abomination. God calls such affections vile and unseemly in Romans 1:26-27. The men of Sodom (where the Biblical term sodomy came from) and Gomorrah were deeply engrossed in this abominable sin and God called them wicked and exceeding sinners that sinned a sin so very grievous that He destroyed both cities because of it. (Genesis 13:13; 18:20) God felt so strongly about this sin that in the Old Testament it carried the death penalty. (Leviticus 20:13) There is no question that God hates the sin of homosexuality! Take note that I said God hates the 'sin' not the 'sinner.' This is to be the stance of the Christian as well. The homosexual agenda is one of tolerance and the Christian should show love towards all people as did Christ, but one who is a follower of Jesus and believes the Bible cannot tolerate a sin that the Bible condemns.

As explained in the 'God – Mercy/Grace/Justice' topic, God is a just God that will judge sin. Romans 1:26-27 is an example of God releasing judgment. It says that He gave them up to their sin and as a result they received the recompense (or consequence) that was meet (or fit the crime). The recompense for this lifestyle is diseases such as AIDS. Another consequence is a breakdown of the family unit which in turn causes a breakdown of society. Homosexuality will be judged according to God's Word. I Corinthians 6:9 refers to those involved in this sin as effeminate and says that they *will not inherit the kingdom of God*. Praise the Lord, however, this is not the end of it for 2 verses later God tells us that those involved any of this list of sins can be saved and sanctified. Homosexuality must be recognized for what it is – a sin that must be confessed and given over to God in order to gain the victory over it.

"For this cause God gave them up unto vile affections: for even their women did change the natural use into that which is against nature: And likewise also the men, leaving the natural use of the woman, burned in their lust one toward another; men with men working that which is unseemly, and receiving in themselves that recompence of their error which was meet."

Romans 1:26-27

"Thou shalt not lie with mankind, as with womankind: it *is* abomination."

Leviticus 18:22

"But the men of Sodom *were* wicked and sinners before the LORD exceedingly."

Genesis 13:13

"And the LORD said, Because the cry of Sodom and Gomorrah is great, and because their sin is very grievous;"

Genesis 18:20

"If a man also lie with mankind, as he lieth with a woman, both of them have committed an abomination: they shall surely be put to death; their blood *shall be* upon them."

Leviticus 20:13

"There is no scientific research or researcher in the world who is willing to admit that people are born homosexuals. People have all kinds of arguments concerning this, but God identifies it as a sin and as a matter of choice." – Clarence Sexton

Idolatry

Idolatry is, "the worship of idols, images, or any thing made by hand, or which is not God," and also includes, "excessive attachment or veneration for any thing, or that which borders on adoration."[1] God is the creator of all things. He gave us all life. He deserves and demands first place in our lives. When God gave the Ten Commandments, the first two were in regards to this. He said, "Thou shalt have no other gods before me. Thou shalt not make unto thee any graven image, or any likeness *of any thing* that *is* in heaven above, or that *is* in the earth beneath, or that *is* in the water under the earth: Thou shalt not bow down thyself to them, nor serve them: for I the LORD thy God *am* a jealous God..." (Exodus 20:3-5) Our response to God in the matter affects more than ourselves too; it affects our families for generations. God continues, "...visiting the iniquity of the fathers upon the children unto the third and fourth *generation* of them that hate me; And shewing mercy unto thousands of them that love me, and keep my commandments." (Exodus 20:5b-6) We see the retribution in verse 5 for those who break God's laws and the recompense or reward in verse 6 for those who obey.

God only wants what is best for us and the one who puts God first in their life will naturally follow in all the other important areas of Christian living. He tells us in I Corinthians 10:14, "Wherefore, my dearly beloved, flee from idolatry." Wherefore refers back to the previous verses which give examples of the trials the Israelites experienced in the wilderness because of their disobedience, including worshipping the golden calf that led them to improper conduct. (Exodus 32) This group of Israelites missed out on seeing the Promised Land because they did not put God first and completely trust Him. How much do we miss out on when we do not put God first? God does not want us to miss out on all the blessings He has for us; this is why He tells us repeatedly to turn from idols and idolatry. (I John 5:21; Leviticus 19:4; Colossians 3:5) Those who allow other gods in their lives only multiply their sorrows. (Psalm 16:4)

Most people believe they are not guilty of breaking this commandment when in fact most people have. An idol does not only mean a physical image or statue of a person or object that one bows and prays to. An idol is anything that comes before God in your life. Hobbies, spouses, children, jobs, entertainment, cars, etc. can all be idols in someone's life. There is nothing wrong with enjoying these things in our lives, but the problem comes when we place too much importance or emphasis on them that they begin to rule our lives. When this happens that 'thing' becomes a master to us and Matthew 6:24 says that we cannot serve two masters. We give the devil a foothold in our lives when we move God out of first place. (Ephesians 4:27)

When the Pharisees asked Jesus what the greatest commandment was, he responded, "...Thou shalt love the Lord thy God with all thy heart, and with all thy soul, and with all thy mind." It is not possible to love God completely when there is something else, an idol, overtaking residence in our hearts. When we love God and put Him first as we should, everything else falls into place. We must strive to *seek ye first the kingdom of God and all his righteousness* and then enjoy the blessed promises of God when we do. (Matthew 6:33)

"Thou shalt have no other gods before me."

Exodus 20:3

"Little children, keep yourselves from idols. Amen."

I John 5:21

"Turn ye not unto idols, nor make to yourselves molten gods: I *am* the LORD your God."

Leviticus 19:4

"No man can serve two masters: for either he will hate the one, and love the other; or else he will hold to the one, and despise the other. Ye cannot serve God and mammon."

Matthew 6:24

"But seek ye first the kingdom of God, and his righteousness; and all these things shall be added unto you."

Matthew 6:33

"Anything that dims my vision for Christ, or takes away my taste for Bible study, or cramps me in my prayer life, or makes Christian work difficult, is wrong for me; and I must, as a Christian turn away from it." — J. Wilbur Chapman

Internet and Social Media

Internet is a global source of information and communication via the exchange of data from interconnected computer networks. Social Media is websites and applications that are operated using the internet and used as tools to communicate and share information from person to person. As with any new technological advance, there are positives and negatives. The biggest advantage to the internet is the global access to an abundance of information and services that are available at just a few keystrokes, whether it be for research, shopping, or news. It has also made maintaining long distance relationships much easier thanks to applications like Facebook and Skype. Above all, there has never been another time in history when the Gospel of Christ has been more readily available to a wide range of people groups all around the world. Along with the positives, however, comes a share of negatives, negatives that have the potential to destroy lives.

The first risk is simply becoming addicted to being on the internet, especially social media sites. They can become very time consuming. I Corinthians 6:12 speaks of this. Using the internet is lawful, and even advantageous at times, but it is not always productive and it can begin to control the user making them a slave to it. God wants us to be good stewards of our time and use it constructively. (Ephesians 5:15-16) There are many other risks that tend to fall under the element of secrecy that is involved in the internet and social media. Being in the comfort and privacy of one's home, and even office at work, results in a loss of inhibition. People will often do and/or say online what they would never do or say in person. This makes it easier for people to assume secret lives and get involved in inappropriate relationships. What must be remembered is that nothing is hid from God, He is omnipresent and omniscient. (Jeremiah 23:24) Even good people with high morals can easily fall into the trap of secrecy that leads to inappropriate communications. (I Corinthians 15:33) The false security of secrecy has also brought a dramatic rise in those involved in online pornography. Heed God's words in Psalm 101:3 and *set no wicked thing before* [your] *eyes*; the consequences are shattered lives because of lost jobs and betrayed loved ones. A risk that can become quite tragic is the gateway that the internet (specifically social media sites and chatrooms) becomes for prowling predators. Predators are very clever on how to lure children (and even adults) into conversations and drawing out the information they need to find, abduct, and/or harm them.

These risks are why caution and balance is of the utmost importance and must especially be exercised among parents of young children that are still in the home. Precautions can be taken to protect against these risks. The first would be to keep the computer in common, high traffic areas with the screen facing the center of the room. Second, don't allow children to aimlessly surf the internet; allow its use on purpose, for a particular purpose, and only for that purpose. Third, parents can also take advantage of one of many applications available to block certain types of websites without a password. It is up to the individual to discern what limits need to be placed on its use. As Christians we are to guard our minds and in so doing we must be careful what influences we allow through internet use. (I Peter 1:13)

"All things are lawful unto me, but all things are not expedient: all things are lawful for me, but I will not be brought under the power of any."

I Corinthians 6:12

"Can any hide himself in secret places that I shall not see him? saith the LORD. Do not I fill heaven and earth? saith the LORD."

Jeremiah 23:24

"Be not deceived: evil communications corrupt good manners."

I Corinthians 15:33

"I will set no wicked thing before mine eyes: I hate the work of them that turn aside; *it* shall not cleave to me."

Psalm 101:3

"Wherefore gird up the loins of your mind, be sober, and hope to the end for the grace that is to be brought unto you at the revelation of Jesus Christ;"

I Peter 1:13

"Every new technology brings with it a myriad of inappropriate uses as well as potentially helpful ones. The potentials of this communication tool for both good and evil necessitate caution and balance." – Paul Chappell

Laying on of Hands

Laying on of hands is a practice conducted by a group of men, usually senior leaders of the church, that place their hands on the receiving individual while prayers are given by several or all of them on that individual's behalf. It is sometimes done in conjunction with anointing with oil. This is simply applying a small amount of oil to one's head while performing the laying on of hands. Exodus 30:23-24 gives the recipe for 'holy anointing oil' used in the Bible, today simple olive oil is commonly used.

The laying on of hands and anointing with oil was once a sign gift given by God in Bible times. (Mark 16:17-18) There was genuine healing that occurred showing forth the power of God. Mark 6:13 and Acts 28:8 are Biblical examples of when divine healing occurred because of laying on of hands and/or anointing with oil. It was also a means of receiving the Holy Ghost. We have the privilege of receiving the Holy Spirit once we are saved, but before Christ's death that was not the case. Ministry was greatly hindered without the power of the Holy Spirit, and those with the ability to bestow that power would, just as Peter and John did to help Philips' ministry once Simon was saved and joined him. (Acts 8:17) We know from I Corinthians 13:8-10 that the signs gifts ceased with the completion of the canon of Scripture (see 'Speaking in Tongues' for further detail), so how is this practice used today?

It is used today as a symbolic practice. When appointing a man to an important office, especially a man into full-time ministry such as in an ordination, a godly group of men will lay hands on the one to be sent out and pray over him. It is a formal recognition and acknowledgment of one's calling. Although symbolic, it is a very serious ceremony that should not be taken lightly and should be approached with much prayer and discernment. I Timothy 5:22 warns the reader to be careful not to be too hasty in appointing men to important offices. Those making the appointment must make sure that the candidate is of good character and is qualified to lead in the capacity that they will be ministering. Today, laying on of hands and anointing with oil is most often thought of to seek healing as given for an example in James 5:14. It must be understood that there is no divine healing power in this method. The use of oil is symbolic of healing because oil was often used for medicinal purposes in Biblical times. Different kinds of oil were even used within the past decade for things like ear aches, constipation, and other such trivial issues. Note also that James 5:14 says that those who are sick are to call for the elders, not those with the power to heal. Even in A.D. 45 when this was written it was intended to be a matter of prayer, not miraculous healing.

Laying on of hands and anointing with oil would once have had divine healing power but has presently become only a symbolic ceremony. The real answer lies in the verse following James 5:14; verse 15 tells us that the *prayer of faith shall save the sick, and the Lord shall raise him up*. It is the prayers of the faithful that are answered and it is only the Lord that has the power to answer those prayers with healing. These practices are merely methods used by God to give us sincere hearts and sober minds and bring us to the point of recognizing the importance and power of prayer.

"And these signs shall follow them that believe; In my name shall they cast out devils; they shall speak with new tongues; They shall take up serpents; and if they drink any deadly thing, it shall not hurt them; they shall lay hands on the sick, and they shall recover."

Mark 16:17-18

"Then laid they *their* hand on them, and they received the Holy Ghost."

Acts 8:17

"And when they had fasted and prayed, and laid *their* hands on them, they sent *them* away."

Acts 13:3

"Lay hands suddenly on no man, neither be partaker of other men's sins: keep thyself pure."

I Timothy 5:22

"Is any sick among you? let him call for the elders of the church; and let them pray over him, anointing him with oil in the name of the Lord:"

James 5:14

"Throughout Scripture oil is the type or symbol of the Holy Spirit; and in connection with prayer for the sick it would have a beautiful significance. ...it is always right for godly elder brethren to meet with the sick for prayer, and it is just as true now – as in the beginning of the dispensation – that God answers the prayer of faith." – H. A. Ironside

Local N.T. Church

The local New Testament church is a local assembly of born-again believers that has a pastor and deacons, observes the two ordinances of baptism and the Lord's Supper, and who have joined themselves together to carry out the Great Commission and encourage and exhort one another. The Bible speaks of two different 'kinds' of churches. One is the global church comprised of all born-again believers in the world; it is the bride of Christ. (Ephesians 5:25-25; Isaiah 54:5) Within this worldwide 'church' are local New Testament Churches, in fact 17 of the 27 N.T. books are letters written to local churches. This smaller church was necessary in order to train and encourage Christians to fulfill the work God had for His 'church.' Many people believe that the very first local N.T. church was formed at the day of Pentecost, but Acts 2:41 suggests differently. This verse says that those who were baptized were 'added unto them' not formed or created. A church had to be present in order for them to be 'added' to something. Christ begun the work of building His church during His earthly ministry, it was empowered at Pentecost, and then established and organized by the Apostles.

God's Word is clear that the local N.T. church belongs to God and He is the head of each individual church. (Colossians 1:18) In Matthew 16:18, Jesus says *I will build my church* and Acts 20:28 tells us that it is the *church of God* and that it belongs to Him because He purchased it *with his own blood*. This is why there should be no board, convention, or other outside hierarchy that determines the beliefs and/or practices of the local church. God and His word is the sole authority of the local church and the One to whom the church is accountable.

God has a plan and purpose for the local church; it is both a place to serve as well as a place of blessings. First and foremost, it is a vehicle by which God evangelizes the world with His Gospel. The local church is a training ground to teach members how to be a witness as well as teaching doctrine. (Ephesians 4:11-16) The local church is to provide for the genuine needs of its members, particularly widows. (Romans 15:26; I Timothy 5:3). It offers an extended family among its members which provide encouragement and comfort to one another. (I Corinthians 12:26) The local church is also used by God to exhort His people and create accountability. (Hebrews 10:25; Galatians 6:1-2) It serves as a safety net (Acts 20:28-29) against the wiles of the devil and helps keep watch over our souls so that we will not be ashamed when it comes time to give an account unto God. (Hebrews 13:17)

No wonder God instructs us in Hebrews 10:25 not to forsake *the assembling of ourselves together*. In other words, we are to be connected to a church and be there and involved when they meet. Church membership is the first step in accomplishing this command. Every Christian should seek out a church that they agree with doctrinally. This is important because it is very difficult to strive together for the cause of Christ when two are not agreed. (Amos 3:3) The local church would be wise to require the same thing of those they take into membership because with each membership comes voting rights in the church's decisions as seen exhibited in Acts 6:5 (the *saying* [decision] *pleased the multitude,* not just the church leaders). The local New Testament church is vital to the Lord's work and a necessary piece for one to serve God fully.

"Then they that gladly received his word were baptized: and the same day there were added *unto them* about three thousand souls. And they continued stedfastly in the apostles' doctrine and fellowship, and in breaking of bread, and in prayers."

Acts 2:41-42

"And daily in the temple, and in every house, they ceased not to teach and preach Jesus Christ."

Acts 5:42

"And I say also unto thee, That thou art Peter, and upon this rock I will build my church; and the gates of hell shall not prevail against it."

Matthew 16:18

"Not forsaking the assembling of ourselves together, as the manner of some *is*; but exhorting *one another:* and so much the more as ye see the day approaching."

Hebrews 10:25

"And whether one member suffer, all the member suffer with it; or one member be honoured, all the members rejoice with it."

I Corinthians 12:26

So we, *being* many, are one body in Christ, and every one members one of another."

Romans 12:5

"Christ is the foundation upon which the church is built, and every born again believer is building upon that foundation." – Oliver B. Greene

Lord's Supper

The Lord's Supper, also known as communion, is a 'meal' observed by born-again believers in remembrance of the price Jesus paid on the cross for our sins. It is one of two church ordinances commanded by Jesus to be observed by the church. It is a 'symbolic' ritual and the elements do not 'become' Christ's body and blood as the Catholics believe. Jesus instituted and demonstrated the first Lord's Supper ceremony on the eve of His crucifixion as an example for us to follow. It was impossible for the elements to become His body and blood at this first Lord's Supper because He was still living and in the very presence of His disciples; why would one believe that the elements perform differently after His death than they did before? Scripture says that communion is done *in remembrance* or as a memorial. (Luke 22:19; I Corinthians 11:24, 25) Furthermore, as with baptism, it is a picture of Christ's death as indicated in I Corinthians 11:26 when it says *ye do shew*. The Lord's Supper is purely symbolic.

The Lord's Supper is reserved for saved, baptized church members. Acts 2:41-42 shows us the correct order of events: first they were saved (*then those that gladly received his word*) then they were baptized (*were baptized*) then they became members of the church (*the same day there were added unto them*) and then they observed communion (*continued...in breaking of bread*). These people were observing communion as part of their local New Testament church and this is demonstrated again in verse 46. Therefore, the Lord's Supper should be observed with one's local congregation during a service designated for the observance, not in one's home on their own. The Bible does not instruct us as to the frequency that communion should be observed. Paul's instructions in I Corinthians 11:26 only says 'as often as' you do observe it do it this way so, it is left up to the church's discretion. Acts 20:7 indicates that perhaps this church observed it every Sunday but this is not a norm today. Many churches will observe on Christmas and/or Easter and then quarterly or monthly. In addition to the who, where, and when aspect, is the two elements used in communion and what they represent. First would be the bread, which spoken of here is unleavened bread made purely of flour and water and baked into a round cake the size of a plate. Some churches will use small cracker wafers made specifically for the observance of the Lord's Supper. The bread represents the body of Christ that was bruised and broken on the cross. The second element is the cup. The drink of choice in the Bible would have been the fruit of the vine or grape juice which is what most churches use today. More significant than what is in the cup however, is the cup itself. Henry Morris commented, "...the 'cup' represent the New Covenant of God with His people, based on the shed blood of Christ offered in substitutionary sacrifice for our sins."[13]

After giving all the instruction and explanation, God gives some warnings. (I Corinthians 11:27-29) He commands us to do a self-examination of our lives and get those things that are not right in order before partaking. One must have their heart right with God and others before they partake. Those who partake unworthily are guilty of irreverence, dishonor, and disrespect to Jesus' death on the cross. (I Corinthians 11:27) Although symbolic, the Lord's Supper is a serious matter that should not be taken lightly.

"For I have received of the Lord that which also I delivered unto you, That the Lord Jesus the *same* night in which he was betrayed took bread: And when he had given thanks, he brake *it*, and said, Take, eat: this is my body, which is broken for you: this do in remembrance of me. After the same manner also *he took* the cup, when he had supped, saying, This cup is the new testament in my blood: this do ye, as oft as ye drink *it*, in remembrance of me. For as often as ye eat this bread, and drink this cup, ye do shew the Lord's death till he come. Wherefore, whosoever shall eat this bread, and drink *this* cup of the Lord, unworthily, shall be guilty of the body and blood of the Lord. But let a man examine himself, and so let him eat of *that* bread, and drink of *that* cup. For he that eateth and drinketh unworthily, eateth and drinketh damnation to himself, not discerning the Lord's body."

I Corinthians 11:23-29

"And upon the first *day* of the week, when the disciples came together to break bread, Paul preached unto them, ready to depart on the morrow; and continued his speech until midnight."

Acts 20:7

"And they, continuing daily with one accord in the temple, and breaking bread from house to house, did eat their meat with gladness and singleness of heart,"

Acts 2:46

"It [Lord's Supper] was appointed to be done *in remembrance of Christ*, to keep fresh in our minds an ancient favour, his dying for us, as well as to remember and absent friend, even Christ interceding for us, in virtue of his death, at God's right hand." – Matthew Henry

Marriage – Equally Yoked

Marriage is, "The act of uniting a man and woman for life...it is a contract both civil and religious, by which the parties engage to live together in mutual affection and fidelity, till death shall separate them."[1] Marriage is an institution created by God for companionship and completing one another. God said in Genesis 2:18 that it was *not good that the man should be alone* so He made *him an help meet for him*. It was here that God instituted the first marriage. Verse 24 says, "Therefore shall a man leave his father and his mother, and shall cleave unto his wife: and they shall be one flesh."

God's plan for marriage is to become one flesh; this is impossible between a saved and unsaved person. God commands us in II Thessalonians 3:6 to withdraw ourselves from the disorderly (unsaved). If we are not to even have close fellowship with unbelievers then why on earth would a believer consider marrying an unbeliever? If that was not enough, God gave plenty of clear cut instruction on the matter in verses like II Corinthians 6:14-18 and Deuteronomy 7:3-4. In the Deuteronomy passage, God's people were being told not to intermarry with the heathen nations listed in verse 1, because they did not believe as they did, they worshipped idols and other gods. A biblical marriage has its foundation on the Word of God and His direction; it is impossible for two people who do not believe on the same God to walk together in unity. (Amos 3:3)

There can even be an unequal yoke between two born-again believers. Care and consideration must also be taken into the maturity level of each in their personal walk with the Lord. In application, consider a literal yoke and how it is used. Imagine two people wearing a yoke and trying to walk across a field. If one of them is trying to walk along at a fast pace (representing a mature Christian), but the other is just walking at a casual pace (representing the immature Christian) there will be problems. One will be trying to pull the other while the other is trying to hold back the one. The mature Christian is on fire for God and tries to revolve their lives around God and the church while the immature Christian will want to hang on to many secular aspects of their life and try to fit God and church around their life. There will be much frustration because of the lack of unity in their walk.

As with everything in God's Word, there are consequences to disobedience. The first consequence to an unequal yoke in marriage is frustration and contention. Marriage is tough even in the best of circumstances. Secondly, there is a high probability that the unsaved spouse will pull the saved spouse away from God. (Deuteronomy 7:4) It is much easier to pull someone down than to pull someone up. The consequences affect others as well. As children grow up and begin to question what they believe and whether they want to attend church, they are pulled in different directions and often end up confused and not living for God. These consequences are scary, but if a believer disobeys God and marries an unbeliever, they have made a life-long covenant which is not to be broken. It is not God's will for an unequal yoke, but divorce is never God's will either. (I Corinthians 7:12-16) One can save themselves from a life of misery and heartache if they follow God's Word and God's plan.

"Therefore shall a man leave his father and his mother, and shall cleave unto his wife: and they shall be one flesh."

Genesis 2:24

"Now we command you brethren, in the name of our Lord Jesus Christ, that ye withdraw yourselves from every brother that walketh disorderly, and not after the tradition which he received of us."

II Thessalonians 3:6

"Be ye not unequally yoked together with unbelievers: for what fellowship hath righteousness with unrighteousness? And what communion hath light with darkness? And what concord hath Christ with Belial? or what part hath he that believeth with an infidel? And what agreement hath the temple of God with idols? for ye are the temple of the living God; as God hath said, I will dwell in them, and walk in *them*; and I will be their God, and they shall be my people."

II Corinthians 6:14-18

"Neither shalt thou make marriages with them; thy daughter thou shalt not give unto his son, nor his daughter shalt thou take unto thy son. For they will turn away thy son from following me, that they may serve other gods: so will the anger of the LORD be kindled against you, and destroy thee suddenly."

Deuteronomy 7:3-4

"Can two walk together, except they be agreed?"

Amos 3:3

"The Christian, married to one not a Christian, is certain to have troubles. Such a marriage should not be broken, and the Christian believer should not depart from his unbelieving mate. The time to do right about that is before marriage. After marriage is too late to avoid trouble. All one can do then is to pray that God will save the unsaved one and try one's best to atone for the sin of yoking up in marriage with an enemy of your Savior and your God." – John R. Rice

Marriage – Husband's Role

Marriage is, "The act of uniting a man and woman for life...it is a contract both civil and religious, by which the parties engage to live together in mutual affection and fidelity, till death shall separate them."[1] Marriage is an institution created by God for companionship and completing one another. God said in Genesis 2:18 that it was *not good that the man should be alone* so He made *him an help meet for him*. It was here that God instituted the first marriage. Verse 24 says, "Therefore shall a man leave his father and his mother, and shall cleave unto his wife: and they shall be one flesh."

Marriage is a picture of Christ and the church and as Christ is the head of the church, so is the husband the head of the wife and home. (Ephesians 5:23; I Corinthians 11:3) There is order to everything in God's creation including marriage. Everything that is successful has order and chain of command: government, business, churches, organizations, AND families. God has placed man as the head of the family organization. This does not mean that the husband is to be a dictator without regard or consideration to his wife and/or families' concerns and opinions. A wise man will ask his wife for her input and opinion before making major decisions and weigh it heavily. There comes a point, however, when a decision must be made and God has given the husband that role and responsibility.

The first responsibility a man has to his wife is to leave his parents and cleave to her. (Genesis 2:24) Of course, God expects us to always be honoring to our parents, but once a boy becomes a man and husband he can no longer be the obedient child to his parents but must dedicate himself to his wife. Part of this dedication is loving his wife *even as Christ also loved the church, and gave himself for it*. (Ephesians 5:25) This love is not an emotion, but rather a decision to express sacrificial love. It is a love that puts the desires and needs of their wife before their own. Every wife has the right to feel cherished by her husband and if he treats her as he does himself, she will. (Ephesians 8:28-29) A good husband will also recognize his wife's delicate emotions and guard against crushing her tender spirit. (I Peter 3:7) Finally, the husband is to provide security for his wife, an important need for women. She needs to feel secure both financially and physically. We see the husband's responsibility to provide financially demonstrated in I Timothy 5:8 and physically in John 15:13.

Men are given a place of honor in the home, but along with that position comes higher responsibility. The success of the home lies in how the man fulfills his role. Dr. Tom Malone wisely stated, "I've heard men say, 'I would be a better man if my wife were a better Christian.' I don't believe that. I'm not a psychologist, but I think I know a little something about human nature. You show me a man who is sold out to God one hundred percent, you show me a man who will put God first in his home, you show me a man who will put the Word of God and soul winning and clean, holy living first in his life, and I will show you a woman who will love him and say, 'I'll follow him to the ends of the earth.' Men, you are the key."[14] If the husband will do their part in being the godly leader of their home and loving their wives as the Bible instructs them to, they will be able to watch their family fall in place behind them!

"But I would have you know, that the head of every man is Christ; and the head of the woman *is* the man; and the head of Christ *is* God."

I Corinthians 11:3

"Husbands, love your wives, even as Christ also loved the church, and gave himself for it;"

Ephesians 5:25

"So ought men to love their wives as their own bodies. He that loveth his wife loveth himself. For no man ever yet hated his own flesh; but nourisheth and cherisheth it, even as the Lord the church:"

Ephesians 5:28-29

"Likewise, ye husbands, dwell with *them* according to knowledge, giving honour unto the wife, as unto the weaker vessel, and as being heirs together of the grace of life; that your prayers be not hindered."

I Peter 3:7

"But if any provide not for his own, and specially for those of his own house, he hath denied the faith, and is worse than an infidel."

I Timothy 5:8

"The role of the head of the home is successfully implemented only when the husband assumes the position of a servant who is motivated by love, as exemplified in the attitude of Jesus Christ toward the church for which He gave Himself in death." – Raymond W. Barber

Marriage – Wife's Role

Marriage is, "The act of uniting a man and woman for life...it is a contract both civil and religious, by which the parties engage to live together in mutual affection and fidelity, till death shall separate them."[1] Marriage is an institution created by God for companionship and completing one another. God said in Genesis 2:18 that it was *not good that the man should be alone* so He made *him an help meet for him*. It was here that God instituted the first marriage. Verse 24 says, "Therefore shall a man leave his father and his mother, and shall cleave unto his wife: and they shall be one flesh." The help meet spoken of in Genesis 2:18 is the foundation for all that is encompassed in the wife's role.

The biggest role of the wife is submission to her husband. (Ephesians 5:22-24; Colossians 3:18) When this is done with the right spirit, every other aspect of the woman's role naturally falls into place. Women must not take this to mean that they are not to voice their opinion to their husband and that it is ok for their husband to walk over them. A man who is loving his wife as he is instructed to do would not treat her poorly and would welcome her input in decision making. Rather, it is voluntarily placing herself under his leadership in obedience to God's Word and desiring God's perfect will and blessings on her life. Ephesians 5:33 instructs that the wife is to reverence her husband, the Greek word for reverence here implying an expression of awe that will lead to humble respect and obedience. A wife who reverences her husband will not nag or preach to him but instead encourage her husband's spiritual walk through her testimony and actions. (I Peter 3:1-5)

Titus chapter two gives a good list of those things that a wife should strive to be and do. Early in the list is loving their husbands. (Titus 2:4) Note that this is something that is to be taught, it is not a feeling but a decision to act in a certain way. Note also that it is listed before loving the children. It is natural and right for a mother to love her children unconditionally, but it must be remembered that it should not be to the neglect of her husband who is to be first in her life second to God. Another role listed in Titus is being *keepers at home*. (Titus 2:5) A godly wife will consider her home her career and put as much effort into making it a haven of peace and happiness as a business women does being successful in her outside career. Meeting her husband's physical needs is also a major role. (I Corinthians 7:2-4) Just as with all the roles of the wife, however, this should not be considered a necessary evil. A wife should glory in those things she is held responsible for doing, doing them with a happy heart.

As mentioned above, the woman's role can be summed up in Genesis 2:18 – she was created to be a help meet for man. Her role is to help her husband succeed at whatever it is God called him to do. A good wife will be of great value to her husband, but a poor wife will cause him shame. (Proverbs 12:4) A husband can have complete trust in a godly wife which lifts a huge burden from his life. He does not have to worry about how she will conduct herself, he can trust her with the deepest concerns of his heart, and he has assurance that she will be there by his side for life. (Proverbs 31:11-12) Being a wife is a divine calling and a godly woman will not rebel against God's plan for her life but embrace it and joyfully be the best she can be.

131

"Wives, submit yourselves unto your own husbands, as unto the Lord. For the husband is the head of the wife, even as Christ is the head of the church: and he is the saviour of the body. Therefore as the church is subject unto Christ, so *let* the wives *be* to their own husbands in every thing."

Ephesians 5:22-24

"That they may teach the young women to be sober, to love their husbands, to love their children, *To be* discreet, chaste, keepers at home, good, obedient to their own husbands, that the word of God be not blasphemed."

Titus 2:4-5

"Nevertheless, *to avoid* fornication, let every man have his own wife, and let every woman have her own husband. Let the husband render unto the wife due benevolence: and likewise also the wife unto the husband. The wife hath not power of her own body, but the husband: and likewise also the husband hath not power of his own body, but the wife."

I Corinthians 7:2-4

"A virtuous woman *is* a crown to her husband: but she that maketh ashamed *is* as rottenness in his bones."

Proverbs 12:4

"The heart of her husband doth safely trust in her, so that he shall have no need of spoil. She will do him good and not evil all the days of her life."

Proverbs 31:11-12

"A wise woman...will realize that her greatest career is the career of a good wife. ...She had no business getting married if she was not willing to submit to her own husband as his helpmeet. Since this is her God-given place, she is to encourage her husband, she is to love him, to honour him, to recognize his leadership in the home." – Hugh Pyle

Modesty/Dress

Modesty in dress is to clothe oneself in a manner that pertains to their sex, is not overtly bold and/or excessive, and covers enough of the body and fits in such a way as not to draw attention to the areas of the body that arouse impure thoughts and desires. After Adam and Even sinned in the garden, they realized their nakedness and attempted to cover themselves. Even then, however, their idea of covering themselves did not meet God's expectations for He replaced their inadequate coverings with more substantial clothing. (Genesis 3:7, 21) Because of sin, nakedness had now become a problem.

So what is God's standard? First, God expects men to look and act like men and women to look and act like women. (Deuteronomy 22:5) A person should not have to wonder when looking at someone what sex they are. When discussing standards of how much should be covered, God's word does establish some minimums. Exodus 28:42 (describing the attire of the high priest) and Isaiah 47:2-3 both reveal God's feelings on the exposure of the thigh and relating it to nakedness. A woman's breasts should also be sufficiently covered as not to be seen even the slightest. Proverbs 5:19-20 describes the pleasure that a husband is to get from his wife's breasts and *only* his wife's. This is a part of the body that is to be reserved only for one's husband to see, not the public. This leaves one to deduce that clothing should be high enough to cover the bosom and low enough to cover the thigh (may I suggest to cover the knee). It would also go to say that clothing should not be too tight as to show the outline of these areas, defeating the point of wearing clothing to begin with. Women who dress improperly must examine their motives. Proverbs 7 gives much detail of a strange woman; how she acts and dresses. Verse 10 says she dresses as a harlot and this is for the purpose of drawing men's eyes to her, to advertise her body and say that she is open for seduction. What is the dress of a harlot? – skimpy, tight, and seductive. One should wear clothing that covers their nakedness and does not bring undue attention to them or shame to God.

God's Word also speaks against being bold and excessive in one's appearance. (I Timothy 2:9-10) Compare this passage with I Peter 3:3. Obviously God wants women to wear clothes, therefore, the idea here is not that women cannot braid their hair or wear jewelry, but that their styles (clothing/hair/makeup/accessories) should not be excessive. Wild and unnatural hair colors, excessive makeup, and overpowering jewelry is not God's idea of modest.

The way one dresses does matter and makes an impact on those around them. People often quote I Samuel 16:7 in argument against dress standards, claiming that it is what is in the heart that matters and that they should not be judged on their outward appearance. While there is an element of truth to that, what is in the heart is indeed what matters, what they fail to recognize is the part of that verse that says that man does look on the outward appearance. We are all human and we will pass judgment (as we should to a certain extent) and all we have to judge someone on is their appearance and actions. Matthew 6:21 holds just as true and your dress is a testimony to what is in your heart. Are you treasuring self and worldliness or is your true treasure found in pleasing and honoring God?

"And the eyes of them both were opened, and they knew that they *were* naked; and they sewed fig leaves together, and made themselves aprons. ...Unto Adam also and to his wife did the LORD God make coats of skins, and clothed them."

Genesis 3:7, 21

"The woman shall not wear that which pertaineth unto a man, neither shall a man put on a woman's garment: for all that do so *are* abomination unto the LORD thy God."

Deuteronomy 22:5

"And thou shalt make them linen breeches to cover their nakedness; from the loins even unto the thighs they shall reach:"

Exodus 28:42

"That they may keep thee from the strange woman...And, behold, there met him a woman *with* the attire of an harlot, and subtil of heart...Let not thine heart decline to her ways, go not astray in her paths. For she hath cast down many wounded: yea, many strong *men* have been slain by her. Her house *is* the way to hell, going down to the chambers of death."

Proverbs 7:5, 10, 25-27

"In like manner also, that women adorn themselves in modest apparel, with shamefacedness and sobriety; not with broided hair, or gold, or pearls, or costly array; But (which becometh women professing godliness) with good works."

I Timothy 2:9-10

"I believe that what is in the heart is more important than what is on the body, but what is in the heart will eventually affect what is on the body." – John Bishop

Music

Music is the art of combining sounds in such a manner to produce melody and harmony and to be pleasant to the ear.[1] God's Word abounds with verses that tell us to sing songs to our Lord. Many of these verses also distinguish that they are to be 'new songs, occurring 9 times including Psalm 40:3, 96:1, 98:1, 144:9, 149:1 and Isaiah 42:10. The music of the Christian should not be the same as that of the world.

The 'new songs' we sing to the Lord have a purpose that goes beyond entertainment; sacred music is for the purpose of worship. (II Chronicles 29:28) While we may enjoy the music, as we should, the main focus of the Christian's music should not be to make them feel good but to be pleasing and honoring to God. For this reason, there should be a reverence and majesty about our music. One of the best ways to praise God and show Him our thanks is through song. (Psalm 147:7, 149:1) Part of worship, is the teaching and admonition we receive. Godly music will be rich in doctrine so that it can fulfill this purpose as well. (Colossians 3:16; Ephesians 5:19) Music plays a vital role in the ministry of church; a vehicle by which we worship God, edify one another, and reveal the truths of God to others.

Sacred music has a proper melody, tone, and rhythm to it as well. The melody must be the prominent characteristic, not the rhythm. You cannot just put doctrine rich words to any kind of music and call it Christian and God-honoring. Music is not any more amoral as the alphabet is. Just as the letters of the alphabet can be combined to form pure words as well as sinful words, so can tones and rhythms be combined to produce compositions that convey either a message of decency and righteousness or the opposite. Music can be composed in such a manner as to be worldly and elicit immorality. (Exodus 32:18-19) One must remember that one of Satan's roles as an angel in heaven was producing music. (Ezekiel 28:13) Music is an art that Satan is a master of and he uses his skill and knowledge to deceive the world. (Revelation 12:9) Satan has twisted something that was meant for sacred purposes to be used for evil and turn people away from God.

Today's secular music styles (especially rock-and-roll) and Contemporary Christian Music (also known as CCM) are all music styles that Satan has his hand on. Most secular music, performers, and performances are geared toward sexuality and other forms of immorality. A look at CCM's sound, performers, and performances will render little, if any, difference from those of the sinful, secular music industry. We are to be a called out assembly, to be different from the world and not blend in. (II Corinthians 6:17) Music should not be used to 'bridge the gap.' God expects us to maintain purity and godliness in all areas of our lives, including music. Unfortunately, the first area to go as a result of compromise in a church is often music. Once compromise begins in this one area, compromise spreads to others areas of the church until it no longer resembles what it once did.

We must refuse to compromise in this area of music. Determine to keep it as pure and holy as the God we sing it to and continue singing as long as we have breath. (Psalm 104:33)

"Praise ye the LORD. Sing unto the LORD a new song, *and* his praise in the congregation of the saints."

Psalm 149:1

"And all the congregation worshipped, and the singers sang, and the trumpeters sounded: *and* all *this continued* until the burnt-offering was finished."

II Chronicles 29:28

"Let the word of Christ dwell in you richly in all wisdom; teaching and admonishing one another in psalms and hymns and spiritual songs, singing with grace in your hearts to the Lord."

Colossians 3:16

"Speaking to yourselves in psalms and hymns and spiritual songs, singing and making melody in your heart to the Lord;"

Ephesians 5:19

"I will sing unto the LORD as long as I live: I will sing praise to my God while I have my being."

Psalm 104:33

"I believe worldly music is the number one stronghold in America." – Byron Foxx

The Occult

The occult is all those religions and practices that revolve around the powers of Satan including Satanism, witchcraft, astrology, fortunetellers, horoscope, voodoo, and other forms of black magic. All of these things are the work of Satan. Those involved in these activities were said to be wroughting evil (II Chronicles 33:2, 6) and witchcraft, which means 'magical arts' can be a broad overlying term for all these things and is listed among the works of the flesh a manifestation of our sin nature (Galatians 5:19-21). Satan is the father of sin and evil, therefore, there is no question that anyone involving themselves in these things are involving themselves with Satan.

The Bible speaks for itself on this matter. I will, however, interpret what some of the terms used in II Chronicles 33:6 and Deteronomy 18:10-12 mean in today's terms. All of them are man's attempt to gain hidden knowledge by supernatural means. Some of them are also used for the simple evil purposes of causing harm to others. Enchantments or enchanters would be today's snake charmers. Those who dealt with, consulted, or had a familiar spirit were those who evoked the dead in order to communicate with them. Observer of times and divination are closely related, having the meaning of seeing the future. They would include fortunetellers as well as those who use astrology to predict horoscopes because they have an ultimate belief that the heavenly bodies are gods that control the destiny of humans. A charmer speaks of those who cast magical formulas and spells. This was often done using a process of binding the recipient with special knots; today's voodoo is closely related in many areas. The biblical necromancer would have connection to mesmerists or hypnotists. Witchcraft, wizards (& in other passages sorcery) are all used to describe those who use these forms of magical arts and are able to elicit results beyond man's power. Oftentimes, you will find mentioned among these evil practices those who required people, most often children, to *pass through the fire*. This was a sacrifice ritual of ancient idol worship. All these things are full of darkness, evil, and the works of Satan.

Today, Satan is still at work and uses subtle ways to deceive many into dabbling in his works of darkness. Satan knows that he has his best chances if he targets the weaker, more impressionable minds of children. Movies about wizards, witches, and sorcery and fantasy role-playing games are marketed for children as innocent entertainment and fun. There is even a so called board 'game' that is used to evoke a response from the dead. In truth, however, these things are not harmless; they are Satan's way of luring and leading as many as he can toward the occult.

All the magical arts of the occult are made possible by the power of Satan. Yes, Satan has much power, but one must always remember that his power is not as great as God's and he is ultimately under subjection to God. (Job 1:12, 2:6; Revelation 20:2) Satan and those who worship him and/or involve themselves in the occult arts will be judged by God. God's Word says that they will not inherit the kingdom of God (Galatians 5:19-21) but will suffer an eternity in hell (Revelation 21:8).

"But did *that which was* evil in the sight of the LORD, like unto the abominations of the heathen, whom the LORD had cast out before the children of Israel. ...And he caused his children to pass through the fire in the valley of the son of Hinnom: also he observed times, and used enchantments, and used witchcraft, and dealt with a familiar spirit, and with wizards: he wrought much evil in the sight of the LORD, to provoke him to anger."

II Chronicles 33:2, 6

"When thou art come into the land which the LORD thy God giveth thee, thou shalt not learn to do after the abominations of those nations. There shall not be found among you *any one* that maketh his son or his daughter to pass through the fire, *or* that useth divination, *or* an observer of times, or an enchanter, or a witch, Or a charmer, or a consulter with familiar spirits, or a wizard, or a necromancer. For all that do these things *are* an abomination unto the LORD..."

Deuteronomy 18:9-12

"But I *say*, that the things which the Gentiles sacrifice, they sacrifice to devils, and not to God: and I would not that ye should have fellowship with devils."

I Corinthians 10:20

"A man also or woman that hath a familiar spirit, or that is a wizard, shall surely be put to death: they shall stone them with stones: their blood *shall* be upon them."

Leviticus 20:27

"But the fearful, and unbelieving, and the abominable, and murderers, and whoremongers, and sorcerers, and idolaters, and all liars, shall have their part in the lake which burneth with fire and brimstone: which is the second death."

Revelation 21:8

"The revival of 'Spiritism,' or 'Demonism,' is one of the signs of the times and should be a warning to every true child of God of the approaching end of the Age." – Clarence Larkin

One Nation Under God

A nation is, "a body of people inhabiting the same country, or united under the same sovereign or government."[1] The United States of America is a nation that was established July 4, 1776 with the adoption of the Declaration of Independence, claiming its separation from England. Its beginning goes back another some 284 years earlier, however, with its discovery by Christopher Columbus. It may be true that some early explorers came for wealth and conquest, but the truth also remains that the first settlers, those who came with the intention of staying and ultimately becoming the original 13 colonies, came to America for religious and political freedom. They came to establish a country where they could serve God as the Bible says they should without dictation and interference from government.

There are many examples within our country that give witness to the beliefs and intentions of America's founding fathers. America's first documents that still hold our nation together are saturated with recognition of the God of heaven being the sovereign ruler under Whom this nation was placed. The Declaration of Independence declares God to be Creator, God of nature, and Supreme Judge of the world. Our money bears the phrase 'In God We Trust' and many of our country's monuments bear recognition and thanks to God as well as scripture references. We sing of our liberty being of God, ask for His protection, and claim God as our great king in our national anthem. The government was ordered in such a way to include God. Men of office, witnesses in a court of law, and the president of our nation are sworn in by solemn oath with God as their witness while placing their hand on a Bible. There is a Chaplain for both the Senate and House of Representatives that starts every session with prayer to seek God's wisdom and guidance in lawmaking. Every branch of our military has Chaplains to provide counsel and comfort and to pray for God's hand in battle. Finally, tax-free status was first given to Christian institutions to encourage their existence because of their value and benefit to the communities and country. The founding fathers of our nation feared God, believed His Word, and recognized the need for God in the success of the nation. Benjamin Franklin said:

> I have lived, sir, a long time; and the longer I live, the more convincing proofs I see of this truth, that God governs in the affairs of men. If a sparrow cannot fall to the ground without His notice, is it probable that an empire can rise without His aid? We have been assured, sir, in the Sacred Writings that 'except the Lord build the house, they labor in vain that build it.' I firmly believe this; and I also believe that without His concurring aid we shall succeed in this political building no better than the builders of Babel.

Evidences of God and the role the Christian faith has had in our country since its start are everywhere and unable to be ignored.

God's Word is clear that the only way a nation will be blessed is if their *God is the LORD*. (Psalm 33:12) Proverbs 14:34 promises that righteousness will exalt a nation but also warns that sin will bring reproach. We must remember that it is God who causes nations to rise and fall and He who gives the power to the leaders. (Romans 13:1) We are called to pray for those leaders if we wish to live a *quiet and peaceable life* (I Timothy 2:1-3). and it is only through prayer and seeking God's face that we can expect our land to be healed. (II Chronicles 7:14)

"Blessed *is* the nation whose God *is* the LORD; *and* the people *whom* he hath chosen for his own inheritance."

Psalm 33:12

"Righteousness exalteth a nation: but sin *is* a reproach to any people."

Proverbs 14:34

"Let every soul be subject unto the higher powers. For there is no power but of God: the powers that be are ordained of God."

Romans 13:1

"I exhort therefore, that, first of all, supplications, prayers, intercessions, *and* giving of thanks, be made for all men; For kings, and *for* all that are in authority; that we may lead a quiet and peaceable life in all godliness and honesty. For this *is* good and acceptable in the sight of God our Saviour;"

I Timothy 2:1-3

"If my people, which are called by my name, shall humble themselves, and pray, and seek my face, and turn from their wicked ways; then will I hear from heaven, and will forgive their sin, and will heal their land."

II Chronicles 7:14

"If we ever forget that we are One Nation Under God, then we will be a nation gone under."
– Ronald Regan

One Way

The way spoken of here is one's means to receive pardon for their due punishment of an eternity spent in hell so that they can have eternal life in heaven. There are many religions that claim to offer a 'way' to heaven. Religion is a system of faith that consists of the belief of a superior power or powers that govern the world and worship of such power or powers.[1] The only true way to heaven, however, is not through religion but receiving Jesus Christ as one's personal Savior.

We will all live for eternity. The question is whether that eternity will be a happy life in heaven or torment in hell. The Bible is clear that unless a person is born again, or saved, they will not have a home in heaven. (John 3:3) The only way to be saved and gain eternal life is to accept God's Son, Jesus, as one's Savior; those who do not will not receive this life. Jesus said, I am 'the' way and I am 'the' door. (John 14:6; 10:9) He did not say 'one' or 'a' door; He is the only way. We also see clearly stated in Acts 4:12 that *there is none other name* by which one can be saved.

The Bible is clear, believing on the Lord Jesus Christ as one's personal Savior is the *only* way to heaven and none of the other religions of the world offer this gift. Nearly every other known religion is a works-based religion, but Isaiah 64:6 explains that *all our righteousnesses are as filthy rags*; there is nothing we can do good enough to earn our way into heaven. Similarly, Ephesians 2:9 and Titus 3:5 specifically tell us that our salvation is *not of/by works*. Besides all the evidences found in Scripture, the fact that no other religion leads to heaven is common logic. Christianity is the only religion whose God was resurrected and is alive today! What power does someone who is dead have for the living? In addition, consider how other religions began. They can be traced back to a common man who one day decided to found a religion: Buddhism by Siddhartha Gautama; Islam by Mohammad; Mormonism by Joseph Smith; Jehovah's Witness by Charles Taze Russell. The God of heaven and His ways have been since before the world began.

Satan uses false religions to deceive people, they are only a counterfeit of the real thing. II Timothy 3:5-7 is a powerful passage that speaks of this exact thing. It tells us, "Having a form of godliness, but denying the power thereof: from such turn away. For of this sort are they which creep into houses, and lead captive silly women laden with sins, led away with divers lusts, Ever learning, and never able to come to the knowledge of the truth." Satan creeps into the homes of people with powerless religions that have just enough of a hint of godliness to fool people into believing. Followers of these religions are very serious about their faith and study and learn all they can but it is all vain for they will never come to the true saving knowledge under these lies. If Satan can get people to follow one of these false religions and die in that state, he will have accomplished his goal of sending yet another person into eternity in his hell. The real truth is that one does not get their name written in the book of life through any other religion but that of Jesus Christ, and those who are not written there will be *cast into the lake of fire*. (Revelation 20:15) Don't be one of Satan's fools.

"Jesus answered and said unto him, Verily, verily, I say unto thee, Except a man be born again, he cannot see the kingdom of God."

John 3:3

"He that hath the Son hath life; *and* he that hath not the Son of God hath not life."

I John 5:12

"Jesus saith unto him, I am the way, the truth, and the life: no man cometh unto the Father, but by me."

John 14:6

"Neither is there salvation in any other: for there is none other name under heaven given among men, whereby we must be saved."

Acts 4:12

"And whosoever was not found written in the book of life was cast into the lake of fire."

Revelation 20:15

"Mohammed founded a religion and died, was buried and remained in the tomb. Can Mohammad give deliverance from sin? NO! Buddha founded a religion and died and was buried and remained in the tomb. Can Buddha give deliverance from sin? NO! Can Confucius? NO! They all leave us in sin and misery. But where they fail, Christ saves." – R. L. Moyer

Persecution

Persecution is, "the infliction of pain, punishment or death upon others unjustly, particularly for adhering to a religious creed or mode of worship, either by way of penalty or compelling them to renounce their principles."[1] God's Word tells us that persecution of Christians is a certainty. (II Timothy 3:12) In fact, He tells us in I Peter 4:12 that we are not to be surprised by persecution or find it strange. The devil is at the root of all the enmity towards Christianity; he hates God and anything or anyone who aligns themselves with God. The hatred that Christians endure is not a personal attack but rather a disapproval of the God they serve. (John 15:18)

Fortunately, the United States of America has been rather free of religious persecution thanks to our forefathers and the constitution they wrote. Our founding fathers had just fled countries that were not allowing them to worship the God of the Bible as the Bible says. They wanted to ensure that they did not see a repeat of those persecutions in this new country that they were forming. Sadly, this is not the case in many foreign countries. Many missionaries are serving in countries where they have to spread the Gospel in secret and/or use 'back door' methods so to speak and cannot even hold open worship services. There are terrorist organizations in the world that have vowed to eliminate all Christians from the face of the earth. One would do well to remember that although we have religious freedom here in the U.S., great persecution does still exist in the world today; we should be thankful for our freedoms while praying for those who are not as fortunate.

There have been many people who have been persecuted for their faith in God. Some have even paid the ultimate sacrifice of giving their lives, thus becoming a martyr for Christ. Jesus was persecuted during His earthly ministry and the persecution against Christians began early in history in the first century Church. Stephen was the first martyr for Christ. We see the story of his persecution in Acts 7:60. The Bible accounts for the martyrdom of John the Baptist in Mark 6:14-29 who was beheaded and James, one of Christ's disciples in Acts 12:1-2 who was killed by the sword by King Herod. You see in verse 3 that Herod arrested Peter assumedly intending on the same fate for him but Peter was miraculously released from prison by an angel. Persecution has never seen an end ever since. *Foxe's Book of Martyrs* is full of accounts of those who gave their life because of their faith. The Holocaust of 1933-1945 was persecution on a very large scale in the form of genocide. Unfortunately, persecution will continue until the Lord returns to set up His Kingdom on this earth.

God's Word tells us that those who are persecuted are blessed because their ultimate fate is an eternity in heaven. (Matthew 5:10) I Peter 3:17 says that persecution for the Lord is better than doing evil and verse 14 goes so far as to say that they are to be happy. Happy, perhaps, because God promises to reward those who are faithful through persecution with a crown of life to be received in heaven. (Revelation 2:10; James 1:12) A crown that they will then have the privilege of setting at the Lord's feet. (Revelation 4:10-11) We can also take comfort in knowing that we glorify God when we are persecuted for His name's sake. (I Peter 4:14,16)

"Yea, and all that will live godly in Christ Jesus shall suffer persecution."

II Timothy 3:12

"Beloved, think it not strange concerning the fiery trial which is to try you, as though some strange thing happened unto you:"

I Peter 4:12

"If the world hate you, ye know that it hated me before *it hated* you."

John 15:18

"Blessed *are* they which are persecuted for righteousness' sake: for theirs is the kingdom of heaven."

Matthew 5:10

"Fear none of those things which thou shalt suffer: behold, the devil shall cast *some* of you into prison, that ye may be tried; and ye shall have tribulation ten days: be thou faithful unto death, and I will give thee a crown of life."

Revelation 2:10

"In which words three things are to be noted: First, that Christ will have a Church in this world. Secondly, that the same Church should mightily be impugned, not only by the world, but also by the uttermost strength and powers of all hell. And, thirdly, that the same Church, notwithstanding the uttermost of the devil and all his malice, should continue." – John Foxe

Personality/Temperament

Personality is, "that which constitutes an individual a distinct person, or that which constitutes individuality."[1] Personality can be thought of as the way one conducts themselves on autopilot, without thinking about it. When considering the different roles which every person has to play in life, one's personality is the role that person is most comfortable with and comes naturally; roles contrary to one's personality require the person to think about and determine to act in such a manner when performing that role. In addition, personality is natural behavior because it is the way God created that individual and cannot really be changed. Temperament, on the other hand, is how one controls that personality in daily interactions and can certainly be changed with the Spirit's help. I Samuel 16:7 speaks of both; it says not to take too much stock in one's countenance (temperament) but explains that what is real (personality) is that which is found in the heart. I Peter 3:4a refers to it as the *hidden man of the heart* and Proverbs 23:7a says that what is in the heart makes up what a person is.

We can observe different personalities in the Bible by studying how different men conducted themselves. In Paul you find someone who was bold, intolerant yet encouraging, a natural leader, and one who got the job done. In Peter you find someone who was impulsive, liked to talk, and didn't mind being 'the man' (which made him perfect for preaching to over 5,000 people on the day of Pentecost). In John (the apostle, not John the Baptist) you find someone who was quiet, humble, kind, and strived to serve. In Thomas you find someone who was analytical and guarded (he was not going to believe a dead person was alive without proof) but ready to follow once any doubts had been resolved. Each man had a different personality, but God used all of them. Each man's unique personality was just what was needed to perform the tasks and roles God had for them to perform.

With every personality comes strengths and weaknesses. It would benefit each person greatly to learn and understand their unique personality and the strengths and weaknesses that come with it. Knowing one's strengths helps them to know what things they should work on developing and will also help them to see how they can best serve the Lord. It is equally important to know one's weaknesses. These are the things that a person must be mindful of in their daily dealings with others so as not to hinder relationships. One's strengths are only such if they are not taken too far and become weaknesses. One's greatest strength is often their greatest weakness as well.

Although our personalities cannot be changed, our temperament can. The power of the Holy Spirit in each person can help them control their personality. I Corinthians 5:17 explains that once a person is saved they become a *new creature*. Consider Paul, for instance, before he was saved he was bold, intolerant, and got the job done of killing Christians. After salvation, he used that same bold, intolerant, and get-the-job-done personality to preach God's word, exhort sinful behaviors, and see souls saved. The key is found in Romans 8:1-4. When a person walks in the Spirit, the flesh and its power over that person is brought under submission which allows the positives of their personality to come through.

"But the LORD said unto Samuel, Look not on his countenance, or on the height of his stature; because I have refused him: for *the LORD seeth* not as man seeth; for man looketh on the outward appearance, but the LORD looketh on the heart."

I Samuel 16:7

"But *let it be* the hidden man of the heart, in that which is not corruptible…"

I Peter 3:4a

"For as he thinketh in his heart, so *is* he…"

Proverbs 23:7a

"Therefore if any man *be* in Christ, *he is* a new creature: old things are passed away; behold, all things are become new."

I Corinthians 5:17

"*There is* therefore now no condemnation to them which are in Christ Jesus, who walk not after the flesh, but after the Spirit. For the law of the Spirit of life in Christ Jesus hath made me free from the law of sin and death. For what the law could not do, in that it was weak through the flesh, God sending his own Son in the likeness of sinful flesh, and for sin, condemned sin in the flesh: That the righteousness of the law might be fulfilled in us, who walk not after the flesh, but after the Spirit."

Romans 8:1-4

"Dealing with another person according to his personality type is like trying to speak another language. If you know how to speak someone's native tongue, you will be able to communicate well. If not, you will be frustrated at best, and at worst you will get nowhere at all!"
– Robert A. Rohm

Pornography

Pornography is the viewing of material that explicitly shows sexual actions with the intention of arousing sexual desires. Everything about pornography is wrong. I will discuss the painful results of viewing it in a moment, but besides those results the activity being viewed itself is wrong. Those involved in the act of pornography are usually not husband and wife and many times homosexual behavior is involved. The Bible is clear that sex is to be reserved for *one* man and *one* woman within the bounds of marriage only (see the topic on sex).

The devil uses many lies to help those who view pornography to justify their involvement. The first lie is that it is only viewing something with the eyes, that there are not any physical actions taking place. God has much to say, however, about what we allow into our heart and minds through the eye gate. Most of our problems begin with what we allow through our eyes. God inspired David to write about not allowing anything wicked into the eye gate in Psalm 101:3. We must be careful what we allow our eyes to see, because we are prone to imitate what we see and watch. (I Corinthians 15:33) Video is a form of communication and I Corinthians 15:33 speaks of how good behaviors are overtaken by evil communications. Furthermore, let us not forget that God said in Matthew 5:28 that a man who looks at a woman with lust is guilty of adultery. A second lie the devil uses is that it will not harm or affect anyone. David explains in the second part of Psalm 101:3 that he is careful what he places before his eyes because of the risk of those things 'cleaving' to him. Those things we see are permanently etched into our mind. Viewing pornography strains marital intimacy because the viewer will judge their mate (even if it is subconsciously) compared to what they have seen and their mate will more than likely not measure up. Yet another lie of the devil is that viewing pornography is private and not known by anyone but the one viewing it. Numbers 32:23 promises that one's sins will always be revealed, more often than not here on earth, but at the least at the judgment. Verses like Psalm 33:13 and Hebrews 4:13 explain that God sees all we do, including what one does in the privacy of their home on the internet. God also gives a warning in Proverbs 28:13 that those who try to cover their sins will not prosper. Don't fall for Satan's lies, the consequences are not worth it.

The sin of pornography boils down to lust of the flesh, lust on the part of the one performing the acts as well as the one viewing it. God says that the lusts of the flesh and eyes are not of Him in I John 2:16 and tells us to flee youthful lusts in II Timothy 2:22. Pornography is a sin that leads to heartache and many times deeper sin, because sin is often a progression. It begins with what one sees, then they begin to think more and more about that thing until they can't stop thinking about it; they begin to fantasize about acting on those thoughts; then they begin to make plans to act on their thoughts, and eventually a very devastating and irreversible action is committed that causes heartache and broken families. Our sinful nature gives us *unstable souls* and when one allows themselves to participate in *covetous practices* such as pornography, filling their eyes with adultery, they *cannot cease from sin*. (II Peter 2:14)

"I will set no wicked thing before mine eyes: I hate the work of them that turn aside; *it* shall not cleave to me."

Psalm 101:3

"Be not deceived: evil communications corrupt good manners."

I Corinthians 15:33

"But I say unto you, That whosoever looketh on a woman to lust after her hath committed adultery with her already in his heart."

Matthew 5:28

"For all that *is* in the world, the lust of the flesh, and the lust of the eyes, and the pride of life, is not of the Father, but is of the world."

I John 2:16

"Having eyes full of adultery, and that cannot cease from sin; beguiling unstable souls: an heart they have exercised with covetous practices..."

II Peter 2:14

"The proliferation of pornography in our society is no light matter. The poison of pornography is having a dramatic effect upon our society, churches and young people. There are numerous examples of pornography producing psychological damage, spiritual bondage, and social deviancy." – Jeff Amsbaugh

Prayer

Prayer is the means by which the Christian communes with God in order to express their love and thanks to Him, confess sins, ask forgiveness, and give supplications for self and others. God the Father loves to hear from His children. He tells us to *pray without ceasing*; we should have a daily prayer life in which we converse with God on everything no matter how small it may seem to us. (I Thessalonians 5:17) Consider what Christ said in Matthew 6:8, "...your Father knoweth what things ye have need of, before ye ask him." God does not need us to tell Him what we need or want, He already knows. God's command to us to be continually in prayer forces us to see our need of Him and remain in a close fellowship with Him.

God's Word gives the child of God assurance that they can expect their prayers to be answered. (Jeremiah 33:3; Luke 11:9) There are some things that must be in place in order for this promise to be fulfilled, however. He will grant the petitions of our prayers so long as they are according to His will. (I John 5:14-15) The main key to accomplishing that is to be in fellowship with the Lord. (John 15:7) When we are abiding in Him, our desires will naturally coincide with His will. We must also have faith in God that He will keep this promise. (Mark 11:24) One must be aware, however, that there is a hindrance to prayer – unconfessed sin. (Psalm 66:18) More specifically: one's self will (I Samuel 15:22-23), unforgiveness (Mark 11:25-26), strained relationships (Matthew 5:23-24), lacking devotional life (Proverbs 28:9), disbelief (Matthew 21:22), self-dependence (James 4:2), and impatience or a lack of perseverance (Isaiah 40:31). Don't despair, however. If one is plagued with any of these hindrances, God gives the answer for removing them in I John 1:9 – confession of sin to Him.

God even gives us a model prayer as a guide in Matthew 6:9-13. It begins with honor given to our Lord, and then asking for His will to be done. After praise is given to the Father, then petitions for one's needs (*our daily bread*) can be given. Forgiveness should then be sought with a final petition for His help in keeping us from future sins. The prayer then closes with recognition of and reverence to an all-powerful God. We see from verse 9 that it is to the Father Whom we ought to pray and John 14:13-14 that it's in Jesus' name we close. Take note that Jesus prefaced this model with an admonition to not use prayer for show or personal glory. (Matthew 6:5-7) God is not impressed with the fancy words of a prayer but answers those with a pure and sincere heart. There can come times in life when trials are so burdensome that one does not know how to pray. Don't fret, God, in His omniscience, has once again made provision. The Holy Spirit makes intercession for us when we pray and He relays our prayers to the Father even when the words don't seem to come to our feeble minds. (Romans 8:26)

There are innumerable things that we could pray for, but there are a few mentioned in God's Word: wisdom (Jeremiah 33:3 and James 1:5), instead of worry (Philippians 4:6), deliverance from troubles (Psalm 34:17), to keep from temptation (Matthew 26:41), and the only thing Jesus specifically told us to pray for - laborers for the harvest (Luke 10:2). Prayer is a powerful thing, but only for those who are right with God and commune with Him in prayer regularly.

"Pray without ceasing."

I Thessalonians 5:17

"Call unto me, and I will answer thee, and shew thee great and mighty things, which thou knowest not."

Jeremiah 33:3

"If ye abide in me, and my words abide in you, ye shall ask what ye will, and it shall be done unto you."

John 15:7

"And when thou prayest, thou shalt not be as the hypocrites *are*: for they love to pray standing in the synagogues and in the corners of the streets, that they may be seen of men. Verily I say unto you, They have their reward. But thou, when thou prayest, enter into thy closet, and when thou hast shut thy door, pray to thy Father which is in secret; and thy Father which seeth in secret shall reward thee openly. But when ye pray, use not vain repetitions, as the heathen *do*: for they think that they shall be heard for their much speaking."

Matthew 6:5-7

"Be careful for nothing; but in every thing by prayer and supplication with thanksgiving let your requests be made known unto God."

Philippians 4:6

"Watch and pray, that ye enter not into temptation: the spirit indeed *is* willing, but the flesh *is* weak."

Matthew 26:41

"God commits Himself into the hands of those who truly pray. Great are the wonders of prayer because great is the God who hears and answers prayer." – E. M. Bounds

Profanity

Profanity is the use of language that accepted standards of morality (both religious and secular) consider blasphemous, obscene, vulgar, rude, indecent, and just down right improper. Exodus 20:7 is often cited when speaking of profanity, but it requires some clarification. The word vain in this verse means emptiness or worthlessness. Therefore any time we use our Lord's name in everyday conversation without the reverence it is due, we are taking His name in vain. Using our Lord's name in conjunction with a curse word is blasphemy. It should be considered as well that there are many slang terms that have become commonplace but are just compromised replacements for known profanity and are just as inappropriate.

Many people try to justify their use of foul language as unharmful and of no concern, but the Bible speaks much differently. God calls the tongue a poisonous evil. (James 3:8) His commands against profanity are numerous. He says to *let no corrupt communication proceed out of your mouth* (Ephesians 4:29), *put off ...blasphemy* and *filthy communication* (Colossians 3:8), *shun profane and vain babblings* (II Timothy 2:16), and not to curse from the same mouth we use to praise God (James 3:9-10). Clearly, God does not want His children to use profanity.

Besides God's commands to not use profanity, there are some practical reasons for refraining from it. The language one uses is a testimony of what is truly in their heart. Those who habitually curse do not have control of their tongue and are a poor testimony to others around them deceiving themselves regarding their relationship with God. (James 1:26) God's Word also tells us that profanity leads to more trouble because of the snow-ball effect of sin. (II Timothy 2:16; Proverbs 21:23) Furthermore, the Bible warns in Matthew 12:36-37 that we will be judged someday according to our words. It reads, "But I say unto you, That every idle word that men shall speak, they shall give account thereof in the day of judgment. For by thy words thou shalt be justified, and by thy words, thou shalt be condemned." We have many reasons to refrain from using profanity.

As children of God, we should strive to make our words acceptable unto Him. (Psalm 19:14) First and foremost, our words should be used to praise and worship God. (Psalm 34:1) Ephesians 4:29 says that our words are to be used to edify fellow believers but the same verse says that our words are to *minister grace*. The goal of edification is to help our brethren not tear them down. We have a great example of what our speech should be in Colossians 4:6. It tells us, "Let your speech *be* always with grace, seasoned with salt, that ye may know how ye ought to answer every man." John G. Butler clearly commentates on this verse saying, "[First] *Grace* does not mean to always be soft, sweet and mild in talk. Christ always spoke in grace, yet He sternly rebuked evil. *Grace* here speaks of high character in speech. Your speech should not be corrupt, unholy, defiled, dishonest. ...[Second] Food without salt is flat, insipid. Symbolically here *salt* means the believer's speech should not be flat, without point, nonsensical, illogical but should reflect good sense, reason, wisdom. ...[Third] Good speech includes being good in declaring one's faith in Jesus Christ."[15] One who is careful to make sure their language is what God expects it to be is less likely to fall into the sin of profanity.

"Let no corrupt communication proceed out of your mouth, but that which is good to the use of edifying, that it may minister grace unto the hearers."

Ephesians 4:29

"But now ye also put off all these; anger, wrath, malice, blasphemy, filthy communication out of your mouth."

Colossians 3:8

"But shun profane *and* vain babblings: for they will increase unto more ungodliness."

II Timothy 2:16

"But the tongue can no man tame; *it is* an unruly evil, full of deadly poison. Therewith bless we God, even the Father; and therewith curse we men, which are made after the similitude of God. Out of the same mouth proceedeth blessing and cursing. My brethren, these things ought not so to be."

James 3:8-10

"Whoso keepeth his mouth and his tongue keepeth his soul from troubles."

Proverbs 21:23

"Filthy and unclean words and discourse are poisonous and infectious, as putrid rotten meat: they proceed from and prove a great deal of corruption in the heart of the speaker, and tend to corrupt the minds and manners of others who hear them, and therefore Christians should beware of all such discourse." – Matthew Henry

Racism

Racism is a belief that a particular race is inferior or superior to another race or races and demonstrating those beliefs by mistreating those races perceived as being inferior. The origin of races began at the Tower of Babel as demonstrated in Genesis 11:1-9. Verse 1 tells us that until this point *the whole earth was of one language*. The Lord was displeased with their disobedience so He mixed up (*confounded*) their languages as a means to force them to disperse and *scatter...abroad upon the face of all the earth*. (vs. 7, 9) The peoples gathered according to their new languages and began migrating to different parts of the earth, nearly isolating themselves from the other groups of languages. This isolation caused genetics to limit certain physical characteristics as dominate genes surfaced creating the races we have today.

Racism is normally against one's physical appearance or ethnicity and has been seen throughout history in different regions of the world. It is demeaning and often times dehumanizing. Jews were killed by the millions in the 1940s by Adolf Hitler. The British introduced slavery into the beginning years of our country which nearly split our nation and cost many lives in a Civil War to end it. Even after the end of slavery and the civil rights movement, however, we still see race riots, shootings, and racists groups today. Racism is an expression of hatred toward others, but God is a God of love and commands us to demonstrate love toward others as well (John 13:34; I John 4:7, 11) even to our enemies (Matthew 5:44).

Some people wrongly suggest that God demonstrated racism in the Bible. They reference the instances in the Bible where God commanded His people to utterly destroy entire nations and people groups. This was not because of race, however, but because of God's command to separate from sin and those engrossed in it. (II Corinthians 6:14) God is not racist towards anyone; however, He is a just God that does not tolerate sin.

For racism to cease, it must be realized that God is the creator of all, loves all, and died for all. John 3:16 says that He died for the entire world and that *whosoever* asked for His salvation would receive it. In Romans 10:12, the word *"Greek"* refers to all those who are not Jews and God is stating that He is the Lord of anyone who calls upon Him. Revelation 7:9 clearly reveals that *all nations, and kindreds, and people, and tongues* will be represented in heaven. God is no respecter of persons when it comes to salvation: rich or poor, with influence or average, young or old, black or white. None of this determines one's value to God or their way into heaven, only that they believe on Him.

We are to judge others to a certain extent, but according to who a person is, what they do, and how they conduct themselves, not on the outward appearance. (John 7:24) We should judge a person by whether they are saved and serving God. Judgment must be reserved only to determine with whom we should fellowship and most importantly so that we can lead those who are not saved to the saving knowledge of Jesus Christ and to prompt them (or backslidden believers) to give their lives to service for the Lord. According to I Samuel 16:7, we fail at this; we must strive to be more like God and judge according to the heart.

"For God so loved the world, that he gave his only begotten Son, that whosoever believeth in him should not perish, but have everlasting life."

John 3:16

"For there is no difference between the Jew and the Greek: for the same Lord over all is rich unto all that call upon him."

Romans 10:12

"After this I beheld, and, lo, a great multitude, which no man could number, of all nations, and kindreds, and people, and tongues, stood before the throne, and before the Lamb, clothed with white robes, and palms in their hands;"

Revelation 7:9

"For there is no respect of persons with God."

Romans 2:11

"Judge not according to the appearance, but judge righteous judgment."

John 7:24

"Jesus loves the little children, all the children of the world, red and yellow, black and white, they are precious in His sight, Jesus loves the little children of the world."
– C. Herbert Woolsten

Revival

Revival is a, "renewed and more active attention to religion or an awakening of men to their spiritual concerns."[1] Often times the blame for the state of our nation is placed on the political system, or lack of. The truth of the matter is, however, that politics are not the answer to our nation's problems and/or current hot topic issues. A personal revival among the people and a turning back to God and His ways is the only answer that will yield lasting results.

II Chronicles 7:14 clearly gives God's recipe for revival. The first ingredient is a humble spirit. In Isaiah 57:15 God promises to revive the humble and contrite. One who is contrite is willing to be crushed and broken. It is only after we are willing to let God truly be God and do with us as He wills that we can expect to see personal revival. The second ingredient is prayer. Prayer is such a powerful resource but is sadly often neglected (see topic on prayer). The third ingredient is a sincere seeking of God. Too many people have a superficial religion and do not earnestly desire to know God and His will. God is accessible to any who would honestly seek Him (Deuteronomy 4:29; Proverbs 8:17) but take heed to the warning in Isaiah 55:6; the farther one gets from God the harder it is to find Him once again. The last ingredient is to turn from one's wicked ways. Ezekiel 33:11 and Isaiah 55:7 echo this commandment. Just as there is no salvation without repentance, revival cannot be seen without repentance either. If each ingredient of this recipe is performed, God promises to forgive and heal or in other words – revive.

God's Word reveals the recipe, but it must be understood that revival starts in the hearts of individual believers. A church-wide revival will never happen without a revival first in the hearts of the congregation of that church. The same goes for the revival of a city which will only come after the revival of its churches and a nation will never see revival without first seeing a revival of its cities. James 4:8 calls for each believer to *draw nigh to God* and to *cleanse* and *purify* themselves before a new spirit spoken of in Psalm 51:10 can become evident. I would challenge the one seeking revival to two things: 1) attend every service of their church and 2) get out of their seat. Church was God's idea because He knew we needed it to grow and remain strong in our faith. One will never get closer to God if they do not surround themselves with sound preaching of His Word and fellow believers. Secondly, remember the first ingredient to revival, humble oneself. When the Lord is working in one's heart through a message they should go to the altar and do business with Him. John R. Rice once said, "Never put much trust in a man who never goes to the altar." If one wants to see a change in the world around them, they must start by making a change in their own heart and life.

Our nation has experienced four great awakenings in our history: 1730s – 1743, 1800 – 1840, 1850s – 1900, and late 1960s – to early 1970s. You will notice that there was never more than 60 years between each one. It is time that we as Christian Americans wake up and realize that we must once again return to God and do our part to begin the fifth great awakening of this nation. Once begun, however, may we not let this one end, but rather live in an eternal state of personal and national revival!

"If my people, which are called by my name, shall humble themselves, and pray, and seek my face, and turn from their wicked ways; then will I hear from heaven and will forgive their sin, and will heal their land."

II Chronicles 7:14

"But if from thence thou shalt seek the LORD thy God, thou shalt find *him*, if thou seek him with all thy heart and with all thy soul."

Deuteronomy 4:29

"Draw nigh to God, and he will draw night to you. Cleanse *your* hands, *ye* sinners, and purify *your* hearts, *ye* double minded."

James 4:8

"Create in me a clean heart, O God; and renew a right spirit within me."

Psalm 51:10

"Turn us again, O LORD God of hosts, cause thy face to shine; and we shall be saved."

Psalm 80:19

"A revival may be expected whenever Christians are found willing to make the sacrifices necessary to carry it on." – Charles G. Finney

Sabbath or Sunday

There is much confusion about what the difference is between the Sabbath and Sunday and without complete understanding of the differences they are sometimes mistakenly blended. They are two distinct and separate days, however. The Sabbath is, "the day which God appointed to be observed by the Jews as a day of rest from all secular labor or employments, and to be kept holy and consecrated to his service and worship. [The Sabbath is observed on the] seventh day of the week, the day on which God rested from the work of creation."[1] The Sabbath was a part of the Mosaic Law and after Christ's death on the cross, the Law was fulfilled. Therefore, "the Christian church very early begun and still continues to observe the first day of the week, in commemoration of the resurrection of Christ on that day, by which the work of redemption was completed. Hence it is often called the Lord's Day."[1] Sabbath is Old Testament Law and Sunday is the day for the New Testament church.

Misconceptions abound surrounding this topic. First is that the Sabbath was to be a day of rest *and* worship but the Sabbath was not a day of worship; rather it was a day purely for rest. (Exodus 20:10) Another is the idea of a 'Christian Sabbath.' Those that hold to this believe that the day the Sabbath is observed merely changed from the seventh day (Saturday) to the first day (Sunday) after Christ's crucifixion. The truth is, however, that Sabbath has always been used in the Bible to mean a specific day of the week – the seventh day and there is no incident recorded in the Bible to suggest otherwise. Misguided people believe that the Sabbath is to be observed by all followers of God, but observance of the Sabbath was meant only for Israelites as part of the ceremonial laws of the Mosaic Law. There is no record of observing the Sabbath before the Mosaic Law or after the Law was fulfilled. The Sabbath was observed by the Israelites as a sign of their coming Savior and was done away, along with the rest of the ceremonial laws, with the death of Jesus on the cross. (Exodus 31:13, 17; Colossians 2:14-17)

The New Testament does not support the observance of the Sabbath, in fact, there is not a single command to keep the Sabbath found in the New Testament. It is actually discouraged in Colossians 2:14-17 and Galatians 4:8-11. Christ, our perfect example, did not observe the Sabbath or command His disciples to and this is one of the very reasons why the Jews sought to crucify Him. (John 5:18) Furthermore, it is the only one of the Ten Commandments that is not repeated in the New Testament. The Sabbath is not for the New Testament church.

The New Testament does support gathering together for worship on the first day of the week, the Lord's Day, or Sunday. (Acts 20:7; I Corinthians 16:2) New Testament Christians have not been commanded to abstain from labor on any particular day or to meet for worship on any particular day, rather it is voluntary and representative of the age of grace we live in. However, we are commanded not to forsake the assembling of ourselves in church. (Hebrews 10:25) If the New Testament disciples found it right and proper to meet on the first day of the week and our New Testament churches have followed that example, then certainly Sunday is the day Christians ought to set aside for the worship of our Lord and Savior.

"But the seventh day *is* the sabbath of the LORD thy God: *in it* thou shalt not do any work, thou, nor thy son, nor thy daughter, thy manservant, nor thy maidservant, nor thy cattle, nor thy stranger that *is* within thy gates:"

Exodus 20:10

"And the LORD spake unto Moses, saying, Speak thou also unto the children of Israel, saying, Verily my sabbaths ye shall keep: for it *is* a sign between me and you throughout your generations; that *ye* may know that I *am* the LORD that doth sanctify you. ...Wherefore the children of Israel shall keep the sabbath, to observe the sabbath throughout their generations, *for* a perpetual covenant. It *is* a sign between me and the children of Israel for ever: for *in* six days the LORD made heaven and earth, and on the seventh day he rested, and was refreshed."

Exodus 31:12-13, 16-17

"Blotting out the handwriting of ordinances that was against us, which was contrary to us, and took it out of the way, nailing it to his cross; *And* having spoiled principalities and power, he made a shew of them openly, triumphing over them in it. Let no man therefore judge you in meat, or in drink, or in respect of any holyday, or of the new moon, or of the sabbath *days*: Which are a shadow of things to come; but the body *is* of Christ."

Colossians 2:14-17

"And upon the first *day* of the week, when the disciples came together to break bread, Paul preached unto them, ready to depart on the morrow; and continued his speech until midnight."

Acts 20:7

"The Bible does not even hint that any other day besides the first should be used as a day of worship. The Lord's Day must be our Sunday. New Testament Christians did not have a day commanded for rest, but they used the first day of the week, not the Sabbath, as a day of worship." – John R. Rice

Salvation

Salvation is the redemption of one's soul from the penalty of sin which is eternal separation from God in hell and instead granting that soul eternal life with God in Heaven as a result of one's belief and acceptance of Jesus' propitiation for their sins on the cross of Calvary. When someone has made this decision they are considered saved. They are saved from the penalty of sin as well as the bondage of sin. The saved person is no longer a servant of Satan but has been freed from the power of sin by means of the presence of the Holy Spirit in their life. (Romans 6:14-18; 8:2) One's salvation is the foundation for the Christian life and that which everything taught in the Bible is built upon. Many people want all their questions answered first before they are willing to put their trust in God. However, they are not going to understand anything until the foundation of salvation is already laid as is revealed to us in I Corinthians 2:14. The things of God are *foolishness* to the unsaved (*natural man*).

The most common verses used to lead someone to the salvation of the Lord is what is known as the Roman's Road (listed on the right). The first thing one must understand is that they are a sinner (Romans 3:23); every person has been born with a sin nature. Adam and Eve sinned in the garden (Romans 5:12). Secondly, there is a penalty for this sin and that is death, both a physical death and a spiritual death – spending eternity in hell separated from God. (Romans 6:23a) The good news is that God made a provision for escape from this penalty – He sent His Son, Jesus, to die on the cross as payment for the sins of *whosoever believeth in him*. (John 3:16; Romans 6:23b, 5:8) In order to be saved, one must believe that: 1) they are a sinner 2) there is a penalty of death and hell for their sin 3) Jesus, God incarnate, died on the cross for their sins and 4) that He rose again on the third day (Romans 10:9; I Corinthians 15:3-8, 14). In addition to believing those things, one must repent of their sins (I John 1:9; Luke 13:3; Acts 3:19), accept God's gift of salvation, and call on Jesus as their Savior (Romans 10:9, 13).

There is one big stumbling block to salvation – people trying to work their way into God's good graces to gain salvation. Salvation is *only* by the grace of God, it is not of works or anything we do to merit it. (Titus 3:5) Isaiah 64:6 explains that anything good we try to do is *as filthy rags* and Ephesians 2:8-9 shows us that if salvation were by works it would allow us to boast of our own achievement. Along the same lines as works, falls religiousness. Believing that there is a God, attending church, and going through all the other motions will not save a person. It requires trusting in His sacrifice, placing your faith in it, and having a personal relationship with God. James 2:19 tells us that *the devils also believe and tremble*, yet they are not saved! Additionally, one must be careful to not begin to feel self-sufficient. Many a well-to-do person believes that they don't need anything, which is why God tells us in Matthew 19:24 that *it is easier for a camel to go through the eye of a needle than for a rich man to enter into the kingdom of God.* One must not be guilty of trusting in their wealth, religion, or good deeds to get them into heaven – these things will not get them there!

Making the decision to trust Christ as one's personal Savior is the most important decision they will ever make. Trust Christ – the *one* and *only* true way to salvation and heaven.

"For God so loved the world, that he gave his only begotten Son, that whosoever believeth in him should not perish, but have everlasting life."

John 3:16

"For all have sinned, and come short of the glory of God;"

Romans 3:23

"Wherefore, as by one man sin entered into the world, and death by sin; and so death passed upon all men, for that all have sinned:"

Romans 5:12

"For the wages of sin *is* death; but the gift of God *is* eternal life through Jesus Christ our Lord."

Romans 6:23

"But God commendeth his love toward us, in that, while we were yet sinners, Christ died for us."

Romans 5: 8

"That if thou shalt confess with thy mouth the Lord Jesus, and shalt believe in thine heart that God hath raised him from the dead, thou shalt be saved. …For whosoever shall call upon the name of the Lord shall be saved."

Romans 10:9, 13

"He saves me from every sin and harm, secures my soul each day; I'm leaning strong on His mighty arm; I know He'll guide me all the way. Saved by His power divine, Saved to new life sublime! Life now is sweet and my joy is complete, for I'm saved, saved, saved!"
– Jack P. Scholfield

Satan

Satan is the fallen angel Lucifer now known as Satan or the devil and prince of the world and darkness; he is the adversary of God and man. Ezekiel 28:12 describes Lucifer as *full of wisdom and perfect in beauty*. Verse 13 then continues to elaborate on all the gems that adorn his covering. Verse 14 gives us his heavenly duties saying that he was *the anointed cherub that covereth*; he had the very honorable position of guarding the throne of God. Unfortunately, like many men do today, he let his beauty, power, and authority overtake him to the point of wanting to be like/above God Himself. (vs. 17; Isaiah 14:13-14) Because of his pride and rebellion, God cast him out of heaven, and he took a third of the angels with him. (Revelation 12:7-9) After the fall, Lucifer became Satan and the angels that went with him became his demons.

Satan is our adversary and his goal is to seek and devour all those he can. (I Peter 5:8) Why does Satan want to destroy us? He lost the battle against God in heaven and when he thought he had succeeded in destroying God's creation in the Garden of Eden, God again defeated him with the provision He made through Christ death and resurrection. Therefore, "There is only one thing left that he can do against God, and that is to *damn the unbelievers* and *slander those who DO believe*, thus grieving the great heart of God and delaying the final consummation of God's blueprint for the ages."[16] The best way for him to grieve God is to keep people from being saved. The devil, which means deceiver, is the father of lies and he uses those lies to complete his main goal – to keep people from the saving knowledge of the *glorious gospel of Christ*. (II Corinthians 4:4) If he fails in keeping someone from being saved, he does all he can to destroy the testimony of the believer in order to keep them from being productive in leading others to Christ. Satan will tempt the believer to do things contrary to the word of God, to defile their body which is the temple of the Holy Spirit, bring circumstances and excuses into the believer's life to cause them to get out of church and backslide in their walk, and break the believer's fellowship with God. One of the biggest attacks of the devil is on the family, the holy unit created by God and the foundation to a successful society. One can be sure, that Satan is the source of all our troubles and the one whom we wrestle against daily. (Ephesians 6:12) The good news for Christians is that we have the power of the Holy Spirit to help us in our fight against the devil. Ephesians 6:10-11 tells us that we have power in the Lord's might and that when we *put on the whole armour of God* we can *stand against the wiles of the devil*. God equips the believer to fight the devil's attacks with the armor described in verses 14-18.

The devil works so hard at destroying God's Kingdom because he knows that his days are numbered. He has a very sad destiny. God sent His Son, Jesus, to this earth to pay the penalty of sin which is *the works of the devil*. (I John 3:8) God created hell specifically for the eternal judgment of Satan and his demons. (Matthew 25:41) God has a specific time in His will that Satan and his demons will be cast into hell and bound there for eternity. (Revelation 20:10; Isaiah 14:15) Be assured that God has always been and always will be on the throne and Satan will someday be defeated for good!

"And there was war in heaven: Michael and his angels fought against the dragon; and the dragon fought and his angels, And prevailed not; neither was their place found any more in heaven, And the great dragon was cast out, that old serpent, called the Devil, and Satan, which deceiveth the whole world: he was cast out into the earth, and his angles were cast out with him."

Revelation 12:7-9

"Be sober, be vigilant: because your adversary the devil, as a roaring lion, walketh about, seeking whom he may devour:"

I Peter 5:8

"In whom the god of this world hath blinded the minds of them which believe not, lest the light of the glorious gospel of Christ, who is the image of God, should shine unto them."

II Corinthians 4:4

"For we wrestle not against flesh and blood, but against principalities, against powers, against the rulers of the darkness of this world, against spiritual wickedness in high *places*."

Ephesians 6:12

"He that committeth sin is of the devil; for the devil sinneth from the beginning. For this purpose the Son of god was manifested, that he might destroy the works of the devil."

I John 3:8

"And the devil that deceived them was cast into the lake of fire and brimstone, where the beast and the false prophet *are*, and shall be tormented day and night for ever and ever."

Revelation 20:10

"The Devil stands ready to fall upon them and seize them as his own, at what moment God shall permit him." – Jonathan Edwards

Separation from the World

Separation is a disconnect, disunion, and/or disassociation from the sinful lifestyles and mindset that characterize this world (moral separation) and from false teachings and doctrinal compromise (ecclesiastical separation). I Peter 2:9 explains that the saved people of God's church are special, we are chosen and are to be holy. This verse also explains why we are to be different. Peculiar here does not mean to be strange like it is often used, but rather the idea of coming into, or having achieved something. We have come into and achieved God's salvation, we have been *called out of darkness* [penalty of hell] *into his marvelous light* [eternity in heaven]. The one called out of darkness, therefore, should no longer have the appearance of those still in darkness – they are a new creature. (II Corinthians 5:17)

God's will is to leave the saved in this world to fulfill His Great Commission, but we are not to be of this world. (John 17:11a, 15-16) This is moral separation – refraining from all the immorality of this world. God commands the saved to not conform to the word's sinfulness. (Romans 12:2) Satan is the god of this world so you can usually count on anything the world promotes as being against God and His statutes. The world's ideas and philosophies so very often do what Isaiah 5:20 warns us about. For example, the world says that the murder of unborn babies in an abortion is right, but that the capital punishment of cold blood murderers is wrong. Worldly music glorifies sinful activity and/or is sensual or arouses sexuality but God calls for the saved to do everything for the glory of God. (I Corinthians 10:31) You cannot mix righteousness with worldliness, therefore, the saved are called to be separate. (II Corinthians 6:14-17)

In addition to moral separation, we are to have ecclesiastical separation. God speaks much in His Word about doctrine, 51 times in fact, so we know that it is important to Him. He says it is *pure*, it is *good*, and that we should *learn* and *understand* it. (Job 11:4; Proverbs 4:2; Isaiah 29:24, 28:9) The Bible also tells us that we are to be wary of *any other thing that is contrary to sound doctrine* and we are to *teach no other doctrine*. (I Timothy 1:10, 1:3) (See Fellowship for more detail) God uses strong language to tell us to avoid biblical error: *shun, purge, turn away, avoid*. (II Timothy 2:16, 21; 3:5; Romans 16:17) Avoiding such error is not to puff oneself up – it is for spiritual protection. Ecclesiastical error can corrupt those trying to follow truth: *will increase unto more ungodliness…eat as doth a canker…overthrow the faith of some* (II Timothy 2:16, 17, 18) and *corrupt good manners* (I Corinthians 15:33). We separate also to not be a stumbling block to the unsaved or baby Christian. (I Corinthians 8:9-13) Salvation is only one element of biblical fellowship, God calls us to separate from those who do not hold to the doctrines taught in the Bible.

The Christian is called to be salt to the earth and to let their light shine to a dark world, but if they are tainted with the things of this world and biblical error, they lose their savor and hide their light. (Matthew 5:13-16) How can one be a witness and testimony to a lost world if they are as dirty and mucky as the world? Why would anyone want to be a Christian if they don't see anything different in the life of a Christian than in their own? Be salt and light!

163

"But ye *are* a chosen generation, a royal priesthood, an holy nation, a peculiar people; that ye should shew forth the praises of him who hath called you out of darkness into his marvellous light:"

I Peter 2:9

"And now I am no more in the world, but these are in the world…I pray not that thou shouldest take them out of the world, but that thou shouldest keep them from the evil. They are not of the world, even as I am not of the world."

John 17:11a, 15-16

"And be not conformed to this world: but be ye transformed by the renewing of your mind, that ye may prove what *is* that good, and acceptable, and perfect, will of God."

Romans 12:2

"Be ye not unequally yoked together with unbelievers: for what fellowship hath righteousness with unrighteousness? and what communion hath light with darkness? …Wherefore come out from among them, and be ye separate, saith the Lord, and touch not the unclean *thing*; and I will receive you,"

II Corinthians 6:14, 17

"But shun profane *and* vain babblings: for they will increase unto more ungodliness."

II Timothy 2:16

"As followers of the Lord Jesus Christ, we must be willing to leave the camp of the world, and the unbelievers, and even false religious professors, and be willing to walk alone with Christ in the path of separation." – M. R. DeHaan

Sex

Sex is the intimate physical relationship between a man and a woman designed by God for the procreation of the human race and to be enjoyed *only* in the bounds of marriage. Although sexual intercourse is a necessity for the survival of the race, God also intended for it to be a blessed thing that is enjoyed by husband and wife. (Proverbs 5:18-19; I Corinthians 7:2-4) It is one way that the two become one, physically and emotionally. Hebrews 13:4 says that sexual intercourse (*bed*) is pure (*undefiled*), but only within the bounds of marriage because of the word *and* which connects this phrase with the previous one which is speaking about marriage and the honor found within it. Unfortunately, the world has taken something pure and holy and perverted it. This perversion has sadly caused many to view sex, whether within marriage or not, as something wrong and dirty.

Probably the biggest abuse of sex is fornication and adultery. Fornication is often referred to as sex between those who are unmarried and adultery as sex between those who are married to other people. Both, however, boil down to sex outside the bounds of marriage. God commanded against adultery in the Ten Commandments (Exodus 20:14) and told us to flee fornication in I Corinthians 6:18. God punished adultery very severely in the Old Testament. Those involved in this sin were subject to death (Deuteronomy 22:22) and David's sin of adultery with Bathsheba cost them the life of the child born from their affair (II Samuel 12:13-23). We may live in the age of grace today, free from such punishments, but that does not erase God's moral law against committing the sin.

There are many other perversions of sex including: incest, pornography, homosexuality, and beastiality. The Bible refers to them as unnatural affections in Romans 1:26 and II Timothy 3:3. Romans 1:26 also calls them vile and continues to condemn homosexuality. Deuteronomy 27:20-23 covers the condemnation of incest and beastiality. Homosexuality and pornography are covered in greater detail earlier in the book. Satan works very hard to turn anything good that God has made into something bad in an attempt to deceive the world and lead it away from God and to himself. Sadly, he has made great strides in destroying the beautiful thing God created in the sexual relationship.

No one is immune to the temptation to fall into one of these sins of sexual perversion. Christian or non-Christian, those raised in a loving supportive home or those from a broken and/or loveless home, bartender or Pastor – anyone can fall if they put down their guard. Every person must decide before temptation arises what their standards are and how they will respond. Every person must be vigilant to prevent opportunities for temptation to arise. The saved person has an advantage. I Corinthians 10:13 says, "There hath no temptation taken you but such as is common to man: but God *is* faithful, who will not suffer you to be tempted above that ye are able; but will with the temptation also make a way to escape, that ye may be able to bear *it*." One must be sure to look for that escape and take it. Christians must flee from these perversions and in so doing, they will be better equipped to maintain a right attitude towards the pure and holy sexual relationship God designed for marriage.

"Marriage *is* honourable in all, and the bed undefiled: but whoremongers and adulterers God will judge."

Hebrews 13:4

"Thou shalt not commit adultery."

Exodus 20:14

"Flee fornication. Every sin that a man doeth is without the body; but he that committeth fornication sinneth against his own body."

I Corinthians 6:18

"For this cause God gave them up unto vile affections: for even their women did change the natural use into that which is against nature: And likewise also the men, leaving the natural use of the woman, burned in their lust one toward another; men with men working that which is unseemly, and receiving in themselves that recompence of their error which was meet."

Romans 1:26-27

"Cursed *be* he that lieth with his father's wife... Cursed *be* he that lieth with any manner of beast. ...Cursed *be* he that lieth with his sister, the daughter of his father, or the daughter of his mother. ...Cursed *be* he that lieth with his mother in law. And all the people shall say, Amen."

Deuteronomy 27:20-23

"Sex is certainly not new, but it is still adultery when it is committed outside of wedlock."
– J. Vernon McGee

Sin

Sin is the transgression and violation of God's divine law either by willfully disobeying those things God commands against doing, or the neglect of those things God commands us to do. (James 4:17) It has been said that sin is anything you think, say, or do that violates God's law. When God finished His work of creation, He *saw every thing that he had made, and, behold, it was very good*. (Genesis 1:31) There was no sin, everything was perfect including His creations of heaven. The Bible does not tell us how much time elapsed between the finished week of creation and the tempting of Eve by the serpent, but sometime between those two events, Lucifer committed the first sin of pride and was cast from heaven becoming Satan (see the topic on Satan). Satan then disguised himself as a serpent and tempted Eve to do the one thing God commanded them not to do – to eat of the tree of the knowledge of good and evil. (Genesis 3) Eve then gave some of the forbidden fruit to Adam who ate as well. Thus the sin nature of all mankind had entered into the world and has passed down to every generation since then. (Romans 5:12)

The sin nature is sometimes referred to as the flesh. It is a disease that wars against the things of the Spirit in our lives every day (Galatians 5:17). We will never be free of it and will continue to fight the sin nature until we get to glory in heaven. Yes, we all sin and can *be sure* [our] *sin will find* [us] *out* if we do not do as God commands us to do (*if ye will not do so*). Not a single soul is immune from the sin nature; we are born with it and *come short of the glory of God* because of it. (Romans 3:23)

The Ten Commandments are one way we see that we *come short of the glory of God*. Sure, God gave us these commandments as a moral law to live by, but they are also a tool to show us that we cannot live up to God's standards and need a Savior. You can find the Ten Commandments in Exodus 20:1-17. Each commandment listed is of equal severity to the Lord. We tend to rank sins, viewing them as little and minor to big and horrific, but to God sin is sin. Often times people see the Ten Commandments as only extreme sins that they are not guilty of committing, but one must realize that each commandment covers an entire family of sins to include all the 'lesser' sins that relate to that particular commandment. For instance, under murder comes the sin of hatred (I John 3:15), under adultery comes lust (Matthew 5:28), and under idolatry comes putting anything above God in one's life. Once this is understood, one can easily see why no one can keep all of the commandments.

God is a holy and just God, therefore there must be a penalty for our sin, our inability to keep the commandments, and that is death – both a physical death and a spiritual death. As soon as Adam and Eve sinned in the garden, their bodies began a physical death. Their sin did something much worse, however, it separated them from an eternity with God and placed them on a path to hell. Nevertheless, God made a provision for that sin debt to be paid so that *whosoever believeth in him* could be saved from that fate and spend an eternity with Him in heaven. (John 3:16) When God looks upon a saved person, He doesn't see the sin; He sees the blood of Christ that was shed on the cross to wash that sin away.

"Therefore to him that knoweth to do good, and doeth *it* not, to him it is sin."

James 4:17

"Wherefore, as by one man sin entered into the world, and death by sin; and so death passed upon all men, for that all have sinned:"

Romans 5:12

"*This* I say then, Walk in the Spirit, and ye shall not fulfil the lust of the flesh. For the flesh lusteth against the Spirit, and the Spirit against the flesh: and these are contrary the one to the other: so that ye cannot do the things that ye would."

Galatians 5:16-17

"But if ye will not do so, behold, ye have sinned against the LORD: and be sure your sin will find you out."

Numbers 32:23

"For all have sinned, and come short of the glory of God;"

Romans 3:23

"For the wages of sin *is* death; but the gift of God *is* eternal life through Jesus Christ our Lord."

Romans 6:23

"Sin will take you farther than you want to go, Sin will keep you longer than you want to stay, Sin will cost you more than you want to pay." – R. G. Lee

Soul Winning

Soul winning is the purposeful act of fulfilling the Great Commission; it is going out to share the Gospel with others in an attempt to lead them to the saving knowledge of Jesus Christ. God's desire is that every person would come to know Him as their personal Savior (II Peter 3:9) so He commanded His people to go out into the world to be a testimony and witness to others of the Gospel of Christ (Mark 16:15). Telling others about Him is our primary responsibility and why the Lord doesn't take us straight to heaven once we're saved but leaves us here on this earth. John 15:16 says that we are ordained to *go and bring forth fruit*. The Great Commission was so important to Jesus that it is the only thing that Jesus Himself specifically told us to pray for. (Luke 10:2) There are various different duties and responsibilities in the church (Pastor, Sunday School teacher, deacon, usher, nursery worker, etc.), but every Christian has the job of being a soul winner.

God does not leave us in the dark regarding how to complete the task. We see examples in His Word that we are to follow. Luke 10:1-12 is a perfect example of a successful soul winning effort. It tells us about a group of 70 people who went before Jesus and the apostles preparing the hearts of those they met for the True Savior who would be coming through behind them. They were more or less door-to-door soul winning and planting seeds. This should be an encouragement for the soul winner who doesn't see immediate fruit. It is not our responsibility to win them (only God can do the saving); God expects us only to tell them. The soul winner may very well just be planting a seed that will one day be watered by someone else and yet another day be harvested by another.

Too many people are satisfied with their own salvation but are not out fulfilling God's command to spread the Gospel because of unwarranted fears or an apathetic attitude. They have their fire insurance, so to speak, but are not concerned enough about the souls of others to tell them the Truth. A great way to gradually work one's way into a soul winning program is to start out as the silent partner. This person can help run interference (entertaining kids, pets, other family members, etc.) while still observing the process first hand. Once they are comfortable, they can step into the lead role. Rejection is a common fear, but one must remember that the person is not rejecting them, rather they are rejecting Christ. (Luke 10:16) One cannot get caught up in those who do not want to hear. (Matthew 10:14) Others worry about what someone will think about them, however, the reality is that most often they will never see the person again, and should the person accept Christ they will be grateful to the soul winner. This is not the case with family members, however, and why it can be difficult to approach them but the feeling of knowing that a deceased family member is spending eternity in hell when you could've done something about it is much worse. The reality of hell should squelch passive attitudes and any fears and compel us all to share the good news with as many people as we can. If Christians don't reach the unsaved, someone else will. God gives warning to those who are ashamed of Him in Matthew 10:32, but promises to bless the church who is not ashamed and is actively and boldly spreading the Gospel. (Luke 2:47)

"And he said unto them, Go ye into all the world, and preach the gospel to every creature."

Mark 16:15

"Ye have not chosen men, but I have chosen you, and ordained you, that ye should go and bring forth fruit, and *that* your fruit should remain: that whatsoever ye shall ask of the Father in my name, he may give it you."

John 15:16

"Therefore said he unto them, The harvest truly *is* great, but the labourers *are* few: pray ye therefore the Lord of the harvest, that he would send forth labourers into his harvest."

Luke 10:2

"Whosoever therefore shall confess me before men, him will I confess also before my Father which is in heaven."

Matthew 10:32

"The fruit of the righteous *is* a tree of life; and he that winneth souls *is* wise."

Proverbs 11:30

"If I had to make a choice to never preach in the pulpit or never win a soul, I say, take the pulpit but let me win souls to Jesus Christ." – Bobby Roberson

Spiritual Gifts

Spiritual gifts are one's special abilities bestowed upon them upon salvation for the purpose of using them for the furtherance of the Gospel and His Kingdom. There is a difference between natural talents and spiritual gifts. William McRae explains, "Talents are possessed by believer and unbeliever alike and are present from birth. God bestows them upon His creatures to benefit mankind on the natural level."[17] I Corinthians 12:7 and 11 both relate the presence of spiritual gifts with the presence of the Holy Spirit, and only a believer possesses the Holy Spirit. McRae continues to tell the reader that these talents can and should be dedicated to the Lord for His service, but that they should not be confused with spiritual talents that are for the benefit of mankind on the spiritual level. There is also a difference between those spiritual gifts that are still present today and those that have ceased. There are the sign gifts of tongues and divine healing which have ceased as we see in I Corinthians 13:8-10 (See the topic on Tongues for further detail) and personal gifts for service which we still see bestowed and used today.

The spiritual gifts given to men for proclaiming God's word to others are found in Ephesians 4:11. The gift of prophecy is the ability to proclaim God's Word publicly; they are dynamic speakers. However, there is no longer the gift of new revelation since Scripture has been completed. (Revelation 22:18) Evangelists are those who go around spreading the Gospel, both locally and abroad as missionaries. Then there are the pastors/teachers who are specially gifted to lead and teach a local congregation of God's flock so that they can go out and reach the community around them. Some are gifted with an ability to study God's Word and impart it to others (teachers), to observe and discern biblical facts in order to explain them to others (word of knowledge/the commentary writers), to bring out biblical truths for life application (word of wisdom/the Christian counselors), and those with the ability to encourage and strengthen the brethren (exhortation). There are also serving gifts like those gifted in leadership and administration (ruleth/government), taking some of the burden from others (helps), sharing their wealth with others (giveth), and comforting and sympathizing with others (mercy). The purpose of all these gifts is *to profit withal* by *perfecting of the saints* and *edifying of the body of Christ*. (I Corinthians 12:7; Ephesians 4:12)

Each believer should make it their goal to discover and develop their God-given spiritual gift(s). The first step in finding your gift is to have a healthy prayer life and to be in fellowship with the Lord. In addition to prayer, one must study – study both God's Word and godly men and women from the past and present. Next, exercise your perceived gift. If it is truly a gift given by God, ability will be present as well as peace and blessings. Exercise is also a tool in the development of your gift. Not many people are a pro at the onset, it requires practice which will improve one's ability. In addition, read appropriate books (recommended by trusted godly mentors) and attend conferences and seminars that will strengthen your gift. Last, regularly evaluate your performance through self-examination and by accepting constructive criticism as well as appropriate praise. God has equipped each one with a specific spiritual gift to help fulfill the Great Commission and His purpose for their life – find it and use it!

"Now there are diversities of gifts, but the same Spirit. And there are differences of operations, but it is the same God which worketh all in all. But the manifestation of the Spirit is given to every man to profit withal. For to one is given by the Spirit the word of wisdom; to another the word of knowledge by the same Spirit;"

I Corinthians 12:4-8

"And he gave some, apostles; and some, prophets; and some, evangelists; and some, pastors and teachers; For the perfecting of the saints, for the work of the ministry, for the edifying of the body of Christ:...From whom the whole body fitly joined together and compacted by that which every joint supplieth, according to the effectual working in the measure of every part, maketh increase of the body unto the edifying of itself in love."

Ephesians 4:11-12, 16

"For as we have many members in one body, and all members have not the same office: So we, *being* many, are one body in Christ, and every one members one of another. Having then gifts differing according to the grace that is given to us, whether prophecy, *let us prophesy* according to the proportion of faith; Or ministry, *let us wait* on *our* ministering: or he that teacheth, on teaching; Or he that exhorteth, on exhortation: he that giveth, *let him do it* with simplicity; he that ruleth, with diligence; he that sheweth mercy, with cheerfulness."

Romans 12:4-8

"As every many hath received the gift, *even so* minister the same one to another, as good stewards of the manifold grace of God. If any man speak, *let him speak* as the oracles of God; if any man minister, *let him do it* as of the ability which God giveth: that God in all things may be glorified through Jesus Christ, to whom be praise and dominion for ever and ever. Amen."

I Peter 4:10-11

"God gave you a gift to equip you for your God-appointed function in the body of Christ, the church." – William McRae

Spiritual Leadership

A leader is, "one that leads or conducts; a guide; or one who goes first."[1] A spiritual leader is one who works by the power of the Holy Spirit to influence people toward personal spiritual growth. Spiritual leadership understands that people cannot be forced into a decision or a life change. It is God's Word and the Holy Spirit that do the work in a person's life, but a good spiritual leader learns how to discern the situation of those they are counseling and will be able to use the appropriate Scripture that will speak to the person's heart. Perhaps the most effective way to guide a person in spiritual growth is through the leader's personal testimony or example. (I Timothy 4:12) When a person looks at the life of a spiritual leader, they should be able to see that their way of life (God's way) is the best. (Psalm 34:8) One can find Bible examples of good spiritual leaders of whom to study in Hebrews 11 – 'The Hall of Faith.' One can learn from their successes and victories, as well as their failures. Even good folks make mistakes, and one would do well to learn from men like Abraham, Moses, and David not to repeat their mistakes and to learn which attributes the spiritual leader should strive for.

Although Pastors and deacons are spiritual leaders, one does not have to hold one of these church offices to be a spiritual leader. There are many good lay people of the church that can serve as spiritual leaders to others. There are some qualifications or character traits that should be evident in the lives of those taking on such a responsibility, however. In Exodus 18:21 we see a list of qualifications Jethro gives Moses in choosing men to help him rule the people. They are to be *able* which speaks of someone who is strong, efficient, and has valor. They are to *fear God* which means they reverence God and His precepts which is the beginning of wisdom according to Psalm 111:10 and Proverbs 9:10. They are honest, being a person of integrity (*men of truth*) and are not greedy for money or possessions (*hating covetousness*). Deuteronomy 1:13 calls for leaders to be wise and have understanding; they should be intelligent and have good discernment and insight. A spiritual leader should not be looking for attention or prestige and care more about the needs of others than themselves. (Philippians 2:3) Another, very important qualification of a spiritual leader is one who is willing to serve. We see this pictured in John 13:2-16 when Jesus washed the disciples' feet. Additionally, Jesus said in Matthew 20:26-28 that those who are great (the leaders) are to be ministers and servants.

There is one thing that is paramount, however, if a spiritual leader wishes to be the most effective – the presence and filling of the Holy Spirit in their life. Every born again believer has the *presence* of the Holy Spirit within them, but not everyone is *filled* with the Spirit. A good spiritual leader will strive to do as the New Testament commands regarding the Holy Spirit in their lives. They will not quench the Spirit (I Thessalonians 5:19) or grieve the Spirit (Ephesians 4:30) but will walk in the Spirit (Galatians 5:16, 25) and be filled with the Spirit (Ephesians 5:18). Being filled with the Holy Spirit is simply acknowledging and repenting of known sins in order to restore fellowship with the Lord and then yielding to His leading in everything one does. A spiritual leader is only a vessel through which God (through the work of the Holy Spirit) guides His people in life's paths.

"Let no man despise thy youth; but be thou an example of the believers, in word, in conversation, in charity, in spirit, in faith, in purity."

I Timothy 4:12

"Moreover thou shalt provide out of all the people able men, such as fear God, men of truth, hating covetousness; and place *such* over them, *to be* rulers of thousands, *and* rulers of hundreds, rulers of fifties, and rulers of tens: And let them judge the people at all seasons: and it shall be, *that* every great matter they shall bring unto thee, but every small matter they shall judge: so shall it be easier for thyself, and they shall bear *the burden* with thee."

Exodus 18:21

"Take you wise men, and understanding, and known among your tribes, and I will make them rulers over you."

Deuteronomy 1:13

"*Let* nothing *be done* through strife or vainglory; but in lowliness of mind let each esteem other better than themselves."

Philippians 2:3

"But it shall not be so among you: but whosoever will be great among you, let him be your minister; And whosoever will be chief among you, let him be your servant: Even as the Son of man came not to be ministered unto, but to minister, and to give his life a ransom for many."

Matthew 20:26-28

"Nobody is fit to be a leader unless he would rather be a follower instead of a leader."
– Jack Hyles

Stewardship

Stewardship is exercising the guardianship of those things one has been given by God; it is the care, maintenance, and management of both the tangible belongings and intangible blessings God gives. Those who are faithful stewards God blesses. (Proverbs 3:9-10)

There is a purpose and need for money. It is a unit of exchange that one uses to provide for those things needed for daily life. (I Timothy 5:8) Those blessed with an abundance of money are so blessed in order to give to others. (Proverbs 28:27) Money is also for the purpose of saving (Proverbs 21:20) and investing. The parable of the talents seen in Matthew 25:14-30 is a perfect example of investing and what good stewardship is. God was pleased with those who made an increased return on what they were given (vs. 21, 23). There is practical need for money.

The first step to good stewardship is in the giving of tithes and offerings. One is to give a *tenth* (Genesis 28:22) of *the firstfruits of all thine increase* (Proverbs 3:9) as a tithe and anything above that would be considered an offering. (See the topic on Tithes and Offerings for further explanation) When one gives, it should be cheerfully as II Corinthians 9:7 says that *God loveth a cheerful giver*. Second, learn to live within your means; in other words, spend only what you have to spend. It is not God's will for us to be in debt. (Proverbs 22:7) The best way to combat debt is to be content with what one has and to not covet those things we do not have. (Philippians 4:19; Hebrews 13:5) Additionally, create a family budget and stay within it. Make sure to figure in savings for large occasional expenses (hospital visits, car repairs, etc.) and allow for some cushion for unexpected things that will inevitably creep in each month. Obedience, contentment, and wise management is the key to good stewardship.

There is reward in being faithful to giving to God and good stewardship. Luke 6:38 shows us that we cannot out give God. One can expect return blessings according to the measure that they give. One cannot expect to be given more if they are not faithful in that which God has already given them. (Luke 16:10-11) The parable of the talents reinforces this as well, those who made an increase with the talents they were given were made *ruler over many things*. It must be noted here that there is no biblical support for the prosperity gospel that many preach today. Sure, there are times that the Lord blesses monetary giving with monetary return, but His blessings are not always earthly. He often blesses the giver and good steward with heavenly blessings. (Mark 10:21) God does this because He knows how much more difficult great wealth makes it for one to turn to Christ, both for salvation and for daily guidance and fellowship with Him. One can be sure that God will supply all their need. (Philippians 4:19)

Good stewardship requires the proper management and use of our time and abilities as well. Take a closer look at the topics on time management and spiritual gifts for discussion on using time and abilities wisely. God commands us to be good stewards of what He gives us because He has a purpose in the blessings. He blesses us with possessions and talents so that we can use them to fulfill the will He has for each individual Christian.

"Honour the LORD with thy substance, and with the firstfruits of all thine increase: So shall thy barns be filled with plenty, and thy presses shall burst out with new wine."

Proverbs 3:9-10

"And this stone, which I have set *for* a pillar, shall be God's house: and of all that thou shalt give me I will surely give the tenth unto thee."

Genesis 28:22

"The rich ruleth over the poor, and the borrower *is* servant to the lender."

Proverbs 22:7

"Give, and it shall be given unto you; good measure, pressed down, and shaken together, and running over, shall men give into your bosom. For with the same measure that ye mete withal it shall be measured to you again."

Luke 6:38

"He that is faithful in that which is least is faithful also in much: and he that is unjust in the least is unjust also in much. If therefore ye have not been faithful in the unrighteous mammon, who will commit to your trust the true *riches*?"

Luke 16:10-11

"For the love of money is the root of all evil: which while some coveted after, they have erred from the faith, and pierced themselves through with many sorrows."

I Timothy 6:10

"Money is one of the many resources God gives us to manage on His behalf. Another is our time; another is our talent...do the best you can as a steward of all of the resources which God has entrusted to you, including your money." – R. B. Ouellette

176

Suicide

Suicide is, "the act of designedly destroying one's own life."[1] The fact that it is one's own life that they are taking does not negate the fact that suicide is still murder which God commands against. (Exodus 20:13) God has a plan and will for each person's life which includes a time line. When one commits suicide, they are stepping outside of that will and putting an end to God's plan before its due time. (Ecclesiastes 7:17) God alone is the one who is to give and take life (I Samuel 2:6) but the one who commits suicide is playing the part of God.

Sadly enough, the average person knows of someone who has committed suicide. The Bible, too, records the suicide of several men. Some people commit suicide because of shame and/or guilt as did Samson (Judges 16:30) and Judas Iscariot (Matthew 27:5). The fear of consequences bring others to their limit as did Saul's armour bearer. (I Samuel 13:5) Still others, like Zimri (I Kings 16:18), commit suicide because of general despair over a situation. The common element among them all is depression. Depression is almost always evident in the life of the suicidal. They have allowed the circumstances of life, and often times their distorted view of the circumstances, drive them over the edge. What they fail to realize, however, is that suicide is a permanent solution to an often temporary problem.

Committing suicide is actually a cowardly and selfish response to one's problems. That person is thinking about their own feelings and completely overlooking the fact that they will be leaving family and friends behind to pick up the pieces. Whether the person believes it or not, every person's life is intertwined with others; this is why a suicide will always affect the lives of others. (Romans 14:7) A suicide never solves a problem, and in fact, it often creates more within its aftermath. Those left behind are left with feelings of guilt and regret. All the opportunities, influence, and good works that surrounded that person are forever gone, not reached, and left undone. When a Christian commits suicide it very much tarnishes the Gospel and Christianity. If a Christian cannot find help, love, and victory why would the unsaved want what they had? For the unsaved, it finalizes their fate to hell and the problems they thought they were dealing with on earth are nothing compared to the eternal torment they enter upon their death. Suicide solves nothing other than give Satan another weapon to use in his war against God's creation.

The reality is that suicide is a refusal to trust God. It does not see God as on the throne in one's life and as the One who has everything under His control. There is hope and help to be found in the Lord for the one who feels life's trials are too much for them to bear. One must cast their burdens on the Lord and lean on God for help and guidance which He promises to give. (Psalm 55:22) To cast one's cares simply means to surrender one's control of a situation over to God and trusting Him to take care of the situation according to His will and in His time. Most of the things in life are not under our control (to whom we were born, where and how we grew up, our physical characteristics, the state of our world today, the sin nature) so we might as well give it over to the One who does have control. One can control their choice to trust God, however, and *choose life*. (Deuteronomy 30:19)

"Thou shalt not kill."

Exodus 20:13

"Be not over much wicked, neither be thou foolish: why shouldest thou die before thy time?"

Ecclesiastes 7:17

"What? know ye not that your body is the temple of the Holy Ghost *which is* in you, which ye have of God, and ye are not your own? For ye are bought with a price: therefore glorify God in your body, and in your spirit, which are God's."

I Corinthians 6:19-20

"Cast thy burden upon the LORD, and he shall sustain thee: he shall never suffer the righteous to be moved."

Psalm 55:22

"I call heaven and earth to record this day against you, *that* I have set before you life and death, blessing and cursing: therefore choose life, that both thou and thy seed may live:"

Deuteronomy 30:19

"Suicide not only affects the one who commits it; it affects an unknown number of other people. The results of suicide do not end with the last breath; they will continue for eternity."
– Randy Raynes

Tattoos

Tattoos are permanent marks put on the body by inserting ink into punctures of the skin. There is not much room for argument regarding God's view on the subject when one looks at Leviticus 19:28. God clearly states that we are not to *print any marks upon you*. A side note here about *ye shall not make any cuttings* is that this would explicitly condemn the practice of 'cutting' which is a repetitive form of self-injury when one cuts their skin. Tattooing is simply a defiling of the body, not a form of art as Satan and the world would have you believe.

One must remember that the saved person's body is not their own. I Corinthians 6:19-20 explains that the Holy Spirit indwells the body of every saved person making their body a temple. The passage goes on to say that the saved are *bought with a price*, the very expensive price of Jesus Christ's life. I Corinthians 3:16-17 echoes that the body of a saved person is a *temple of God*, but goes farther to say that anyone who defiles that temple is subject to God's wrath. Imagine for a moment that I asked you to spray paint your favorite person's name, animal, or even Bible verse on the side of a church building. Would you comply? Of course not – it would be defiling the house of God. In comparison, if one's body is the temple of the Holy Ghost, why would they defile it by marking it up with permanent ink. The biblical answer is that one's body should be treated with the same respect and honor as the house of God is.

II Corinthians 6:14 asks *what communion hath light with darkness*, I John 2:15 tells us to *love not the world, neither the things that are in the world*, and I Thessalonians 5:22 tells us to *abstain from all appearance of evil*. Herein lies a second problem with tattoos – it is associated with the world and rebellion. As Pastor Chappell's quote on the right states, the origins of tattoos are anything but godly. The context of Leviticus 19:28 is God condemning heathen practices done as an act of mourning. Throughout time, tattoos have been a mark of rebellion as seen in the first case of a tattoo mentioned in the Bible which was placed on a murderer to mark him as a rebel against God. It is seen in Genesis 4:15 after Cain killed his brother Abel. It remains today that the average crowd associated with tattoos are rebellious, rough, rowdy, and simply worldly – those things we are to distance and abstain ourselves from. It could be noted here as well, that the practice of body piercings would be condemned under these same grounds because its' roots are found in witchcraft and false religions and today is primarily associated with the same crowd. The negative connotations surrounding tattoos are why the presence of tattoos can hurt one's testimony and/or ministry. Others make judgment on that person and many times will not put much confidence in what they say. One should be mindful of making such rash judgments since there is a possibility that the tattoo(s) were gotten before that person was saved, but that does not change the reality of judgments (permanence being yet another argument against tattoos). There is nothing righteous or wholesome about tattoos.

As was established above, the body of the saved person belongs to God and we are to present our bodies to the Lord for His work. (Romans 12:1) Tattooing one's body defiles the temple of God and hinders one's testimony. One should make it their goal to be a member of God's church that can be presented without spot, wrinkle, or blemish. (Ephesians 5:27)

"Ye shall not make any cuttings in your flesh for the dead, nor print any marks upon you: I *am* the LORD."

Leviticus 19:28

"What? know ye not that your body is the temple of the Holy Ghost *which is* in you, which ye have of God, and ye are not your own? For ye are bought with a price: therefore glorify God in your body, and in your spirit, which are God's."

I Corinthians 6:19-20

"Know ye not that ye are the temple of God, and *that* the Spirit of God dwelleth in you? If any man defile the temple of God, him shall God destroy; for the temple of God is holy, which *temple* ye are."

I Corinthians 3:16-17

"I beseech you therefore, brethren, by the mercies of God, that ye present your bodies a living sacrifice, holy, acceptable unto God, *which is* your reasonable service. And be not conformed to this world: but be ye transformed by the renewing of your mind, that ye may prove what *is* that good, and acceptable, and perfect, will of God."

Romans 12:1-2

"That he might present it to himself a glorious church, not having spot, or wrinkle, or any such thing; but that is should be holy and without blemish."

Ephesians 5:27

"If you research the history of tattoos, you will find that barbaric nations, criminals, heathens, and godless people turned to the practice of marking their bodies for idol worshipping, witchcraft, and many other reasons. Therefore, the origination of tattoos is godless."
– Paul Chappell

Testimony

One's personal testimony is their, "open attestation or profession," of their faith in God and the, "witness, evidence, or proof of some fact," that others see as a result of how they live their life.[1] There are two aspects to one's testimony. First, there is one's personal salvation testimony. This is the account of how a Christian came to the knowledge of Lord as their personal Savior. There is also your living testimony. This is the public manner in which a saved person conducts themselves and lives their life which reflects Christ and Christianity to the world around them.

Luke 8:39 exhorts us all to tell everyone we can about all God has done for us. The most important thing He has done for us is provide a way of salvation from our sin and eternal punishment in hell. Every believer has a personal salvation testimony they can share with others. It is a good practice to write out one's salvation testimony as it will help when it comes time to witness and share the Gospel with others. Every Christian can also testify to others of all the blessings God has bestowed on their lives. God is exceeding good to His children which should compel them to share their testimonies uninhibited and unashamed. (Psalm 119:46) Matthew 10:32 promises us that, "Whosoever therefore shall confess me before men, him will I confess also before my Father which is in heaven," but continues in verse 33 with the warning, "But whosoever shall deny me before men, him will I also deny before my Father which is in heaven."

Another important aspect of one's testimony is the example they exhibit by the way they live their lives on a daily basis. (I Timothy 4:12) How one lives their life will reflect positively or negatively on their testimony determining how the world views Christ. It is important for the Christian to remember that they represent Christ to unbelievers and the world is watching to see if how they act matches what they believe God's Word teaches. The world knows that Christians are to be different than unbelievers. I Peter 2:9 refers to this difference as being a *peculiar people*. The Christian is called to be salt and light to the world in Matthew 5:13-16. The passage explains that if the Christian is no different than everyone else around them, they will make no impact for God just like salt that has lost its savour. The passage continues to use light as an analogy of one's testimony, explaining that the light must be exposed just as our testimony cannot be hidden by a poor or silent testimony. When one is the light and salt God calls them to be, they glorify God.

One's testimony is a lifelong endeavor, something one is to be mindful of until the end of their days. Too many people take a back seat in this area as they near the end of life. Psalm 71:15-18 is a great passage that reflects how we should approach our testimony. It speaks of telling all one can about how good God is and how He saved them. The Psalmist speaks of continuing his testimony when he is *old and grayheaded* and pleads with the Lord to not stop teaching him so that he can in turn teach *this generation* and *every one that is to come*. May we all be like the psalmist and yearn to continually be growing so that we can be a godly example to the world around us.

"Return to thine own house, and shew how great things God hath done unto thee. And he went his way, and published throughout the whole city how great things Jesus had done unto him."

Luke 8:39

"I will speak of thy testimonies also before kings, and will not be ashamed."

Psalm 119:46

"Let no man despise thy youth; but be thou an example of the believers, in word, in conversation, in charity, in spirit, in faith, in purity."

I Timothy 4:12

"Ye are the salt of the earth: but if the salt have lost his savour, wherewith shall it be salted? it is thenceforth good for nothing, but to be cast out, and to be trodden under foot of men. Ye are the light of the world. A city that is set on an hill cannot be hid. Neither do men light a candle, and put it under a bushel, but on a candlestick; and it giveth light unto all that are in the house. Let your light so shine before men, that they may see your good works, and glorify your Father which is in heaven."

Matthew 5:13-16

"My mouth shall shew forth thy righteousness *and* thy salvation all the day; for I know not the numbers *thereof*. I will go in the strength of the Lord GOD: I will make mention of thy righteousness, *even* of thine only. O God, thou hast taught me from my youth: and hitherto have I declared thy wondrous works. Now also when I am old and grayheaded, O God, forsake me not; until I have shewed thy strength unto *this* generation, *and* thy power to every one *that* is to come."

Psalm 71:15-18

"God doesn't have to have an expensive vessel, but He does have to have a clean vessel."
– Lester Roloff

Time Management

Time management is the prioritizing and organized planning of the time one has been given of God in order to be the most effective and productive in fulfilling God's will. We are called to be good stewards of what God has given us including our time. There are 1,440 minutes in a day, 10,080 minutes in a week, 43,829.1 minutes in an average month, and 525,949 in a year. We all have the exact same amount of time each day; there is no way to add more to your day and you cannot carry any unused or wasted time over to another day. There are those that accomplish more in a day/week/month/year than others, however, and that is simply because they are better managers of their time.

The first step one must do in order to be successful at time management is to monitor where their time is going. We are instructed in Psalm 90:12 to *number our days* and in Psalm 39:4 to know the *measure of my days*. These verses are telling us that we are to be mindful and aware of the time we have and what we are doing with it. Both verses continue to explain *why* it is important to do so – to *apply our hearts unto wisdom* and to keep us mindful of how short our life really is in the spanse of time and eternity (*that I may know how frail I am*). It is a necessity for one to determine where it is that they are spending their time and from there determine if there are areas of life that are getting too much or too little of their time.

Once a person has identified where there time is currently being spent, they can begin to prioritize the areas of their life and determine the correct amount of time to be spent in each area. There is great importance in the things of God, family activities, and work responsibilities, but they must be balanced properly for one's life to be happy and productive. God commends a studious worker and chastises the sluggard (Proverbs 6:6-11), but one can put too much priority on money and work that they neglect their families and God. A proper attitude toward work can be found in the one who views it as a means to provide for their financial needs and not in pursuit of great riches. We see in Ecclesiastes 3:4 that there is a time to *laugh*; God wants us to be happy and enjoy life occasionally, but there are too many people today that live for fun and entertainment to God's displeasure. Unfortunately, God tends to get the bottom of the barrel of people's time today. The Christian's life should center on God. At the least, family activities should be scheduled around the regular services of the church. Beyond that, however, it is a good practice to schedule around the church's activity calendar. Church activities often incorporate fellowship with the church family, but are also great family time as well. It is also very important for the Christian to plan and schedule time to pray and read the Bible just as they do for everything else in their life. The priorities one sets will reveal what they truly treasure in life. (Matthew 6:21)

God says that those who are *redeeming the time* are wise. (Ephesians 5:15-16; Colossians 4:5) C. T. Studd wrote, "Only one life, 'twill soon be past, only what's done for Christ will last." The world flaunts the reality that 'you only live once' as an excuse to sin, but the Christian sees that as motivation to manage their time wisely in order to make an eternal impact for God.

"So teach *us* to number our days, that we may apply *our* hearts unto wisdom."

Psalm 90:12

"LORD, make me to know mine end, and the measure of my days, what it *is; that* I may know how frail I *am*. Behold, thou hast made my days *as* an handbreath; and mine age *is* as nothing before thee: verily every man at his best state *is* altogether vanity. Selah."

Psalm 39:4-5

"I must work the works of him that sent me, while it is day: the night cometh, when no man can work."

John 9:4

"See then that ye walk circumspectly, not as fools, but as wise, Redeeming the time, because the days are evil."

Ephesians 5:15-16

"Walk in wisdom toward them that are without, redeeming the time."

Colossians 4:5

"I believe that we need to pay very close attention to our time so that we balance all...areas of our life and succeed in the will of God in each area." – Jeffery J. Fugate

Tithes and Offerings

Tithe simply means a tenth, therefore giving of a tithe is giving back to God a tenth of the monetary gain God has blessed one with. An offering is, "that which is presented in divine service; an animal or a portion of bread or corn, or of gold or silver, or other valuable articles …as a return of thanks for His favors."[1] Examples of giving found in the Bible would suggest that tithes and offerings are to be the church's *only* source of income, excluding yard sales, bake sales, car washes, etc. Verses such as I Corinthians 16:2 and II Corinthians 9:7 show that funds should be voluntary contributions. We see also in Mark 11:15-18 and John 2:13-16 how angered Jesus was when the temple was used as a place of business. It is through the tithes and offerings that God runs His church and the ministries the church supports.

As the definitions suggest, a tithe is ten percent of one's earnings. Jacob set the first precedent of a tenth in Genesis 28:22. It should be noted that this was before the Mosaic law was given which negates arguments that the ten percent figure was just to the Israelites as a part of their law and has been done away with. Proverbs 3:9 tells us that we are to give of our *firstfruits* which conveys that the ten percent should be on one's gross earnings, before deductions. Insurance and taxes are nothing more than bills (just like all the others) that are deducted from one's paycheck by their employer. Any giving above the ten percent would be considered an offering. Missions giving is an offering, therefore, allocating a portion of one's tithe to go towards missions is not biblical. It is also not biblical to send money to various Christian organizations and consider that one's tithe. The tithe is to be given to the local church for use at their discretion. Malachi 3:10 speaks of bringing the tithe *into the storehouse* which means a treasury. This language is also seen in I Corinthians 16:2 (*lay by him in store*) as well as the instruction to give *upon the first day of the week* which was when the local church gathered together. It really is rather simple; a tithe is ten percent of one's earnings before deductions to be given to the local church and offerings are giving above and beyond one's tithe given to the local church or any organization or ministry as one feels led by the Lord.

Besides the what and where of giving, there is the how and why. Above all, we are to give to the Lord out of love and appreciation, not pure obligation. II Corinthians 9:7 says that the Lord *loveth a cheerful giver*. We are also to give sacrificially. We are to give of the *firstfruits* not just what is leftover. Sacrifices given in the Old Testament had to be of the best of the flock and without blemish. (Exodus 12:5; Deuteronomy 17:1) These were the animals that cost the farmers to let go, not the lame or sick that were of no use to them anyway. This is likely one reason why God did not accept Cain's sacrifice. Genesis 4:4 specifically says that Abel gave *of the firstlings of his flock* meaning that he brought his best. No such specifications are made of Cain's sacrifice. We are to give our best and give it cheerfully.

God blesses the cheerful, generous giver. It is impossible to out-give God as seen in verses like Luke 6:38 that promises return blessings in proportion to the measure one gives. On the other hand, God chastens those who withhold their giving, charging them with robbing God. (Malachi 3:8) May we give like our churches depend on it, because they do.

"Every man according as he purposeth in his heart, *so let him give*; not grudgingly, or of necessity: for God loveth a cheerful giver."

II Corinthians 9:7

"Honour the LORD with thy substance, and with the firstfruits of all thine increase:"

Proverbs 3:9

"Bring ye all the tithes into the storehouse, that there may be meat in mine house, and prove me now herewith, saith the LORD of hosts, if I will not open you the windows of heaven, and pour you out a blessing, that *there shall* not *be room* enough *to receive it*."

Malachi 3:10

"Give, and it shall be given unto you; good measure, pressed down, and shaken together, and running over, shall men give into your bosom. For with the same measure that ye mete withal it shall be measured to you again."

Luke 6:38

"Will a man rob God? Yet ye have robbed me. But ye say, Wherein have we robbed thee? In tithes and offerings."

Malachi 3:8

"When giving of our material possessions becomes another way of serving the Saviour, it is indeed a joyful experience." – Don Sisk

Tobacco

Tobacco is a plant that is used for smoking, chewing, and in snuff that has a disagreeable smell and an acrid taste; however, the practice of using it in any form soon conquers distaste and forms an addiction that is extremely hard to break.[1] The unpleasantness of tobacco would make one wonder why anyone would ever partake of it. The primary reason is conformity; people do what they feel is necessary to fit in with the crowd, but soon become addicted. Howbeit, I John 2:15-17 tells us that the things of the world are not of God and Christians are not to involve themselves in them. Supposed stress relief is an excuse for some, but we are to relieve stress through prayer and meditating on God and His Word. (Philippians 4:6; Isaiah 26:3) Popularity means nothing and stress levels are only magnified, however, once tobacco has taken its toll on one's body.

The Christian must remember that their body is not their own, rather it belongs to God and is the temple of the Holy Spirit. (I Corinthians 6:19-20) Using tobacco in any form (cigarettes, pipes, cigars, and smokeless tobacco such as chew/snuff and snus) destroys the body. Cigarette smoke is full of poisons, nineteen to be exact, and several of them deadly in small pure doses. Nicotine increases blood pressure because of constricted blood vessels.[18] The CDC has numerous reports that show the increased risk of cardiovascular and respiratory disease as well as several different cancers. There is no way of escaping the harmful effects tobacco has on the body. Christians are to take care of the temple of God in their bodies and strive for good health. (III John 1:2)

Another major problem with tobacco is its addictive nature. I Corinthians 6:12 says that we are not to be *brought under the power of any*. The one who is addicted to tobacco has allowed themselves to be brought under the power of that substance and has lost control of their person. As Jesus explains in John 8:34, the one who sins becomes a servant to sin. The Christian, however, is to be under the power of the Holy Spirit (Romans 8:14; Galatians 5:16) and serve only Christ (Luke 4:8; Matthew 6:24). There are many things in life that are not illegal according to our judicial system nor are they spelled out in Scripture as 'Thou shall nots,' but as I Corinthians 6:12 clearly states, that does not mean that all things are *expedient* or profitable/good. Take note that this was so important to God that he repeats these words a few chapters later in Chapter 10 verse 23. Tobacco is one of those things. It is not illegal or spelled out as wrong in the Bible but it is not good for you and is wrong according to other Bible principles that are clear.

Lastly, one must consider one's testimony to others. Most of the unsaved world view tobacco use as an unholy activity and something that Christians should not partake of. Therefore, when a Christian uses tobacco it tarnishes their faith and hinders their influence. This is the kind of thing spoken of in I Corinthians 8:9-13; becoming a stumbling block to another is a sin. Consider also Hugh Pyle's quote on the right, tobacco use will impede soul winning efforts. The Christian must make the safe and righteous choice and *abstain from all appearance of evil* so that they can represent the Lord honorably. (I Thessalonians 5:22)

187

"What? know ye not that your body is the temple of the Holy Ghost *which is* in you, which ye have of God, and ye are not your own? For ye are bought with a price: therefore glorify God in your body, and in your spirit, which are God's."

I Corinthians 6:19-20

"Beloved, I wish above all things that thou mayest prosper and be in health, even as thy soul prospereth."

III John 1:2

"All things are lawful for me, but all things are not expedient: all things are lawful for me, but I will not be brought under the power of any."

I Corinthians 6:12

"Jesus answered them, Verily, verily, I say unto you, Whosoever committeth sin is the servant of sin."

John 8:34

"Depart ye, depart ye, go ye out from thence, touch no unclean *thing*; go ye out of the midst of her; be ye clean, that bear the vessels of the LORD."

Isaiah 52:11

"The wise Christian wants to be his best, look his best and smell his best as he endeavors to bring others to Christ. If we are dominated by binding habits, we do not impress others that we have the real thing." – Hugh Pyle

Tongues/Ceased Sign Gifts

Tongues by its Greek definition is simply the language or dialect of a people group that is distinct from other people groups. Therefore, the gift of tongues is the miraculous ability for one to speak in a foreign language that they have never learned. The gift of speaking in tongues in the Scriptures had a defined purpose. I Corinthians 14:22 clearly explains that the gift was *for a sign...to them that believe not*. They were used to validate the preaching of the men of God because they did not have completed Scripture to use as a standard. It was also a sign to the nation of Israel of the judgment they would receive because of their unbelief. (Isaiah 28:11; I Corinthians 14:21) Both of these purposes were fulfilled, therefore there is no longer a need for the gift. God used the Romans to judge Israel and the canon of Scripture is complete. The completion of Scripture is the *'that which is perfect is come'* spoken of in I Corinthians 13:10. The fulfillment of its purpose and this verse is why the gift of tongues has ceased as I Corinthians 13:8 says it would.

The Bible also defined the proper use of the gift of tongues. The Charismatic movement and what some people call tongues today does not follow these biblical guidelines and would not have been permitted in the early churches. There were four main rules to the gift's use. The first three are found in I Corinthians 14:27-28. First, there were to be no more than three men using the gift in any given service (*let it be by two, or at the most by three*). Second, they were not all to speak at the same time, they were to take their turn (*that by course*). Third, there was to be an interpreter (*let one interpret*). All three of these rules were set to avoid confusion because confusion is not of God. (I Corinthians 14:33) The fourth rule is seen in I Corinthians 14:34 forbidding women to *speak*, in other words, this gift was not given to women. The supposed tongues that are spoken today are not biblical and nothing more than gibberish.

Another misconception of the gift of tongues is that its presence is evidence of the presence of or being filled with the Holy Spirit. One receives the Holy Spirit at the moment of salvation. Peter explained this to the men of Israel in Acts 2:38. If this misconception were true, every believer would have the gift. A note of clarification here would be that this verse does not support the belief that one does not receive the Holy Spirit until the moment of or after baptism (see God the Holy Spirit for further explanation). Another truth that negates the correlation of tongues and the Holy Spirit is that God commands all believers to be *filled with the Spirit*. (Ephesians 5:18) Clearly, God is not commanding every Christian here to use the gift of Tongues. The gift of tongues in the Bible was not the evidence of the Holy Spirit nor does it show evidence of such in today's claims of the gift.

All the other sign gifts (prophecy, divine healing, and miracles) have ceased as well along with the gift of tongues. The gift of prophecy as known in the Bible has ceased, but exists today in a new way (see Spiritual Gifts). We still see miraculous healing today, but it is the work of God alone; He no longer does so through human touch or word. Our means of healing today is through prayer to an all-powerful God. (James 5:14-15) God used these spiritual gifts for an appointed time as a sign to the early church, but Praise God we now have His perfect Word!

"Wherefore tongues are for a sign, not to them that believe, but to them that believe not: but prophesying *serveth* not for them that believe not, but for them which believe."

I Corinthians 14:22

"Charity never faileth: but whether *there be* prophecies, they shall fail; whether *there be* tongues, they shall cease; whether *there be* knowledge, it shall vanish away. For we know in part, and we prophesy in part. But when that which is perfect is come, then that which is in part shall be done away."

I Corinthians 13:8-10

"If any man speak in an *unknown* tongue, *let it be* by two, or at the most *by* three, and *that* by course; and let one interpret. But if there be no interpreter, let him keep silence in the church; and let him speak to himself, and to God."

I Corinthians 14:27-28

"For God is not *the author* of confusion, but of peace, as in all churches of the saints."

I Corinthians 14:33

"Then Peter said unto them, Repent, and be baptized every one of you in the name of Jesus Christ for the remission of sins, and ye shall receive the gift of the Holy Ghost."

Acts 2:38

"We do not need 'signs' in this glorious day of grace, in this day when we have that which is perfect." – Oliver B. Greene

Victorious Living

Victorious living is a Christian living their life in a manner that shows evidence that they have overcome the power of Satan and sin in their lives. It is living with the recognition that they are children of the One who conquered death and hell and overcame the world. (I John 5:4) It is being successful at living the Christian life according to the precepts and principles God teaches in His Word. The first and most important victory one must make is that over the grave. We can gain this victory through the Lord Jesus Christ alone. (I Corinthians 15:57) The one that puts their faith in Jesus becomes a child of God and can become victorious over every area of their life because the Holy Spirit that lives within them is greater than any other. (I John 4:4)

God gives the Christian the tools needed to live victoriously. Ephesians 6:11 refers to them as the *armour of God*. The key, however, is that the Christian must use them in order to *stand against the wiles of the devil* and be victorious. The passage continues through verse 19 and starts with the belt of *truth* (vs. 14). This is seeking after the truths of God and who He is, but is also being honest and fair in one's doings. The second piece of armour is the *breastplate of righteousness* (vs. 14). A pure life and godly character is necessary to protect against evil and enables one to withstand accusations hurled against them. *Feet shod with the preparation of the gospel of peace* follows in verse 15. This conveys the importance of preparing oneself to share the wonderful gospel of peace with others. Next we see the *shield of faith* (vs. 16). One must not allow their trust in God, His Word, and His promises to waver. *The helmet of salvation* (vs. 17) is simple yet vital. One must accept Christ as their savior to protect their soul from an eternal death. The last piece of armour mentioned is the *sword of the Spirit* (vs. 17). Evil is defeated by the Word of God, but one cannot use Scripture unless they are a student of the Bible. Although not assigned a piece of armour, the passage rightly ends admonishing the Christian soldier to be in prayer (vs. 18). The Christian can *put on* every piece of the Lord's armour, but it will do little good without praying for God to go with them into the battle.

Another very important key to living a victorious life is being filled with the Spirit. It is commanded in Ephesians 5:18 and Galatians 5:16 explains why. The one who is filled with and walking in the spirit will be less likely to fall into temptation and fulfill the desires of the flesh. Victorious living is the result of winning the battle between the spirit and the flesh. A steadfast faith is also key in victorious living. Hebrews 11:6 tells us that it is impossible to please God without faith. Faith in God and who He is, is the foundation that everything else in one's life is built upon. As II Corinthians 5:7 so clearly declares, *we walk by faith, not by sight.*

One day God will return to set up His Kingdom on earth, and His saints will rule and reign with Him. (see topic on End Times) This truth alone should lead the Christian to a positive attitude and to be content with *whatsoever state* they are in. (Philippians 4:11) One cannot allow themselves to become a victim because of a poor outlook on their current circumstances. The Christian is a child of the one who has *overcome the world*. (John 16:33) One's position with salvation, use of the Lord's armor, ability to be filled with the Spirit, and disposition in life, will decide if they are a victim or victor.

"For whatsoever is born of God overcometh the world: and this is the victory that overcometh the world, *even* our faith."

I John 5:4

"But thanks *be* to God, which giveth us the victory through our Lord Jesus Christ."

I Corinthians 15:57

"Ye are of God, little children, and have overcome them: because greater is he that is in you, than he that is in the world."

I John 4:4

"Put on the whole armour of God, that ye may be able to stand against the wiles of the devil."

Ephesians 6:11

"*This* I say then, Walk in the Spirit, and ye shall not fulfil the lust of the flesh."

Galatians 5:16

"Nay, in all these things we are more than conquerors through him that loved us."

Romans 8:37

"The reason why many fail in battle is because they wait until the hour of battle. The reason why others succeed is because they have gained their victory on their knees long before the battle came. Anticipate your battles; fight them on your knees before temptation comes, and you will always have victory." – R. A. Torrey

War

War is, "a contest between nations or states, carried on by force, either for defense, or for revenging insults and redressing wrongs, for the extension of commerce or acquisition of territory, or for obtaining and establishing the superiority and dominion of one over the other. These objects are accomplished by the slaughter or capture of troops, and the capture and destruction of ships, towns, and property."[1] War is fought between two or more disagreeing nations because negotiations are not successful and peaceable resolutions cannot be reached. Because war is between nations, the loss of life resulted from it is not considered murder. The sixth commandment is *thou shalt not kill* (Exodus 20:13) but Moses later gives instruction to the same people in Deuteronomy 7:2 to *smite them, and utterly destroy them*. There is no contradiction here, rather the first deals with individual conduct while the second deals with the conduct of nations. God tells us in Ecclesiastes 3:8 that there is *a time of war*. God is the righteous judge and cannot and would not instruct His people to do something that goes against His Word.

If God says there is a time for war, what are the justifications for it? An obvious justification would be for protection. We see this demonstrated in Nehemiah when they were rebuilding the walls around Jerusalem while being threatened by the Samaritans of an attack. Verses 17-18 explain that they built with a tool in one hand and a weapon in the other. Another biblical justification for war would be to squelch evil. This was the case in the command given in Deuteronomy 7:2. The nations of Canaan were engrossed in every imaginable sin and the only way to purify the land was to destroy them. Similar instances are seen in I Samuel 15:1-23 and Joshua 10:40. Romans 13:3-4 explains that God uses government as a judge against evil. This pertains not only to executing judgment domestically (see topic on Capital Punishment), but also the evil of other nations. Wherefore, war is sometimes necessary as a measure of protection and is also the means by which government judges the evil of other nations.

It is important to understand that war is something declared and carried out by government which was instituted and is ordained by God as is explained in Romans 13:1-2. We see here that we are commanded to be in subjection to the government and that those who do not are actually resisting God. For someone to object to military service or war for conscience sake is not biblical and is answered in verse 5 which says we *must needs be subject...for conscience sake.* The only exception is when that government goes against God's commands. It is at this point that one *must obey God rather than men* as Acts 5:29 says. For example, God makes a covenant with Abraham in Genesis 12:3 promising to *bless them that bless thee and curse him that curseth thee*. It is for this reason that the Christian should never support a war against Israel and be ready to defend them against those who would desire to harm them.

Because of sin, war is unavoidable. We will see and *hear of wars and rumours of wars* and should not be surprised when we do. (Matthew 24:6-7) Verse 6 tells us, however, that *the end is not yet*. Glory to God, there will come a day when wars will cease – when Christ returns and creates a new heaven and new earth. (Revelation 21:4)

"A time to love, and a time to hate; a time of war, and a time of peace."

Ecclesiastes 3:8

"They which builded on the wall, and they that bare burdens, with those that laded, *every one* with one of his hand wrought in the work, and with the other *hand* held a weapon. For the builders, every one had his sword girded by his side, and *so* builded. And he that sounded the trumpet *was* by me."

Nehemiah 4:17-18

"Let every soul be subject unto the higher powers. For there is no power but of God: the powers that be are ordained of God. Whosoever therefore resisteth the power, resisteth the ordinance of God: and they that resist shall receive to themselves damnation. For rulers are not a terror to good works, but to the evil. Wilt thou then not be afraid of the powers? do that which is good, and thou shalt have praise of the same: For he is the minister of God to thee for good. But if thou do that which is evil, be afraid; for he beareth not the sword in vain: for he is the minister of God, a revenger to *execute* wrath upon him that doeth evil. "

Romans 13:1-4

"And ye shall hear of wars and rumours of wars: see that ye be not troubled: for all *these things* must come to pass, but the end is not yet. For nation shall rise against nation, and kingdom against kingdom : and there shall be famines, and pestilences, and earthquakes, in divers places."

Matthew 24:6-7

"Yes, a Christian should bear arms in obedience to the commands of the government, for the government is authorized by God to 'bear the sword,' hence that government may delegate any of its citizens as its representatives in its military or naval obligations." – Robert L. Moyer

War Between Spirit & Flesh

The Spirit is the righteous way a saved person knows they should live because of the Holy Spirit living within them. The flesh is the sinful nature that every person is born with. The war between them, therefore, is the daily struggle one faces in wanting to do right yet still having the desires and tendency toward sin. The result of winning this war is victorious living while the result of losing it is living in a backslidden condition. The Christian should strive to win the war because Revelation 3:16 tells us that God does not like the lukewarm Christian. He is pleased with the one who is sold out and on fire for Him and His work.

The devil and the sin nature are to blame for this war. I Peter 5:8 explains that he is our *adversary* and that he *walketh about seeking whom he may devour*. This war is not a physical war but rather a spiritual one. (Ephesians 6:12) In many ways, this spiritual war is harder to fight because one cannot see their opponents, opponents that are cunning and more powerful than any physical adversary. If the devil cannot keep someone from gaining salvation, his next goal is to make them lose this war so that they are not productive for the Lord.

An examination of one's life will reveal if the spirit or the flesh is winning this battle. Galatians 5:22-23 gives us the fruit of the spirit. The one who is right with the Lord and filled with the Spirit will display these characteristics in their life: *love, joy, peace, longsuffering, gentleness, goodness, faith, meekness, temperance.* On the opposite side you find the works of the flesh which are given in verses 19-21. They include: *adultery, fornication, uncleanness, lasciviousness, idolatry, witchcraft, hatred, variance, emulations, wrath, strife, seditions, heresies, envyings, murders, drunkenness, revellings*. If one sees a pattern of these things in their life, it means they are losing this battle and need to seek God for His power to overcome the flesh.

God gladly gives power to win this battle to the one who earnestly seeks and asks for it. First, one must resolve to submit themselves to God and His ways while rejecting the devil and the worldly living he encourages. (James 4:7) When a Christian is walking in the Spirit and living a righteous life, they will not feel as strong of a temptation toward sinful behaviors. (Galatians 5:16) This means avoiding places, people, and situations that encourage sin or offer increased temptation. One can succeed at living a righteous life if they will only use the armour God provides asking God to fill them with His Spirit. (see Victorious Living) The Christian has an arsenal of spiritual weapons at their disposal that are *mighty through God*. (II Corinthians 10:4)

Unfortunately, this is a daily battle that every Christian must deal with until they reach glory. No one is exempt and one should not feel like a failure because they struggle so much with it. Even Paul expressed his frustration with the battle in Romans 7:15-20. It was not that he did not *want* to do right, but the sin that dwelled within him pulled him to do evil. We are reassured in Revelation 21:27 that the day will come when we will sin no more – the moment we enter heaven. Only once the sin nature is gone will the battle between the Spirit and the flesh be truly won.

"Be sober, be vigilant; because your adversary the devil, as a roaring lion, walketh about, seeking whom he may devour:"

I Peter 5:8

"Put on the whole armour of God, that ye may be able to stand against the wiles of the devil. For we wrestle not against flesh and blood, but against principalities, against powers, against the rulers of the darkness of this world, against spiritual wickedness in high *places*. Wherefore take unto you the whole armour of God, that ye may be able to withstand in the evil day, and having done all, to stand."

Ephesians 6:11-13

"Submit yourselves therefore to God. Resist the devil, and he will flee from you."

James 4:7

"*This* I say then, Walk in the Spirit, and ye shall not fulfil the lust of the flesh. For the flesh lusteth against the Spirit, and the Spirit against the flesh: and these are contrary the one to the other: so that ye cannot do the things that ye would."

Galatians 5:16-17

"(For the weapons of our warfare *are* not carnal, but mighty through God to the pulling down of strongholds;)"

II Corinthians 10:4

"When we are born again, a new life - the life of God - is put into us by the Holy Spirit. But the old self-life, which is called in Scripture the flesh, is not taken away. The two may coexist in the same heart." – F. B. Meyer

Women's Role in the Church

The women's role in the church is the influence and responsibilities that are acceptable or not acceptable in the church according to God's plan and organizational structure. It is very important to understand that this is only a matter of order, not value. Everything in God's creation has a perfect order, and when we follow God's plan, we find that things work much more smoothly. Take note to I Corinthians 11:3 which says that *the head of Christ is God*. We know that Christ is God and equal in power and importance, yet He places this person of Himself under authority of the person of God.

God's chain of command, so to speak, is clearly written out in I Corinthians 11:3: God first, men second, and women third. His plan for order is for men to have the leadership role. This is called for in the marriage and family relationships. Ephesians 5:22-23 instructs the women to submit themselves to their husbands and calls for the husband to be the *head of the wife*. Evidence of their leadership role within the family is seen in I Timothy 3:12 (qualifications for deacons) which says these men are to be *ruling their children and their own houses well*. If this is so in the marriage and family relationships, so much the more it holds true within the church as well. I Timothy 3:2 and 12 give the qualifications for bishops (what we would also refer to as ministers or pastors) and deacons. Both verses call for these roles to be men by the qualification that they be a *husband of one wife*. A woman cannot fulfill that qualification for they cannot be someone's husband. I Timothy 2:12-14, however, is perhaps the passage that best relates God's will in this matter. It clearly states that a woman is not to teach a man which is indicated by the use of the word *nor*. This conjunction connects the first command with the second which commands women not to *usurp authority over the man*. God even gives an explanation why in verses 13 and 14. First, God created man first placing men above women in status. Second, Eve was the one deceived in the garden indicating that women are more vulnerable to deception. God clearly places man above women in position and responsibility.

A verse often misinterpreted is I Corinthians 14:34. This verse is sometimes taken out of context to tell women that they are to hold no roles at all in the church, to teach literal silence of the women in church. The context of this verse, however, is in regards to the gift of tongues. This verse simply shows that there are certain areas of the ministry that are reserved for men only. Similarly, I Timothy 2:12 does not teach that women cannot teach at all. This verse only restricts women from teaching (which would obviously include preaching) any class with men in attendance. Women are certainly qualified to serve God by teaching children and other ladies.

All this does not diminish the great value of women. God's Word is filled with admiration of good godly women and the importance they hold. (Esther; Ruth; Proverbs 31; Titus 2:3-5) The church very much needs women and women can have a big part in other areas of the church including: choir, nursery, bus ministry, Sunday School teachers, and secretarial to name a few. Above all, women are needed to be the helpmeet God created them to be. There is a great need for women to be serving alongside their husbands in the ministry, helping their husbands fulfill what it is God is calling them to be or do in their lives.

"But I would have you know, that the head of every man is Christ; and the head of the woman *is* the man; and the head of Christ *is* God."

I Corinthians 11:3

"A bishop then must be blameless, the husband of one wife, vigilant, sober, of good behaviour, given to hospitality, apt to teach;"

I Timothy 3:2

"But I suffer not a woman to teach, nor to usurp authority over the man, but to be in silence."

I Timothy 2:12

"Let your women keep silence in the churches: for it is not permitted unto them to speak; but *they are commanded* to be under obedience, as also saith the law."

I Corinthians 14:34

"When the assembly is gathered together in a Scriptural way, then a woman's place is one of silence so far as ministry is concerned...a woman must not set herself up as an authority in matter of doctrine...a woman must not be put in a place of authority in the church. ...It is not a matter of superiority or of inferiority, but it is a matter of order." – M. R. DeHaan

World Missions

World missions is the process by which one is called by God and sent out by a church and/or other organization to propagate religion and evangelize the lost. The nature of their work is such that they depend on the support of local New Testament churches. They will often spend several years before ever leaving for their field on deputation raising the support they need to sustain their living expenses and ministry. Most missionaries' goal is not only to evangelize an area, but to establish churches and train local pastors to lead them. We see a great example of this in Paul, likely the greatest missionary example we have recorded in Scripture. He traveled on several missionary journeys preaching the gospel to thousands and establishing churches along the way. Sadly, Paul suffered much persecution for his faith as do many missionaries today. Many missionaries (particularly those on foreign fields) give up the common American comforts we enjoy and put their lives in danger for the cause of Christ.

We are living in a world that is in dire need of a Savior. The Bible is clear that there is only one way to heaven and that is through the Lord Jesus Christ. (John 14:6) The problem is that not everyone knows about this good news. The United States may be predominantly Christian (although the majority is losing ground even here), but most other countries of the world are engrossed in false religions and have very little or even no Christian population or influence. Truth be told however, no one has an excuse not to realize there is an intelligent creator. Everything around us is evidence to this fact. (Psalm 19:1) That being said, Christians cannot let something as grave as where others will spend eternity depend on lost ones recognizing a creator from their surroundings. The most sure fire way to ensure that people will know the truth is for them to hear the Word of God preached to them, but that cannot happen without people willing to go and churches willing to support them. (Romans 10:14)

Christ is fully aware of the need; missions holds a very dear place in the Lord's heart and holds a very high position on His priority list. The Bible is filled with verses telling the Christian to tell others about God and to praise His name abroad; those on the right are but a few. Furthermore, of all the things Christ could have said to His people just before He ascended into heaven, He chose to urge His people to tell the world about the Gospel. (Mark 16:15) There is only one thing that God ever specifically asked His people to pray for and that is laborers for the harvest, showing the Lord's passion for missions. (Luke 10:2)

The average person thinks of a missionary as those who spend their lives preaching the gospel to particular people groups, and most often to those on foreign fields, on a full-time basis. God calls us all to be missionaries however. Missions is not something that is only done on the remote foreign fields of faraway countries. We are to be concerned with our hometowns and surrounding areas as well. Acts 1:8 speaks of witnessing in *Jerusalem, and in all Judea, and in Samaria* as well. One's hometown is their Jerusalem and the towns surrounding them are their Samaria. According to Luke 24:47 we are to begin at Jerusalem. We must be concerned about the souls of the countries abroad but not to the neglect of the areas around us. Preaching the Gospel to every creature includes your neighbor across the street.

"And he said unto them, Go ye into all the world, and preach the gospel to every creature."

Mark 16:15

"But ye shall receive power, after that the Holy Ghost is come upon you: and ye shall be witnesses unto me both in Jerusalem, and in all Judea, and in Samaria, and unto the uttermost part of the earth."

Acts 1:8

"Declare his glory among the heathen, his wonders among all people."

Psalm 96:3

"For so hath the Lord commanded us, *saying*, I have set thee to be a light of the Gentiles, that thou shouldest be for salvation unto the ends of the earth."

Acts 13:47

"Then opened he their understanding, that they might understand the Scriptures, And said unto them, Thus it is written, and thus it behoved Christ to suffer, and to rise from the dead the third day: And that repentance and remission of sins should be preached in his name among all nations, beginning at Jerusalem. And ye are witnesses of these things."

Luke 24:45-48

"I believe missions has always been the very heartbeat of God." – Charles Keen

Worry

Worry is to be anxious, have grave concern, and/or be apprehensive over a situation or circumstance in one's life. Often times the situations or circumstances one is worrying about are completely out of their control. This lack of control is a big contributing factor to worry. It can intensify small concerns into much stronger feelings of worry that if allowed to strengthen can be debilitating. What is so ironic, is that majority of the things one worries about never happen.

Worry is a sin. It is a ploy of the devil to keep a believer from trusting the Lord and to hinder or even destroy their life so that they will not be effective for the Lord. Most people do not naturally look at worry as a sin but God commands us to *be careful for nothing.* (Philippians 4:6-7) Matthew 6:25a instructs the believer to *take no thought* for their physical needs for life such as food and water or what they should wear. He then says in verse 34 to not worry about tomorrow for it will take care of itself. This can be commanded because God promises to supply all our needs in Philippians 4:19. When one worries they are not trusting God to fulfill the promises He gives in His Word.

Worry has no benefit, rather a long list of adverse side effects. Foremost, it steals one's joy. It is evident through verses like John 14:27, Romans 15:13, Philippians 4:4, and I Thessalonians 5:16 that God wishes for His children to have joy and to radiate that joy to others so that they will want what they have. Excessive and uncontrolled worry in the life of a believer destroys their testimony. The lack of joy in one's life can lead to depression and suicidal thoughts or actions. Worry also affects one's body physically. Proverbs 17:22 explains that *a merry heart doeth good like a medicine: but a broken spirit drieth the bones.* There is an unending list of health problems that are associated and/or aggravated by stress such as high blood pressure, ulcers, shingles, headaches, insomnia, rashes, heartburn, chest pain and difficulty thinking to only name a few. There is nothing good that comes from worry; it only wreaks havoc on the mind and body of the person worrying.

There is a remedy to worry; it is putting full trust and faith in the Lord Jesus Christ and the promises He has given us in His Word. One must come to internalize that God loves them and cares for them. I Peter 5:7 instructs us to cast all our cares on Him. Most understand that the idea of casting is throwing something upon another, but it also implies giving up or letting go of the thing you are casting. One can cast their cares by keeping their mind on God and being in His Word. Isaiah 26:3 tells us that peace is found when we keep our minds stayed on God. Worries can also be cast onto God through prayer. After exhorting us not to worry in Philippians 4:6, He says instead to be in prayer. Furthermore, consider the awesome truth that every believer is a child of the King of Kings who has overcome the world. (John 16:33; see also Victorious Living) Worry is not of God. II Timothy 1:7 declares that *God hath not given us a Spirit of fear; but of power, and of love, and of a sound mind.* There is no mistaking that God's desire for His children is not to be under the bondage and destruction of worry, but to have control over their thoughts and feelings and to display love and joy to those around them.

"Be careful for nothing; but in every thing by prayer and supplication with thanksgiving let your requests be known unto God. And the peace of God, which passeth all understanding, shall keep your hearts and minds through Christ Jesus."

Philippians 4:6-7

"Therefore I say unto you, Take no thought for your life, what ye shall eat, or what ye shall drink; nor yet for your body, what ye shall put on...Take therefore no thought for the morrow: for the morrow shall take thought for the things of itself. Sufficient unto the day *is* the evil thereof."

Matthew 6:25a, 34

"But my God shall supply all your need according to his riches in glory by Christ Jesus."

Philippians 4:19

"Casting all your care upon him; for he careth for you."

I Peter 5:7

"And we know that all things work together for good to them that love God, to them who are the called according to *his* purpose."

Romans 8:28

"For God hath not given us a Spirit of fear; but of power, and of love, and of a sound mind."

II Timothy 1:7

"Worry, like a rocking chair, will give you something to do but it won't get you anywhere."
– Vance Havner

Plan of Salvation

You must accept that you are a sinner

Romans 3:10, "As it is written, There is none righteous, no, not one:"

Romans 3:23, "For all have sinned, and come short of the glory of God;"

Where did sin come from? Romans 5:12, "Wherefore, as by one man sin entered into the world, and death by sin; and so death passed upon all men, for that all have sinned:"

You must accept that as a sinner you owe a major penalty

Romans 6:23, "For the wages of sin is death; but the gift of God is eternal life through Jesus Christ our Lord."

John 3:18, "He that believeth on him is not condemned: but he that believeth not is condemned already, because he hath not believed in the name of the only begotten Son of God."

I Corinthians 15:22, "For as in Adam all die, even so in Christ shall all be made alive."

You must accept that you cannot pay your penalty yourself in order to go to Heaven

Ephesians 2:8-9, "For by grace are ye saved through faith; and that not of yourselves: it is the gift of God: Not of works, lest any man should boast."

Titus 3:5, "Not by works of righteousness which we have done, but according to his mercy he saved us, by the washing of regeneration, and renewing of the Holy Ghost;"

You must accept that Jesus Christ has already paid your sin debt

Romans 5:6, "For when we were yet without strength, in due time Christ died for the ungodly."

Romans 5:8, "But God commendeth his love toward us, in that, while we were yet sinners, Christ died for us."

John 3:16, "For God so loved the world, that he gave his only begotten Son, that whosoever believeth in him should not perish, but have everlasting life."

II Corinthians 5:21, "For he hath made him to be sin for us, who knew no sin; that we might be made the righteousness of God in him."

Christ was not a sinner, and the Bible teaches that God took all of our sin and placed it on Christ. While Christ was bearing all of our sins in His own body, God punished Him in our place to pay the debt we owe.

You must accept that He arose from the grave and is alive today

Matthew 28:6, "He is not here: for he is risen, as he said. Come, see the place where the Lord lay."

Acts 1:3, "To whom also he shewed himself alive after his passion by many infallible proofs, being seen of them forty days, and speaking of the things pertaining to the kingdom of God:"

I Corinthians 15:17, "And if Christ be not raised, your faith is vain; ye are yet in your sins."

You must accept by faith what Jesus did for you and ask Him to save you

Romans 10:9, "That if thou shalt confess with thy mouth the Lord Jesus, and shalt believe in thine heart that God hath raised him from the dead, thou shalt be saved."

Romans 10:13, "For whosoever shall call upon the name of the Lord shall be saved."

Acts 2:21, "And it shall come to pass, that whosoever shall call on the name of the Lord shall be saved."

John 1:12, "But as many as received him, to them gave he power to become the sons of God, even to them that believe on his name:"

Action is required

If you understand and accept these 6 points, you must then put your faith into action and call on Jesus Christ to be your Savior. Below is a prayer you may use (it is not a specific prayer that saves you) to help you express to the Lord Jesus a genuine heart concerning the truths above.

PRAYER

Dear Lord, I know I am a sinner. I believe in my heart that Jesus, your Son, died on the cross and shed His blood for the remission of my sins and that He rose from the dead. Please forgive me of my sins and come into my heart. I receive Jesus Christ as my personal Savior. I commit my life to you today and ask you to help me to live for you from this day forward. In Jesus name, Amen.

Bibliography

1 – Noah Webster. *Noah Webster's First Edition of an American Dictionary of the English Language.* (San Francisco, CA:Foundation for American Christian Education, 1967).

2 – James Orr. *The International Standard Bible Encyclopedia.* (Grand Rapids, MI:Wm. B. Eerdmans Publishing Co., 1939) p. 132.

3 – John R. Rice. *Saved For Certain.* (Murfreesboro, TN: Sword of the Lord Publishers, 2008) p. 14.

4 – Paul Chappell. *The Value of Christian Education.* (Lancaster, CA:Striving Together Publications, 2011) p. 27.

5 – David W. Cloud. *Way of Life Encyclopedia of the Bible & Christianity.* (London, Ont.:Bethel Baptist Print Ministry, 2008) p. 157.

6 – Ibid., p. 153.

7 – Do Demons Possess People Today? (n.d.). Retrieved December 2, 2015, from http://truthfortheworld.org/do-demons-possess-people-today

8 – Curtis Hutson. *Divorce and Remarriage.* (Murfreesboro, TN: Sword of the Lord Publishers, 1987) p. 15.

9 – "Substance Use." *Centers for Disease Control and Prevention*. Centers for Disease Control and Prevention, 10 Sept. 2015. Web. 03 Nov. 2015.

10 – J. B. Buffington. *Legalized Gambling: A house of card.* (Murfreesboro, TN: Sword of the Lord Publishers, 1985) p. 5.

11 – "Understanding God's Will." *Fundamental Baptist Institute*. N.p., n.d. Web. 03 Nov. 2015.

12 – Walter L. Wilson. *A Dictionary of Bible Types.* (Peabody, MA: Hendrickson Publishers, 1999) p. 291.

13 – Henry M. Morris. *The Henry Morris Study Bible*. (Green Forest, AK:Master Books, 2012) p. 1751.

14 – Tom Malone. *For Men Only.* (Murfreesboro, TN:Sword of the Lord Publishers, 1999) p. 13.

15 – John G. Butler. *Analytical Bible Expositor. Volume 13.* (Clinton, IA: LBC Publications, 2009) p. 213.

16 – Oliver B. Greene. *Why Does the Devil Desire to Damn You?* (Greenville, SC:The Gospel Hour, Inc. 1966) p. 30.

17 – William McRae. *Dynamics of Spiritual Gifts.* (Grand Rapids, MI:Zondervan Publishing House, 1976) p. 20.

18 – John R. Rice. *Tobacco.* (Murfreesboro, TN:Sword of the Lord Publishers, n.d.) p. 13.